*f*P

A HANGING OFFENSE

The Strange Affair of the
Warship *Somers*

BUCKNER F. MELTON, JR.

FREE PRESS

NEW YORK   LONDON   TORONTO   SYDNEY   SINGAPORE

*f*P

FREE PRESS
A Division of Simon & Schuster, Inc.
1230 Avenue of the Americas
New York, NY 10020

For information about special discounts for bulk purchases,
please contact Simon & Schuster Special Sales: 1-800-456-6798
or business@simonandschuster.com

Designed by Jan Pisciotta

Manufactured in the United States of America

1   3   5   7   9   10   8   6   4   2

Library of Congress Cataloging-in-Publication Data

Melton, Buckner F.
A hanging offense : the strange affair of the warship Somers / Buckner F. Melton, Jr.
p. cm.
Inclides bibliographical references (p.) and index.
1. Trials (Mutiny)—United States. 2. Courts-martial and courts of inquiry—United
States—History. 3. Somers (Brig : 1842–1846). I. Title.
KF7653.S66 M45 2003   343.73'0143—dc21

ISBN 0-7432-3283-6

Contents

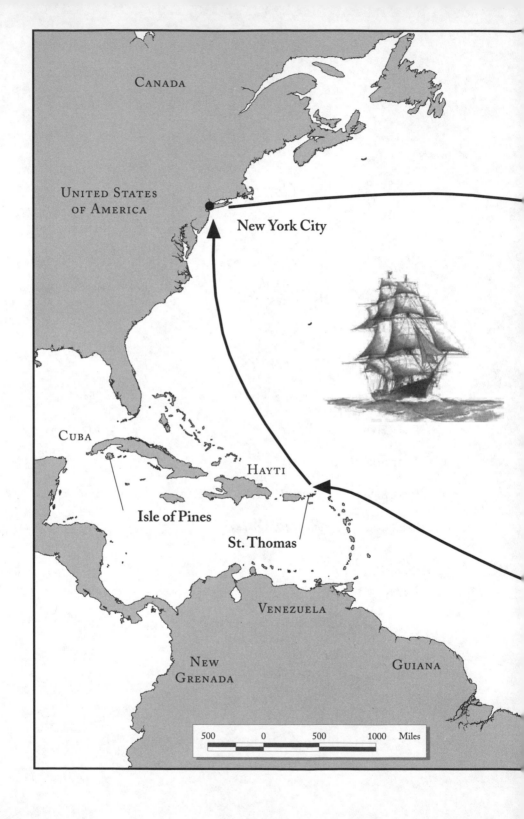

CANADA

UNITED STATES
OF AMERICA

New York City

CUBA

HAYTI

Isle of Pines

St. Thomas

VENEZUELA

NEW
GRENADA

GUIANA

500   0   500   1000   Miles

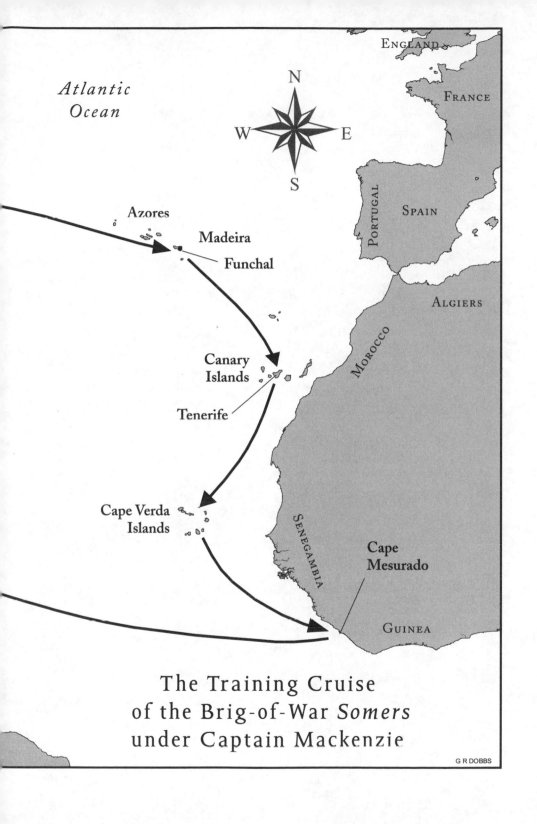

Atlantic Ocean

Azores

Madeira

Funchal

Canary Islands

Tenerife

Cape Verde Islands

ENGLAND

FRANCE

PORTUGAL

SPAIN

ALGIERS

MOROCCO

SENEGAMBIA

Cape Mesurado

GUINEA

The Training Cruise
of the Brig-of-War *Somers*
under Captain Mackenzie

G R DOBBS

A Hanging Offense

A navy is essentially and necessarily autocratic. . . . Whilst the ships sent forth by the Congress may and must fight for the principles of human rights and republican freedom, the ships themselves must be ruled and commanded at sea under a system of absolute despotism.

—John Paul Jones

The most amazing wonder of the deep is its unfathomable cruelty.

—Joseph Conrad, *The Mirror of the Sea*

What are you doing out here all alone? Aren't you afraid of me? . . . There isn't anyone to help you. Only me. And I'm the Beast.

—William Golding, *Lord of the Flies*

One of them was a troubled young man—a boy, really, still in his teens, with the demons of adolescence deep in his soul. Another was a longtime professional officer who had risen to one of the most powerful posts that the human mind has ever conceived: command of a warship. The rest were junior officers, young men, and whiskerless children who could never have imagined what waited for them far out upon the face of the waters.

Chance or fate had brought them all here, thrown them together on a man-made island of wood, a little self-contained planet whose orbit would take it into an alien realm, beyond society's view and control. Here the elements ruled, the elements lying without and within—the wind, the water, the stars, and darker, less controllable things. In this insular world, forces would collide, in the end provoking a maelstrom. The result, according to some, was murder. But according to others it was even more dreadful than that: it was a mutiny at sea. A mutiny in the United States Navy. A mutiny aboard a brig-of-war named Somers.

PART ONE

Somers

EVEN TIED UP AT DOCK, she gave the impression of speed. Her sharp bow, her tall, swept-back masts, made her seem as if she were a sprinter poised to fly across the white wave tops. Low, flush-decked, smallish in size, she had a touch of yacht about her. Even a casual eye could tell with just a glance or two that when she slipped the leash that held her alongside the land, she would take to the ocean with the swiftness and grace of a greyhound.

She was not, strictly speaking, a ship, although she was large enough: a hundred feet in length between her perpendiculars and a beam of twenty-five, an eleven-foot depth of hold, and more than two hundred fifty tons burthen. A good many acres of trees, everything from oak to pine, had given their lives to bring her forth. But she had only two masts, not a ship's requisite three, although both were square-rigged as a ship's masts were.

By the standards of her day, her armament was on the light side. In the old British classification system, she would hardly have rated. The ships of the line, the battleships of the wooden world, were floating fortresses, the equal of almost any land-bound castle in fire-power. They carried seventy-four, ninety, a hundred and ten artillery pieces, while she carried scarcely a dozen. A single broadside from even a third-rate line-of-battle ship would have blown her to flinders. But first the battleship would have to catch her, and that could never happen. With the press of sail that she could carry on those tall masts of hers, she was one of the fastest things afloat.

She was first cousin to a Baltimore Clipper; the relationship showed in her sharp lines, her narrow, knifelike hull, and her rather broad beam. Forerunners of the true clipper ships, the Baltimore Clippers were quick and handy sailers. They carried small cargoes but carried them nimbly, in deep and shallow water alike. Slavers and buccaneers liked them; they were good at running and hiding, and at chasing down poorly armed prey.

But Baltimore Clipper was only part of her heritage. Technically she was a brig, given her rig and her number of masts. The name stems from *brigand,* in honor of the North African raiders who first used vessels of her sort. She had piracy in her bloodlines. But it was a domesticated piracy. She was on the side of the angels. She was designed to take on the slave ships and the corsairs, and to beat them at their own game. She was weatherly; she could sail very close to the wind, and easily into the shallows, following her enemies wherever they went, and she could sail as fast as they. She was over-sparred, like a modern-day hot rod with too much engine for its own good. Of course, all those sails could make her very hard to control. If someone handled her carelessly, the wind that she used for power could turn on her and tear her to pieces. But in the right hands, more firm than gentle, she could respond as no other ship did. And if her master knew his business, he could use what she had to hunt down his prey and bring her to the culmination of battle.

Given what she was hunting, her ten to twelve guns were enough. They were medium thirty-two-pounders, which was fairly heavy artillery. She was over-gunned, in fact, as well as over-sparred, the guns' thousands of pounds of weight adding to her handling problems. But in exchange for the loss in stability, those weapons gave her a serious punch. They were heavier than any field pieces, and of longer range, too. No army field artillery regiment of the day had anything close to her striking power, to say nothing of her mobility. A single broadside from her would send a hail of solid shot into an enemy hull, tearing it open to the sea and blowing its wood into shards that would shred human flesh to hamburger. If a round happened to hit a man it would take off his arm, or his leg, or his head, in less than an eyeblink. The guns could also be loaded with grapeshot, clusters of small iron balls, turning them from anti-ship weapons to purely anti-personnel pieces. A broadside of grape was like a blast from a bank of giant shotguns. It could sweep clean an enemy deck in seconds. The guns could even be loaded with chain and aimed at the enemy's rigging, robbing him of the ability to maneuver or even make headway. Then, after his likely surrender, her boarding parties could take him in hand. She was a potent device.

Swift and sharp, graceful and powerful, she stood at the pinnacle of six thousand years of sailing ship development, resting there at the New York Navy Yard in the spring of 1842, a few months after her birth. Good American ships were the best in the world, even better than England's, perhaps, and her maker had built her well. She was the epitome of her kind. No one could know that for all her newness and eagerness, she had a terrible flaw: this brand-new warship, this United States Brig-of-War *Somers*, was nearly obsolete.

The sea never changes. Its details may differ, to an amazing degree, from time to time and from place to place. Anyone who spends even a little while on or around the world's oceans knows that. The sea can be calm and as flat as a pond, and if the light is just right, the water can turn to milk, difficult to distinguish from skies the color of powder. In the north the sea can be hard, changing to liquid gunmetal with cold steel highlights or dead, leaden hues. The waters can sparkle like sapphire under a tropical sun, or green like a washed-out emerald closer to shore, or too black to make out on a dark, storm-tossed night. The sea can get angry, working up into a rage of white foam, spawning waves so high and troughs so deep that they can swallow a tanker, and winds that can drive raindrops so hard that they sting like a swarm of needles. But for all of these changes of aspect, the sea's essence remains the same. It always consists of water, which lies beneath air, which in turn lies beneath sun and stars. The tides are predictable, and the water is always as salty as teardrops. The sea, in short, is as constant as human nature.

But human technology changes. And in the mid-nineteenth century, a half-dozen transformations of naval technology changed the nature of ships and of war at sea more than all the developments of the previous half-dozen millennia put together. Yet, for all of that, *Somers* still had things in common with her earliest ancestors.

Ships are as old as human society. Perhaps they are even older. Technology is one of the signs of civilization, and technology is what ships are all about. A ship is a device that turns an impassable barrier—a river, a lake, an ocean—into a highway for travel and trade. Without ships, some of these barriers are absolute. But ships transmute them, like magic, into the world's greatest channels for exchanging every building block of society from food to ideas. When ships began, so, too, did civilization.

The Mediterranean was the earliest ocean frontier, along with the Red Sea and the Persian Gulf, which together surrounded the Fertile Crescent. Calm and flat, with light and predictable winds, it was perfect for oar power. Egyptians were perhaps the first to reach out into its waters, although they began their lessons on the Nile. The currents of Egypt's river ran against the prevailing wind, so that air and water were always at battle, so maybe this was the place where humans first took to sail, using the breezes to fight the Nile's northward flow. This gave Egyptian sailors experience, so that when the time came for them to expand their horizons and set out into the open ocean and out of the sight of land, Egypt was up to the challenge. It had learned the ways of both oar and sail, the two sources of power that would rule, in tandem, for thousands of years.

The earliest sailing rigs were simple. Ancient depictions of sailing ships show single square sails on a single short mast, driving long hulls with uplifted ends. Such a rig wouldn't have let a captain do anything flashy or fast, especially in the Eastern Mediterranean's light winds. But it let him do things on the cheap, and that was what merchantmen wanted. Human beings, whether free men or slaves, cost money. They (or their labor) are expensive to buy, and they are expensive to feed. A ship is expensive, too, but once built, if powered by sail, its costs of operation are low and its cargo capacity relatively high, at least without many men on board. Even today, ships carry most of our cargo, and carry it more cheaply, pound for pound, than any other system of transport. This was a lesson that merchants picked up on almost as soon as there were merchants. So sail began to flourish, and Egypt moved outward, as did others—the Cretans, the Phoenicians, the Greeks. But ships, in addition to helping these peoples build maritime empires, threatened their commerce as well, for pirates could use ships, too.

A lumbering merchant ship can be slow, especially if it uses sails in the Mediterranean. Pirates had to be faster, in order to catch their prey, so they usually relied on oar power. Oars are much more expensive to run than sails, for they need lots of men, and those men need food and fresh water. An oar-propelled ship tends to be longer and leaner than its sail-powered counterpart. All of this cuts down on cargo capacity, and thus on range. Oar-propelled ships were tied more closely to land, since they needed constant resupply. But as payback for all of these downsides, the oar-propelled ship got one huge advantage: a built-in power source that a captain could call on at whim. He could use it in motionless air; he could use it to move against an in-your-face wind. His ship did his will, his brain directing the rowers' muscles; all that his men supplied was animal power. And having harnessed that power, he could use it to overhaul and grab the fat merchant prizes. This was a dynamic that stayed the same until *Somers*'s day. To a degree it is still true in our own. The only difference is that today the machinery is more complicated than oars.

The oar never fully conquered the sail, at least in merchant shipping. But the tactical edge that it gave meant that the struggle for command of the sea more often than not took place between oar-powered ships. It was oar, not sail, that fought at Salamis in 480 B.C., where Athens stopped the Persian invasion of Europe, forever changing history. It was oar power that wrenched command of the sea from the Carthaginian Empire in the last of the Punic Wars, when Rome, already a magnificent land power, crushed Carthage's fleet on the water. When Carthage lost command of the sea, it lost its maritime buffer zone, and thus its national security. Not long after that, it lost everything else as well. It ceased to exist, the Romans eradicating it utterly. It was oar power that, not many years later, gave Octavian the victory and the emperor's crown in his seaborne clash with Mark Antony in the Battle of Actium. The Egyptian queen Cleopatra's fleet was with Antony's; but her ships were driven by sail. At the battle's crucial moment, having the weather gage, the benefit of being upwind, her ships charged Octavian's fleet, bearing down on it in a rush. Octavian quickly opened up a gap in his oar-powered line, and Cleopatra's ships sailed neatly through. Too neatly, in fact: she never engaged Octavian. An instant later she was downwind, with no easy way of coming about and making another attack. Her force, slave as it was to the winds, had wasted itself. So she kept sailing on, away from the battle and home to Egypt. Behind her Antony and his fleet came to ruin, Octavian's forces setting fire to her lover's ships. The ancient Mediterranean belonged to oars.

With the death of Carthage and the end of the Punic Wars—certainly with Antony's death—Rome came to rule the sea unchallenged, and the naval peace called the Pax Romana commenced. The only real danger at sea was the threat of small-scale piracy, and Rome's fleet soon took care of that. Even the dangers that came from the sea itself—squalls, shoals, and lee shores—were slight in the calm and sunny Mediterranean. Oar may have won the wars, but it had won them to make the sea safe for sail, as the merchantmen plied their trade.

But not all seas are calm and flat. To the west, beyond the Pillars of Hercules, beyond Gibraltar and Mount Acha, lay a far vaster, more tempestuous ocean, the ocean that *Somers* would sail nearly two thousand years later. Now and then the ancient ships had sailed beyond this place that marked the end of the world, into the unknown sea; but this was merely prelude. And in the following centuries, mariners learned that neither their long, oared ships nor the simple Mediterranean sailing rigs were a match for Atlantic and North Sea gales, or the high walls of water that the deep ocean could thoughtlessly throw at ships. Something more was needed. As Rome crumbled and fell, and the barbarians of Northern and Western Europe began to build a new world, seafaring technology began to evolve.

The Mediterranean is a very small sea, barely a million square miles in all. The North Atlantic alone is thirty times bigger than that, and the North Atlantic is just one of a half-dozen true oceans, most of which are still larger. Because of the size of those oceans, the possibilities that they offered for trade and expansion dwarfed those of the Mediterranean—but only for ships that were up to the task. Gradually, very gradually, over a span of nearly a thousand years, Europe learned how to build such ships. And those ships were powered by sail.

But the sailing ship of the North Atlantic was far different from those of the Mediterranean. It had to be able to sail into the wind, not just with it, and to keep the currents and waves from pushing it off its course. Over the centuries the mariners there devised the technology that would let them do these things. The centerline rudder; the bowsprit; displacement hulls that bit well down into the water—all of these things made ships better able to live in high winds and tempestuous seas. Sail plans grew more complex; one sail per mast became two, then three, then more. More sails meant more complexity, and more crew, too, but they also meant more speed and more flexibility. These were the rigs that could carry ships on voyages of nearly impossible distance, voyages around the Cape of

Good Hope and eastward from there to India, voyages westward from Spain to American coasts, even voyages, by 1520 or so, completely around the world. By the end of the high Middle Ages, the technology was finally in place. The deep-ocean ship had finally come to be.

Europe, which had brought forth that ship, was now the mistress of the winds and the waters, which in turn gave her control of the planet. She used them to discover a new world to exploit. And, in time, a country of that new world would become one of the greatest maritime powers in history.

In August 1834, a young man with troubled eyes set foot on another brig that was tied up in Boston Harbor. He was new to *Pilgrim;* he had just come from Harvard, where he'd overdosed on his books. He needed a taste of fresh air and work to restore him to health, and in the next few years he would get them.

Being a landsman, Richard Henry Dana, Jr., managed to capture on paper for other landsmen and women something of what being a seaman meant, for the difference between the two was huge. His voyage was a long one, to California and back, and in his book *Two Years Before the Mast,* he painted quite a picture of the seagoing life. One of its highlights was his description of the sails of his vessel. One night in the South Atlantic he was far out on the bowsprit, and he turned and took in the sight of his ship. The night was calm, and nearly all of the sails were set. The sight took his breath away.

> There rose up from the water, supported by only the small black hull, a pyramid of canvas, spreading out far beyond the hull, and towering up almost, as it seemed in the indistinct night air, to the clouds. The sea was as still as an inland lake; the light trade-wind was gently

and steadily breathing from astern; the dark blue sky was studded with the tropical stars; there was not a sound but the rippling of the water under the stem; and the sails were spread out, wide and high—the two lower studding-sails stretching out on each side, twenty or thirty feet beyond the deck; the top-mast studding-sails, like wings to the top-sails; the top-gallant studding-sails spreading fearlessly out above them; still higher, the two royal studding-sails, looking like two kites flying from the same string; and, highest of all, the little sky-sail, the apex of the pyramid, seeming actually to touch the stars, and to be out of reach of human hand. So quiet, too, was the sea, and so steady the breeze, that if these sails had been sculptured marble, they could not have been more motionless. Not a ripple upon the surface of the canvas; not even a quivering of the extreme edges of the sail—so perfectly were they distended by the breeze. I was so lost in the sight, that I forgot the presence of the man who came out with me, until he said (for he, too, rough old man-of-war's-man as he was, had been gazing at the show) half to himself, still looking at the marble sails—"How quietly they do their work!"

Dana's reverie reminds us of one of the most vitally important things about a sailing ship. It is a thing of great beauty. Rarely in human invention has pure functionalism had such an exquisite form. But the beauty is happenstance. A ship has a job to do. And a warship's job is the projection of force beyond its home country's shores. Until the Wright brothers flew, warships were the only means of projecting force across water barriers. And when force projection is the objective, beauty must take a back seat.

Sail was always the choice of merchants, but by the 1500s it was the choice of most navies, too. Oared galleys survived until 1800 or so, but by the time they finally died out, sail had held center stage for centuries. The reason was simple: guns had appeared.

Navies are different from armies, in almost every imaginable way, from strategy and tactics to matériel and logistics. In the Age of Sail, a warship was an excuse for its guns, the guns the reason for the rest of the ship. While armies traditionally arm the man, in the words of one strategist, navies man the arm. The officers, the crew, the sails, the rigging, the hull—everything serves the weapons. The ship's *raison d'être* is to bring those weapons to bear on the target that the national will has selected.

The more firepower, the better. And with heavy, slow-firing artillery pieces, that meant putting a lot of guns along the sides of the ship, instead of just in the bow and the stern, where only a few could fit, and where they could only point forward and aft. Broadside arrangement of the guns, therefore, made a ship far more powerful. But the sides were where the oarsmen sat, so the oarsmen, and the oars, had to go. The transition began in the 1500s, as artillery first took to the sea in a serious way, and before long it was nearly complete. By 1600, oars, though still around, were passé. Thus did navies finally embrace the power of sail.

Now that warships relied on the wind, both tactics and strategy changed. A warship, to attack, had to be upwind of the enemy, to be able to pursue and to catch it. In nautical terms, it had to have the weather gage. When enemy ships met each other at sea, chance usually decided which one of them held the weather gage, and so chance played a big role in combat. In the string of Anglo-French wars that raged from the Glorious Revolution in 1688 to Waterloo in 1815, England's Admiralty constantly feared that a momentary, contrary wind would sweep its fleet from the Channel, giving Louis XIV or Napoleon the window he needed to invade, and thus smash, England, just the way that Rome had smashed Carthage. All this was the price of sail. And navies adapted, but always they remembered the day when they carried their driving force aboard the ship itself.

Then, in the nineteenth century, that day returned, when an American inventor first came up with the idea of putting a steam engine aboard a ship. And suddenly the game was never the same again.

Steam engines had been around for years before Robert Fulton began working with them. They had even been on boats before, but never successfully. In 1807 Fulton made them work, linking them to paddle wheels and thus changing the relationship of ships to the elements, and to manpower, too. At first the arrangement was primitive, but each passing year saw greater efficiency, and brought more experience. Before long steam moved from rivers to oceans, first in the service of merchants, and then, slowly, into naval vessels.

Steam power at sea worked a huge revolution. In a way it was closer to oars than to sails, but it was different even from them. It freed a ship from the slavery of the winds and the tides, but at the same time it tied the vessel to shore, limiting its range because of the need for coal. Shiphandling and tactics changed drastically. Even geography itself seemed to alter, since steam-powered ships could travel from place to place in more or less a straight line, instead of having to follow the paths of the winds. Room had to be made for engines and fuel, and engineers and their magical science became major forces aboard. With the arrival of steam power, in short, hundreds—even thousands—of years of nautical knowledge began to grow obsolete; and so did the sailors who knew and practiced the old ways.

The changes came fast when compared to the centuries of slow technological evolution that had been the usual way of the ship, but they still weren't instant. For now—for 1842 at least—sail still had something to offer. *Somers* was not obsolete, not quite, not just yet. Her days were numbered from the moment her keel was laid down, for she was one of the last ships of the United States Navy—of any navy, in fact—to be designed and built as purely a vessel of sail. But she still had some things to offer that steam couldn't possibly match. She was handy, and she had long legs. Given a capable crew, she could sail completely around the world, the way Magellan and Drake had done, with few supplies and no help. She could show the Stars and Stripes on nearly any sea on the planet, off the shore of any continent. All by herself she could project more power beyond American shores than the whole of the U.S. Army, which could cross no sea on its own. Though the sun was about to set, her day, and that of her sail-driven sisters, was not over.

Yet for all her advantages, there was one thing she had to have— one thing, without which she would lie as dead in the water as a steamship empty of coal. She needed men to work her. She needed officers who knew the ways of the sea, who knew how to tack and wear ship and take bearings, able seamen who knew the ropes, hands who could climb the rigging like monkeys. She needed a crew with cast-iron stomachs who had the art of sail in their bones, an art much harder to learn than the labor of shoveling coal toward a boiler. And in mid-nineteenth-century United States, unbelievably, such a crew could be terribly hard to find.

"Seeing how energetically the Anglo-Americans trade, their natural advantages, and their success, I cannot help believing that one day they will become the leading naval power on the globe," Alexis de Tocqueville wrote in 1835, at the height of the Golden Age of American Sail. "They are born to rule the seas, as the Romans were to conquer the world."

He was right. The United States is a maritime nation, and it has been so from the beginning. Its eastern coast fronts on the sea that links it to Europe; its bays and fine harbors, its many deep rivers, invited exploration and settlement, welcoming the Old World's peoples. Its innumerable hardwood stands were perfect for hulls and for masts, while its forests of pine supplied pitch and tar. When the colonies gained independence, Yankee traders swept out all over the world, from Mahon to Mauritius, from Canton to Liverpool, hawking the wares that North America grew in abundance: corn, rice, wheat, cotton, and a hundred other products. In time the United States gained a foothold on the Pacific Rim, on the continent's western shores, looking across the world's largest ocean to the Orient's massive markets and limitless raw materials. Between San Francisco, New Orleans, and New York—the three great ports through which so much wealth flowed—the whole landmass was filled with resources of its own, resources that no other maritime power has ever commanded within its own borders. And with the end of the War of 1812, the country began to exploit these things as it never had before.

Of all of the tonnage that America sent to sea in the years after 1812, only a small amount was naval. A navy is a means of power projection, and today America's navy is one of the bases of America's strategic power projection capability. But a navy is only a means, not an end. A major reason for its existence is to protect its country's vital trade, to safeguard its merchant marine. Commerce is the root of maritime greatness; naval power is merely its guardian.

It can be an expensive guardian, too. Right after the War of 1812, Congress expanded the navy. It was a big investment for its day, a million dollars a year, guaranteed for six years, for upkeep and new construction, and after the burst of postwar national pride had worn off, the price tag sank in and Congress backed off. Trade may increase the country's wealth, but except for the merchants and shipowners, once a ship slipped below the horizon, out of sight was out of mind. "No more ships of war than are requisite to the protection of our commerce," declared President Andrew Jackson in 1829, with all the assurance of a frontiersman who had never once gone to sea. "Our best policy would be to discontinue building ships of the first and second class." Others agreed. America's early version of the military-industrial complex, they feared, would become an expensive engine that could wipe out the country's finances.

Big ships were costly, and so Congress tended to skimp on them, authorizing only smaller vessels, when it authorized any at all. But as bad as this problem was, it wasn't the worst one. Even with the navy's small size, it faced a perpetual manpower shortage. Without well-trained sailors, the ships might as well lie alongside the wharves and rot. And well-trained sailors were rare in the mid-1800s, and they seemed to be getting still rarer.

One of the first to notice the problem, or at least one of the first to say something about it, was Matthew C. Perry. Perry was a remarkable man. He was a member of America's most prominent naval family, and a highly capable officer in his own right. His appearance was nothing unusual: medium height, brown hair and eyes, rather strong features that most often wore a humorless, sober expression. By age twenty he was already a battle-hardened veteran of the War of 1812, which helps explain the gaze. Still, he wasn't a typical officer. He had many of the usual qualities: an ability to lead men, a devotion to duty and country, and a deep, bellowing voice that was so perfect for issuing orders in a howling gale that he won the nickname "Old Bruin" before he turned thirty. But he had other traits, too: an understanding of tactics and strategy much deeper than that of most of his fellow officers, a deeply religious perspective that stood in stark contrast to the torrent of blasphemies that could often be heard aboard ship, and a thoughtful, even temperament that was a sure recipe for success. He believed in the use of the navy in scientific expeditions. He helped found Liberia, the humanitarian experiment in colonizing Africa with freed American slaves. And he was always interested in improving the navy's efficiency, especially when it came to personnel and education.

In 1851, Perry would command the squadron that called on Japan, opening relations between that country and his. By then he would have sailed nearly all of earth's oceans, doing everything from pushing the navy to make the move to steam power and high-tech explosive shells to commanding the naval forces off Vera Cruz during the Mexican War. But in the mid-1820s he was just another lieutenant commandant serving in the pirate-infested Caribbean, in command of the schooner *Shark*. He gave the pirates a very rough time, and they returned the favor. But the real enemy was different. His men dropped like flies from the fevers. Disease could mow down men by the hundred, and sometimes it did. This, no doubt, made him realize just how important it was for the navy to have a supply of good sailors, a supply that it just didn't have. Not long after the end of his tour, while he was serving at Brooklyn Navy Yard, he decided to try to do something about this dangerous shortage.

He himself had once felt the pull of the American merchant service, with its better pay and better living conditions, but he hadn't given in. Still, he knew that many men did. Life in the Old Navy wasn't usually an adventure; it was a job, one that wasn't very high-profile or respectable, and the service lost out on a lot of nautical talent that went to the private sector. In Perry's eyes, that trend compromised national security. The problem bothered him enough to make him leapfrog the chain of command, complaining directly to Secretary of the Navy Samuel Southard in early 1824. "The sources from whence we have heretofore drawn our choicest seamen are partially dried up," he said, lamenting the lingering effects of the War of 1812. "Unless some plan is adopted to improve the number and condition of our seafaring population, we shall find too late, that although we may have ships in abundance, yet our government in case of emergency would have to contend with insuperable difficulties in *procuring crews for them*."

Perry even tried to go over the secretary's head, and the president's, too. Officers of the Old Navy often did things that way. They were so good at making decisions, bawling out orders from their quarterdecks, and watching their crews leap to obey them, that they tended to behave the same way whenever they stepped ashore. Perry was no different, and now he appealed to the public. Four years after he first approached Southard, and with nothing having happened, he began writing letters to the newspapers. He was for a strong navy in general: "By maritime means only can we be approached," he said, using words that government reports would soon echo, "and by such means must we be principally defended." He offered many suggestions, one of them touching on the training of a corps of young seamen. "My proposition is to enter boys as apprentices to the Navy, until they shall be twenty-one years of age," he wrote in one issue of the *National Gazette*. He made a compelling case. "It is an object of national importance to increase the number of our seafaring population," he argued. "Doing so would not clash with any other interest in the community." And using boys would help not just the boys, by teaching them valuable skills, but the service as well. "The moral and intellectual condition of seamen generally," he wrote, "might be greatly improved by early attention to their education."

Southard quickly picked up on the idea of using boys to make up for the lack of trained men, and he mentioned the idea to Congress in an 1825 report. But Congress was slow to decide. Four years later, all it had done was to ask Southard for further details. So Southard submitted another report on the shortage, spelling out all the reasons that enlistments stayed down. The terrible pay; the lack of a social security system for aging and infirm seamen; the exciting lure of life as a privateer or in a Latin American navy; Southard listed these things and more. He suggested recruiting in the nation's interior, and again he brought up the subject of boys. He hammered on this point, suggesting a scheme to enlist young teenagers who would serve until they turned twenty-one. By then, he observed, the apprentices would know much about sailing a ship. It would be a great education for them; it would produce hundreds of hands right away; and in the long run it would give the navy a new group of able seamen who had first served as apprentices before signing on again as grown men. Ten years after the Congress established an apprentice system for boys, Southard predicted, the nation's reliance on foreign-born sailors would end; the boys, now grown sailors, would supply "all our petty officers of every description," and they would "make the navy what it ought to be, in every thing—American." With that last nationalistic flourish, Southard again left the matter with Congress.

It was like towing a battleship with a rowboat. Ten years later, at the point when Southard had hoped to see an established corps of professional sailors, Congress was still dragging its feet. It refused to be hurried, especially when it came to spending the money. Southard and others claimed that the measure would be cost-effective, but either Congress didn't believe them or else it didn't care. But the chatter in the newspapers about it gradually increased the momentum. Eventually a viable bill emerged from committee. At last, more than a decade after Southard first proposed it, Congress enacted it into law.

It came at the very end of the Twenty-fourth Congress, in March of 1837, as if the legislature feared a public backlash. It was close to what Southard had first suggested. It allowed the enlistment of boys between thirteen and eighteen years old, to serve, with their parents' permission, until they turned twenty-one. But it didn't expressly provide for their education, or how, exactly, the navy was to use them. These were things that the law left to the navy.

At first the navy decided to segregate the boys, putting them all aboard school ships, and training and teaching them there. But sometimes this caused problems. These school ships rarely left port, and their ports were all good-sized cities, Boston, New York, and Norfolk. Big-city life lured more than one boy to desert. On top of that, the boys and their families often found the program a big disappointment. There was no naval academy at Annapolis in the 1830s, and many people had gotten the idea that this new law was designed to turn out young officers, the same way that West Point did. They were wrong. The way that Congress imagined it, and the way that the navy ran it, it was a system for making seamen, not officers. Once people figured this out, they grew disenchanted.

So the program started to falter, almost as soon as it started. Southard had once predicted that twelve hundred boys would join up in the first year or so, but he was nowhere close. The total number of boys to have enlisted had barely reached that number even six or seven years after Congress first passed the law.

But the program wasn't a total debacle. Some officers, among them Matthew C. Perry, thought that it was doing all right. He claimed that when a trained boy came off a school ship and helped crew a regular vessel, he usually proved a better young sailor than most of the rest of the seamen. Of course that, too, caused problems. A ship's crew was literally a pretty rum bunch, soused in spirits, in love with foul words and tobacco, and happy to pass on its ways to teenagers. Perry liked the apprentices, but even he could see the need to keep the men from corrupting them.

By 1841 Perry was a commodore, in command of the New York Navy Yard and all of its ships, when he got an idea that seemed brilliant. Why not get the boys out of their school ships and send them on a training cruise, a whole crew of them, with just enough older hands, specially picked, to help the youngsters learn what they needed to learn? The prospect of a sailing adventure, perhaps in tropical waters, on a smart man-of-war, would interest boys and their parents and with luck help boost enlistments. It would show the truth of what Perry was claiming, that the apprentices were fine young sailors. And it would avoid the danger that impressionable boys would pick up older men's bad habits. Only a few trusty sailors would ship with them. For the most part, the boys would be associating only with other boys, all of them equally innocent. What harm could possibly come of that?

Quite simply, the plan seemed perfect.

Of course Perry had to make sure. This was to be a high-profile cruise, and he didn't want a single thing to go wrong. So he planned everything very carefully. *Somers* was fitting out in New York, brand-new and ready to go, freshly commissioned in April. The new steamships were coming along, but their bleeding-edge technology was inelegant and uncertain. *Somers,* on the other hand, was a smart, handy brig, one that would draw a lot of admiration, and small enough for a crew of boys to handle. Perry even gave her an official mission, just to add to the voyage's prestige. He bade her sail to the African coast and find the ship *Vandalia,* engaged on anti-slavery duty there, and deliver important dispatches. He carefully chose her officer complement, each officer with years of experience, but each of them young—this was to be a ship of youth, from her keel to her captain—and two of them related to Perry. These were men whom he knew and trusted. Finally, he even helped choose the *Somers's* four midshipmen, one of whom was also his son, and two others of whom had ties to him by marriage or family friendship. The problem was with the fourth.

Because midshipmen, as junior officers, were important, Perry wanted to be careful in choosing them, just as careful as he was being in every other respect. But it was in choosing midshipmen that he made his mistake, the mistake that would help bring a nightmare to pass, although he could never have known it. And so it happened that his picture-perfect training cruise, on a spanking-new warship, this showcase of naval ability, this triumph in the making that was to show American sea power at its best, included a young man who should never have set foot on the deck of a ship.

His name was Philip Spencer.

PART TWO

Spencer

MAYBE HE DID what he did because of testosterone, the hormone, the drug that made men become hunters, seeking conquests of sex and of blood. Possibly it was due to his parents, one whipping too many, one spanking too few. It might have been something that didn't yet have a name, a term of art that still awaited invention: transference, or repression, or obsession. Perhaps it was simply a mean streak, a manifestation of original sin; perhaps he was simply no good. Maybe, just maybe, it was nothing at all—nothing, that is, but others' perceptions, others' overactive imaginings. But *something* caused it. And whatever the cause, it all turned, in the end, on young Philip Spencer.

To another teenager, of course, he wouldn't have seemed young at all. He was eighteen, nearly nineteen, in 1842. Today we would hesitate to call someone that age a "boy." The word is nearly pejorative, almost as bad as "girl." They wouldn't have called him a boy back then either. By then he would have been considered a man—a young one, yes, but a man nevertheless. Still, he lacked a certain maturity, an experience of life. Psychologically he was still developing, more so than men just a few years older than he. The newly awakened hormones were touching his blood with fire, a new and powerful fire that he would have found hard to control. Man . . . boy . . . call him what you will, he had not yet fully escaped the cyclonic days of his youth.

And he was a youth adrift in a world of youth. One recalls the motto Captain Nemo chose for his remarkable submarine *Nautilus: Mobilis in mobili,* mobile within a mobile element. For America, too, was a youth, an adolescent. Many a woman, many a man, was still alive, having been born in the colonies, a subject of His Majesty George III. Many recalled the days of the War of Independence, if only as a childhood event. Still more recalled the frontier: the place, the existence, where the lights of civilization grew dim and everything, even human life, was in flux. That frontier still thrived, though now much farther inland, in the continent's secret heart, and the nation was now its own. And everyone knew of the coming of industry, and reform, and democracy, the wild rush of the common citizen to take his place on the nation's stage. America was changing radically, just as an adolescent changes radically, in body, mind, and soul. Spencer was change in a country, a world, of change. And even when he was a very small child, events were occurring that would shape—perhaps warp—his nature.

In a way it all started in the Caribbean, the place where it might have ended up if things had gone according to young Spencer's plans. That's where some people said that William Morgan was hanged as a pirate.

That was almost certainly gossip. Morgan had been kidnapped from the Canandaigua jail in the night in western New York in the late summer of 1826; but despite all the stories of what happened to him afterward, we have no proof that anyone but his abductors ever saw him alive again.

Canandaigua's officials had imprisoned him on a pretext, his failure to make good on a debt of less than three dollars. Then, after sunset, three men appeared at the jail, paid the debt, and escorted Morgan away. The jailer's wife remembered hearing a shrill whistle and looking out through her window to see what was happening. She saw Morgan struggling in the street with two men, yelling "Murder!" at the top of his lungs. Then there were more men, and a carriage rolled up. The men threw Morgan inside, and it flew off into the darkness. That, it appears, was the last of William Morgan.

In reality he was probably killed and his weighted-down body thrown into the Niagara River, somewhere below the falls. But no clearly identifiable corpse was ever found; hence the rash of Morgan sightings in the following years, everywhere from Cuba to the Ottoman Empire.

The men who'd sprung Morgan were Masons, members of the secret society that dated all the way back to the cathedral stoneworkers' guilds of medieval times, or even (according to some) to those who had built the Temple of King Solomon's day. Morgan, too, was a Mason, or at least he'd posed as one. But when times got hard, and he simultaneously found himself ostracized by his brethren for his rambunctious behavior, he got an idea. He'd write an exposé, a book describing all of the secret, intricate rituals, the signs and the passwords, of the Masonic Order. That would make him some money, and it would show the Masons that they shouldn't have messed with him.

People had already beaten him to it. Books like the one that he wanted to write were already available in England and the United States, too. But Morgan seemed not to know. Neither did the Masons themselves. When they found out what he was up to, they started a campaign of intimidation against him: arson attempts, spurious criminal charges, and threatening newspaper notices were all part of their program. Finally came Morgan's jailing, followed by his abduction.

The result was a steadily gathering wave of resentment and anger toward Freemasonry. Americans, who'd built for themselves a new quasi-religious faith—a faith based upon patriotism, self-reliance, and tolerance for dissent—were intolerant of anything that seemed to threaten that worldview. Freemasonry, with its private lodges and rituals, its deeply rooted and well-connected "Old Boy network," seemed quite undemocratic, and the America of the late 1820s was getting more democratic with every passing day. The Masons just didn't fit into the American faith. Never mind that George Washington himself had been a Mason. Such cults were un-American. And in the wake of Morgan's abduction, people decided to get the Masons under control, and to ferret them out, removing them from political and ministerial office.

The immediate outcome was a series of criminal kidnapping trials of four men accused of Morgan's abduction. After that came a social pressure aimed at the heart of Freemasonry, and then a political party dedicated to the Masons' destruction. Congregations demanded that clergymen give up either their Masonic memberships or their pulpits. Women banned their daughters from marrying Masons and forced their husbands to quit the society. It was all part of a highly emotional time, in a part of New York that was wracked by religious revivalist spirit, a region that folks called the "burned-over district." It spread outward from there, toward the West and New England, propelling young Anti-Masons into successful high-profile lives, men such as Thurlow Weed, Thaddeus Stevens, and William H. Seward, who would later become secretary of state.

Seward wasn't the only Anti-Mason to make it into the national Cabinet. Another was John Canfield Spencer. Fifteen years later, this New Yorker of high social standing, an accomplished attorney, would become President John Tyler's secretary of war, and then his secretary of the treasury. He would even win nomination to the federal Supreme Court, although the Senate wouldn't confirm him. But in 1827 he was just a lawyer who got in on the ground floor of Anti-Masonry by prosecuting some of the Morgan kidnapping cases.

Spencer had a young son at this time, a boy of three or four named Philip. For the next few years, as the child grew toward adolescence, he probably had a chance to see his father denounce Freemasonry and the idea of secret societies, likely even before he could fully understand what it was all about. Maybe, later on, he even read Morgan's book. His father probably had a copy somewhere. It is even possible that at some point he heard Morgan's name mentioned in connection with Cuba and piracy. It would explain a great deal.

John Canfield Spencer may have been an Anti-Mason, but children often rebel, not just against their parents, but against society, too. Eighteen twenties and 1830s America was a place and time of rebellion against unofficial connections and power, things that it thought it saw in Freemasonry. But for an alienated, restless young spirit who was approaching his teenage years during the height of the Anti-Masonic movement, the things about Freemasonry that angered and scared other people—the secrecy, the signs, the sense of belonging—would have been a perfect magnet, especially if that spirit were troubled. And there were definite signs, long before he ever came aboard *Somers,* that Philip Spencer was troubled indeed.

He seemed a very bright boy, enrolling in Hobart (then called Geneva) College in 1838 at the age of fourteen or fifteen, and he impressed more than one person, not merely with his intelligence but with how he failed to use it. "The ease with which he mastered the Greek and Latin is remarkable," a fellow student later remembered. But he seemed quiet to his teachers and classmates, and he had problems with his grades, two of the classic signs of troubled youth. "Such a mind, properly trained, is capable of doing great things in life," said another acquaintance. "Left to itself it runs to a tangle of rose briars—a waste all the same even if it does smell sweet in June."

Tall, pale, with a certain delicacy about him, he could be nice enough. Some people spoke of him warmly, at least many years later, as having been pleasant and kind. Still, there was something about him, something about the look in his eyes. "He would have been thought good-looking, if not handsome," an acquaintance recalled—if it hadn't been for those eyes of his. And though he could be sociable, at heart he seemed to have that classic sign of gravely disordered youth: he was a loner. "He seemed to live very much by himself and to mingle little with the other students," wrote a former schoolgirl who'd known him. "If he had any intimates I do not know who they were, and my belief is that he had none."

He was a cutup, showing little regard for authority. He knew better than that, or should have known it, given his intelligence. But though he could do well when he wished, he often avoided his books, leaving him plenty of time for mischief. He "was quite a favorite with many of his schoolmates," admitted a former associate, "though his queer stories and sharp tricks made him unpopular with others." One professor remembered the spectacle that Spencer had made of himself at a commencement ceremony. The boy himself wasn't graduating; in fact he never would. But he joined the procession anyway, at the tail end, wearing a comical, conical hat, a dunce's cap, with a streamer attached that read "Patriarch of the Freshman Class." Sometimes he left campus and went into nearby Canandaigua—the site of Morgan's abduction—without official permission. He played a role in a minor election day student riot in 1840. But his greatest obsession was with piracy.

He had a volume of grisly stories called *The Pirates Own Book,* and he talked now and then to a classmate about his plans to go west and become a freebooter, a land pirate, somewhere on the western rivers. The Ohio had once been a great place for that, but now the frontier was moving on, and Spencer had the Mississippi in mind. The frontier, of course, had always drawn malcontents. But he never got the chance. After three years of disciplinary actions and unacceptable grades, his father pulled him out of the college.

The world still had a lot of education in store for him, some of it brutally tough, but only a little of it would come from schoolbooks. John Canfield Spencer, still trying to make something of his son, now enrolled him in Union College, his own alma mater. The president there, Eliphalet Nott, was known for riding herd on his students, and that was clearly what Spencer needed. Maybe Nott could do something with him.

It was no use. Spencer was still more interested in his fantasies and his dreams than in his studies. Arriving at Union, he took one look at its fraternities and decided he didn't like them. He wanted his own instead, consisting of people of his own choosing, a society rich in secret and ritual . . . something resembling the Masons.

Within a month of his coming, he had one. Seeking out nine other students, he proposed, and then helped initiate, what is today Chi Psi fraternity. One of his co-founders later wrote of Philip's main interests. "Spencer, who gave most of his time to the business of organization, devised the signs, grips, and passwords, and made arrangements for the badge of Chi Psi to be worn by the members," he recalled. It was almost obsessive. "He always took a great delight in the[se] initiations, grips, signs, and passwords, and studied how to make them more mysterious and impressive."

Something was wrong with him. At least people later said so. One Union acquaintance cast him as a Byronic sort, one of those people who "become morbidly sensitive, renounce allegiance to a false order of things, are commonly misunderstood, or whether misunderstood or not imagine themselves to be so." And whatever his problem, Union College was unable to fix it. Having stayed just long enough to found his fraternity, he was then on his way again, this time seeking adventure for real. He would find far more than he wanted.

America wasn't lacking in opportunities for adventure. The east was starting to grow tame, domesticated, by now. Everything to the Mississippi's Atlantic side was getting very "civilized." But there was still half a continent open, unsettled, ungoverned by anything more than tribes and self-restraint and brute force. The freebooting life that Spencer envisioned was no fabrication; people were living it just a few weeks' travel away from the colleges he gave up on. People were going west. They had always done so, chasing the fleeing sun, in search of something elusive: conquest, happiness, peace. Spencer could try for that life if he wanted; all he had to do was head into the heart of the continent and put everything at risk. The western frontier was one limitless possibility.

But there was another frontier as well, not to west but to east: closer, less friendly, more deadly, so old that it had been ancient when the continents had been young.

It was the sea.

It was the sea that most young Americans chose when they set out in search of adventure and fame, at least until the Gold Rush. It was accessible from the big eastern cities, where most people lived. It put the adventurer in touch not with just one continent but with nearly every part of the globe. And, even more than the landward frontier, it forced a man to come to terms with himself, his society, and his demons. There, a seemingly infinite distance out on the face of the deep, there is no escape, not from shipmates or captain or tempest or self. The sea, God's powerful servant, ruthlessly ordains the conditions of life, isolating a ship and having its way with both it and its denizens. All they can do is react. Life at sea is the ultimate crucible.

The isolation and discipline of that life both can be advantageous, and life aboard a nineteenth-century ship, with its great isolation, demanded utmost discipline. And if things went wrong—if unpleasant incidents happened—they happened far, far from genteel New York and Washington drawing rooms, out of the sight of polite society. Given what young Spencer seemed to be turning into, one can imagine that these advantages would appeal to his father, the politician.

Spencer himself seemed to have chosen the sea. Within a few weeks of leaving Union College, he signed on to a Nantucket whaler, planning on shipping "before the mast," as the phrase went—that is, as a common sailor. But even now he lacked the resolve to apply himself. He backed out at the last minute, hiring a substitute to take his place. At any rate, *someone* hired a substitute. His friends, perhaps, or maybe his parents, might have had something to do with it. But the whaler sailed without Spencer.

Then came weeks of drifting, followed by another attempt. John Canfield Spencer was secretary of war by now, well connected in New York and sitting in the same Cabinet as the secretary of the navy, Abel P. Upshur. By November 1841, Philip reported to a receiving ship at the New York Navy Yard with a warrant as acting midshipman signed by Upshur himself. He was accompanied by his uncle, Captain William A. Spencer, who was already an accomplished naval officer. Philip was joining up, and at a level that showed his status and family ties at work. This wouldn't be life before the mast. He was now an officer-in-training.

America, at the time, had no naval academy. It never had had one. It had a school for army officers, dating from Thomas Jefferson's time, and other nations, notably France, had similar schools for officers in the naval service. But Great Britain did not. His Britannic Majesty's Navy relied upon on-the-job training for both its men and its officers, instead of cooping them up in classrooms. This had always been the American way, for at least a couple of good reasons. First, although France had sometimes influenced America, the United States always looked mainly to England when it came to matters of law, and culture, and military organization. British ways were familiar.

The second reason was even more compelling. The British usually won at sea, and the French usually lost. Quiberon Bay, the Saints, the Nile, Trafalgar, and a hundred smaller engagements spoke to the success of the British approach. So that was the approach that America took when training its young naval officers.

This meant that midshipmen, the junior officers in the making, learned their craft on board ship. The American service offered practically no formal education on land, and it had no system at all for selecting and screening potential human material. The approach was trial and error. By hook or crook—or by pulling political strings—boys got hold of midshipmen's warrants; they then went to sea, and they, and the navy, found out what they were made of. If they took to the seafaring life, then in time they might earn lieutenants' commissions and later move up from there to the respectable rank of commander and then to the rarefied heights of post-captain. Otherwise they stayed midshipmen forever, or they simply left the navy. But if they stayed they could, if negligent or incompetent or a dozen other things, cause serious mischief.

This was the system that Philip Spencer had entered, largely through his family's connections, while other boys scrabbled in vain to get in.

Unfortunately—for both him and the navy—nothing much in him changed. He was still a rebel, and he even got worse. By now he'd discovered alcohol, and before long came a drunken brawl. Fights happened among common sailors sometimes, but officers, even ones as junior as Spencer, were supposed to set good examples.

Passed Midshipman William Craney had the deck when Philip Spencer first reported aboard the receiving ship, and the newcomer's uncle asked Craney to take Spencer in hand. Craney was glad to do so, or so he later said. Having the son of a cabinet member as a friend, after all, couldn't hurt anyone's career.

As a passed midshipman, Craney was almost, but not quite, a commissioned officer, a lieutenant. As such he had his own stateroom; midshipmen and acting midshipmen did not. So, as part of his cultivation of Spencer, Craney let him make use of his quarters, a valuable commodity on board ship where personal space was a rarity.

Spencer used it freely, at all hours, often leaving a light burning when he shouldn't have. And he stored liquor there, too, several bottles of it. None of this was good. The navy wasn't a social or drinking club. Still less was it a democracy, whatever may be happening on shore. Spencer was ignoring the rules, and Craney started issuing warnings.

They didn't accomplish much. Spencer went on unauthorized

liberty, often got drunk, and ignored Craney's orders to stop. Finally someone reported Craney to the ship's first lieutenant for having a light in his stateroom after hours. That was the final straw.

One night Craney awakened to find Spencer in his room, rummaging around for a hidden bottle. Craney ordered him out; Spencer, drunk again, told the senior midshipman that he would go when he was ready.

Craney told him again to get out, and this time Spencer hit him. Craney sprang out of his bunk and threw himself at the boy, hurling him into the wardroom. A minute later other officers were on the scene, separating the two and ordering Spencer below to the berth deck.

Craney's impulse was to report Spencer. Striking a superior officer was a hanging offense. But the ship's first lieutenant warned him not to go through with it, in light of Spencer's connections. Then, not too long afterward, another fight happened. Craney was down in steerage, teaching the younger midshipmen how to use his sextant, a sophisticated device for measuring angles and making lunar observations. While he was looking along the instrument—it was of very high quality—Spencer, without warning, came up from behind and went after him, knocking him and his chair to the floor.

Craney leapt up and jumped in Spencer's direction; it took several people to hold him back. Others, meanwhile, grabbed Spencer and dragged him away. For his part Craney calmed down, but only somewhat. This time he did write a report to the Navy Department, describing all that had happened between Spencer and him, and he then sent it in.

The next thing he knew, he'd been summoned before Commodore Matthew C. Perry, who commanded the New York Navy Yard. Perry began by asking the passed midshipman not to pursue the matter. Craney replied that he couldn't do that. Spencer had committed a grave offense, and more than once, the second time in front of a crowd of witnesses. Reporting it was a matter of duty, and it was also a matter of honor. But that wasn't enough for Perry. The commodore pulled out Craney's report and handed it back to him; he hadn't sent it onward to Washington. He also told Craney that Spencer had drawn an assignment on the U.S. frigate *John Adams*.

Craney saw what was happening, or at least he thought that he did. The son of the secretary of war was getting a break from the system. With that he gave up. He was so disgusted, in fact, that within days he resigned from the navy.

His estimate was probably right. But at least Spencer had enough sense to make appropriate statements of sorrow, though he refused to take all the blame. "I would respectfully represent that the aggravation which induced the assault was of such a character that my feelings were highly excited," he wrote Perry. "Laboring under the imputation of being a liar, I was led to an act of insubordination and breach of discipline, which reflection has taught me was highly improper."

That was it, then. Spencer claimed that Craney was the bad guy, and given the latter's own spotty record—he'd once been dismissed from the service—it wasn't a clear-cut case. So Perry probably decided to get Spencer out of the way, assigning him to a warship that would take him deep into the South Atlantic. There, at least, if he kept cutting up, not many people would see it.

The navy was small, but as protector of America's mercantile interests, it had to show the flag all over the world. It didn't really have a fleet as such, an organized unit of ships of the line whose duty it was to sail into battle together and slug it out with an enemy fleet. It had few ships of the line at all, and they sailed singly, lone wolves of the sea. Its real power lay in smaller-size vessels—its frigates, its sloops and its brigs, faster, lighter, and cheaper to operate than massive battleships. They were more useful in peacetime, too, when enemies were likely to be pirates, slavers, or small non-European states, and not the world's Great Powers. In the absence of fleets, and to coordinate naval activity, the Navy Department had broken things down into squadrons, centering them on areas where the nation had strategic and mercantile interests: the Mediterranean Squadron, the West Indies Squadron, the Africa Squadron, the far-flung Pacific Squadron. Spencer's new ship *John Adams* was setting forth to join the Brazil Squadron, weeks and thousands of sea miles away from American shores.

A squadron was under the command of a commodore, but he was more administrative head than fleet commander. Each squadron's operating area was so large, and its number of ships so small, that the vessels almost never sailed in a single group, going their separate ways instead. This led to a lot of autonomy among individual ships' captains. The officers and crew of a ship, of course, always had the "old man" to watch out for—his power over them in practical terms was near-total—but they, too, were aware of just how isolated they were from society. That knowledge may have led to more breaches of discipline, since (according to congressional laws, at least) a captain could go only so far in punishing those who served under him. So it was just bad luck for Spencer that when he went on a drunken spree while in Rio de Janeiro in May, quite soon after *John Adams* arrived on station, the squadron's commodore was nearby, and he heard all about it a few days later.

Alcohol was a staple in the American navy, the high point of most sailors' day, the medication of choice for thousands. When Winston Churchill, early in the following century, curtly dismissed British naval tradition as "rum, sodomy, and the lash," he might as well have been talking about the American service. It was hyperbole: by the 1900s, things had changed greatly. But this was 1842, and the grog flowed freely.

Spencer, however, was young, and an officer in training as well. Officers were supposed to be gentlemen, of a better class than the men they commanded. And public drunkenness, especially when it was extreme, was frowned on. And Spencer had gotten stinking, disgustingly drunk, possibly even on duty, and gotten into a fight with some locals. He admitted as much to Commodore Charles Morris after his arrest. "I . . . drank considerably," he confessed. "When I went on shore for the day, by permission of the first lieutenant, I was overcome by the liquors I had drank. . . . I am perfectly sensible, sir," he continued, "that I behaved in a manner highly disgraceful to myself and the service." But others in the squadron had done the same before, he argued. He shouldn't be singled out.

Morris wasn't interested in the defense. He wanted to make an example of someone, and Spencer was it. He knew who Spencer was. The boy himself, perhaps trying to intimidate him, had reminded him of the fact. But what better example than someone special? It would show other officers that they couldn't expect anything different. Morris, unlike Craney, had nothing to fear. He was a post-captain, a commodore, a squadron commander, near the hierarchy's very top.

Still, he wasn't without leniency. Spencer had asked him for permission to resign rather than having to face a court-martial. Very well. So be it. For the good of the service, replied Morris, "I have concluded to withdraw the charge . . . upon receipt of your resignation, and to forward your resignation to the secretary of the navy with the facts in the case and to direct your return to the United States, there to receive his decision upon your conduct."

Morris had called Spencer's bluff, if that was what it had been. Spencer now had no option, and he sent his resignation to Morris. Morris himself lacked the authority to accept it. All he could do was send it on its way to the secretary, which he promptly did. But that would take months, and meanwhile here was Spencer, still under arrest. By sending him home, the commodore could wash his hands of the problem completely. He had a ship preparing to sail for North America, so he would send Spencer with it. "You will report yourself," he ordered the acting midshipman, "to the commanding officer of the U.S. Frigate *Potomac* to return to the U. States in that ship—there to receive the decision of the secretary of the navy."

It was a reprieve, though Morris might not know it. As long as his resignation hadn't actually been accepted, maybe Spencer could still get out of this jam. He wanted to and he thought that he could. The voyage home was undoubtedly hard, with him probably living carefully under the captain's watchful eyes. Upon returning to Boston he wrote his brother John an upbeat letter, describing the beauty of the tropics—the fruit there, he said, was "the most delicious in the world"—and asking for a loan of some money. He also said that he was ready to apply for sea duty again as soon as he was detached from *Potomac*. He wrote Upshur, too, expressing contrition for what he had done, and he now waited to hear the answer.

His father's fellow Cabinet minister was stern, but not totally unforgiving. "I am mortified to learn that one more young officer of the navy and one brought up as you must have been has been guilty of the degrading and disqualifying vice of drunkenness," he told Spencer. But given the expressions of sorrow, the secretary decided, he would give the acting midshipman one final chance. He was now on probation. If his conduct henceforth was what "the country has a right to expect from one who wears her uniform," Upshur wrote, "what has passed will be forgotten, but if otherwise it will be remembered against you." With that he concluded, returning Spencer's resignation and telling the youngster that he would be getting some orders soon. But Spencer had been warned, and in no uncertain terms.

Upshur was as good as his word. Barely a week later Spencer received his next message.

Report to Capt. M. C. Perry for duty on board the U.S. brig *Somers*.

PART THREE

Mackenzie

THE UNITED STATES NAVY was still in its youth in 1842. Its infancy lay behind it; already it had seen action in three small-scale wars and it had fought a good many other battles as well, not counting the American Revolution. But still, it was young. Its ways were those of canvas and rope, of sun and squall, of stiff breezes nearly unclouded by the vapor and smoke of steam engines, or fouled by the radiation of nuclear power. A century beyond *Somers* it would become the mightiest collection of fleets the world has ever known. The thrust across the Pacific in the campaign against Japan was the most stunning projection of force on a planetary scale that can be found in the annals of history, yet it took place even as the navy was helping to wage another Herculean campaign in the Atlantic, on the other side of the world. Rome's sustained assault on Carthage; the Armada; the deployments of Desert Storm; even, perhaps, the British Empire's subjugation of Napoleon at sea; all these pale in comparison. The American service of 1842 bears the same relationship to that later, globe-girdling navy that a gawky adolescent boy has to himself as a full-grown man in his prime. It was a very small force, with just a few handfuls of vessels. Its administration was outmoded and clumsy, its officer corps small, its body of regular professional seamen nearly nonexistent. Its mission was only vaguely understood, either by itself or its civilian masters, and its funding was minuscule.

Even with all of these shortcomings, though, the 1840s navy was growing, witnessing reorganization, technological breakthroughs, and refinements of mission. All these changes hinted at what it would someday become. But growth is rarely painless. And the small group of officers who were the heart of the navy were the ones who would have to endure that pain. One of them was a thirty-nine-year-old commander named Alexander Slidell Mackenzie.

"Commander" was his rank in the early 1840s. He was a notch below the exalted level of "post-captain," the commission to which all officers aspired. Yet he commanded warships, and so he often was called, by courtesy, "captain." And, more important, as a commanding officer, he assumed an almost godlike power over any ship he skippered, whatever his actual rank.

Herman Melville, who would go on to write *Moby-Dick* and still later *Billy Budd*, was at sea around this time. He spent several months before the mast on the frigate *United States*. A few years later he drew on his time in the navy to describe "The World in a Man-of-War" to readers in his partly autobiographical novel *White-Jacket*. And one of the things he described for an ever more democratic society was the captain's total authority. "A ship is a bit of terra firma cut off from the main; it is a state in itself; and the captain is its king," he explained. "It is no limited monarchy, where the sturdy Commons have a right to petition, and snarl if they please; but almost a despotism, like the Grand Turk's." That would have been good enough for most folks to get the point, but Melville wanted to be quite sure. "The captain's word is law," he continued. "He never speaks but in the imperative mood. When he stands on his quarter-deck at sea, he absolutely commands as far as the eye can reach. Only the moon and the stars are beyond his jurisdiction. He is lord and master of the sun."

Mackenzie, however, didn't seem to fit the mold. "A man of medium height," wrote one observer, "with a fine head covered rather thinly by light auburn hair, a high forehead, and of an amiable and pleasing rather than stern and commanding presence." He doesn't sound like the right kind of character to play the role of a Captain Bligh, which is how some people later tried to portray him. Another acquaintance concurred, remarking upon Mackenzie's "calmness, gentleness, and refinement." Many others agreed; Mackenzie's behavior was that of a well-mannered gentleman. "Lawyers, I suppose, were children once," wrote Charles Lamb, the English essayist. He might have said the same thing of captains of warships. Whatever Mackenzie ended up doing, he began life in the usual way.

He began it, though, under a different name. He was officially Alexander Slidell; only later did he legally add the "Mackenzie" to perpetuate the name of his mother's childless brother. And though he would rise to command more than one warship, his career had to start several rungs below that, as a lowly midshipman in a new, mostly peacetime, navy.

Eleven-year-old Alexander Slidell joined up on the first day of January in 1815. Two days later the navy made its first tactical use of a steam-powered vessel. The coincidence tells us a lot. Steam was fairly new to the seas, and as a force in naval warfare, it would skew the narrow, crabbed world that the boy had just entered. He was coming of age in a season of little giants. The navy's handful of ships, consisting of a few frigates and smaller vessels of war, every last one of them powered by sail, often managed great feats in the service's early years. Isaac Hull, in the famous forty-four-gun *Constitution;* Stephen Decatur in the frigate *United States* and David Porter of *Essex:* during the War of 1812, on those rare occasions when the odds against the British were even, American ships tended to give excellent accounts of themselves.

But things never do stay the same. As 1815 dawned, the war that had spawned these commanders, these ship-on-ship actions, had officially ended. A good thing, too, since by then the little American navy, outmanned and outgunned by sixty to one, had been forced back into its ports, blockaded into near-total humiliation. The glory days were gone, at least for the time being. And steam would change nearly everything.

The war was technically over, but a battle remained to be fought, just below the crucial town of New Orleans, gatekeeper of the American west. Andrew Jackson, the famed frontier general, was in command there, and on January 3 he spotted Henry Shreve's *Enterprise,* a merchant side-wheeler, one of the first on the Mississippi. Driven by steam, she could easily travel upriver, a commonplace thing today but a marvel in 1815. Quickly Jackson seized on her power to treat the currents and winds with contempt, turning her into a transport. She became a useful weapon in the final Anglo-American battle.

Useful: revolutionary, even. Slowly, almost imperceptibly, steam had started undoing thousands of years of maritime history. Two generations after Slidell joined the American service, it would scarcely resemble the navy that people had known in the 1812 years. Even one generation removed, it would be different in many respects. That final generation to be dominated by sail would be peopled by a race of sailors and officers who were a dying breed, nearly the last of their kind, who watched as their ways came under siege. Alexander Slidell was one of them.

His likeness shows an alert intellect and a genuine cheerfulness. Nothing in it suggests a quarterdeck tyrant. He was a healthy man, too. Conditions in the navy can be rough, and Slidell served everywhere, in his time, from the germ-ridden Caribbean to the tempestuous, ill-named Pacific. As far as we know, the decades of rough duty did nothing to alter his constitution or character, but beyond doubt they tempered his steel. No one who served as a line officer in the American navy was a stranger to the requirements of discipline. Officers had to subject themselves to it constantly, and they also had to mete it out.

The navy was out of step that way. It hadn't always been; before the rise of republicanism, before the rise of democracy, life in the

Western world was a class-based thing, even in North America. There was not a lot of social mobility. In the British Empire, in the France of the Bourbons, in the principalities throughout the Old World, a commoner simply couldn't rise to be king, no matter how smart or skilled or industrious he was. His bloodlines—or lack of them—predestined him, if not to a precise slot in life, at least to a general category. It worked the other way, too, of course; around 1600, Shakespeare has Henry V ruing the ceremony that is the only reward for wearing the heavy crown, and even as late as the 1930s, Edward VIII drew heavy censure for abandoning the duty imposed by his birth for the sake of a selfish, forbidden relationship.

The United States *was* different, though, at least to a degree. The fluidity of frontier life—and in the beginning the frontier was all of America—was a great leveling influence. On North America's shores, the second son of an earl would starve just as fast as the meanest pauper unless he was willing to till the forest's soil, to girdle and cut down its trees, to hunt its elusive game. Nevertheless, the old ways died hard. With the coming of the Jacksonian age, with social reform, with the rise of the common woman and man, further barriers fell. White male voting became widespread. Vested legal property rights came under assault. Women began to campaign for an equal political voice, and equal social footing as well. But there were still classes. There were still places where no debate was allowed. There were still institutions in which one man could whip another to ribbons if that was his wish. One was the plantation world of slavery. Another was young Slidell's realm, the world of the United States Navy.

On the rare occasions when Americans stopped to think of their navy, they tended to picture a service that had begun in the rich, noble English tradition, with two castes of men: the officers, the small elite class whose members held their commissions from the Crown, and the common sailors, the skilled and unskilled laborers, the brute force that conquered the elements and made everything work. The army had this arrangement, too, of course. But in America the army was small, and the state militias, much more democratic than the national corps of soldiers, were the dominant part of the military. The navy, on the other hand, was a powerful standing force, in charge of the world's most powerful weapons systems, beyond the control or even the view of the citizens, under the command of post-captains and commodores who, while out on the deep, answered to no one but God. America didn't even have admirals. The nearly royal pomp and perquisites of the office were too much for a republic to stomach. Post-captains were bad enough, especially when they commanded whole squadrons, thus earning the honorific of commodore. Below post-captain came the rank of commander; then came lieutenant, and then the nether regions of midshipmen and passed midshipmen, the latter waiting, sometimes for years, for promotion, until a lieutenant's slot finally opened up. Below the midshipman was the acting midshipman, appointed at will by ship's captains. Midshipmen, acting or not, were officers in training, usually (though not always) young. Far below these were the warrant officers, and then, at the bottom, came the various flavors of sailors.

As far as advancement went, anything below a midshipman was nearly inconsequential. Almost nobody came up from the ranks and got a commission, just as very few midshipmen ever got close to reaching post rank. But for those who became post-captains—indeed, for any man who rose to the command of a warship, no matter how small and modest she was—the power was awesome and heady. True, command of a warship meant endless responsibility. But it also meant control of one of the world's most lethal devices, an extraordinarily expensive thing of strength and beauty and speed and death and destruction, which obeyed the whim of its master. Command of a warship meant de facto, and often de jure, life-or-death power over every living thing aboard her and within range of her guns, over anything she happened upon out on the sea. Melville was so right. If warship commanders weren't aristocracy, then nobody else on earth was.

This was the world that eleven-year-old Alexander Slidell had joined.

His rise in the service was fast enough. Entering as a midshipman, a natural start for the son of a well-to-do New York merchant-banker fallen upon hard times, he had a shot at the top, unlike the common sailors before the mast—if he showed that he had what it took. And he seemed to show it quickly. Ten years after signing on, he became a lieutenant, and then only after taking a leave of absence. He put that leave to good use, commanding a merchant ship for a time while he was in his early twenties. That sort of experience was good for upward mobility. It also didn't hurt that his sister Jane had married up-and-coming naval officer Matthew C. Perry, just days, in fact, before Slidell became a midshipman. By the mid-1820s, Perry was beginning to make waves and really get himself noticed. Before too long he would be in a perfect position to help his contacts and relatives.

Slidell had other connections, too. His brother John had gone to New Orleans and made it big there, eventually coming back east as a member of Congress. Naval officers needed good patronage, and being a Slidell, related by marriage to Perrys, was probably advantageous. But Alexander Slidell had plenty of merit. He was a studious sort, and a naval officer—if he were to rise to command—had to be not merely conversant, but an accomplished expert, in many things: seamanship, shiphandling, tactics, navigation, diplomacy, and gunnery, to name just a few. We have almost no indication that Slidell was lacking in any of these, with one or two big exceptions. But to them he added a talent for writing that few naval officers shared.

In 1829 Lieutenant Slidell published a two-volume book, *A Year in Spain,* a travelogue recounting his sojourns there while on leave from the navy. An author with a nautical background wasn't unheard of in Jacksonian America; Melville, James Fenimore Cooper, and Richard Henry Dana, in whose circles Slidell moved, were in the same category. But, unlike them, Slidell was a professional sailor and not just a man with some sailing experience, which made him a rarity. And he wrote of his profession. In 1833 he published his second book, *Popular Essays on Naval Subjects*.

Although he was friend and relative to the reform-minded Perry, at heart Slidell had a traditional streak, much like the bulk of the naval officer corps, and *Popular Essays* shows it. While discussing naval history, up-to-date ordnance, and new methods of shipbuilding, the book mentions steam power barely at all. Slidell, like most of his brother officers, had little experience with the new technology and little appreciation of what it might accomplish.

One thing Slidell did discuss, though, was the Battle of Lake Erie. As naval battles went it had been on the small side, but for strategic effect it was large, and for propaganda purposes it was huge. It had happened on September 10, 1813. Matthew C. Perry's older brother, Oliver Hazard Perry, had taken on a British squadron commanded by a veteran of Trafalgar. The contest was one of flylike vessels on a miniature ocean: Perry commanded a total of fifty-four guns, scarcely more than a single heavy frigate. The British guns were still fewer, but they had longer range. Perry had the weather gage, and in the early afternoon, battle flag flying from his ship, he led his squadron downwind. Taking volley after volley from the British artillery, he finally got within range, loosing a broadside that tore enemy spars and lines to pieces. After two hours he managed the classic, long-sought, and rarely achieved maneuver that obsessed officers during the gunnery age from the Armada to World War II: he crossed the enemy's T, presenting all of his line-ahead broadsides to the line-ahead British bows at right angles, delivering maximum possible firepower onto a row of ships that couldn't shoot back.

Because of Perry's fine tactics, his opponent became the first English commander in history to surrender an entire squadron. That surrender gave the United States undisputed control of all the Great Lakes, and thus security along its whole northwestern flank, ending the threat of invasion there, as well as terminating British-backed

Indian raids. It was one of the more heroic moments of a messy and unheroic war, at least from the American viewpoint.

That battle eventually led to a different kind of conflict, one between Slidell and James Fenimore Cooper. The two men were oddly similar. Both were New Yorkers; both had backgrounds as sailors and writers. Both had an uneasy relationship to America's newfound democracy; both lauded the common man while continuing to flirt with elitism's attractions. And both, despite that flirtation, were self-made men, so much so that each formally changed his name, remaking himself in a way that reflected the American frontier spirit.

But there were big differences. While Slidell, now Mackenzie, was kind and affable, Cooper was a hard-bitten critic of the American way of life. The latter's writings had made him into a celebrity. But those writings were uneven, and some of his books were flops. Mackenzie, on the other hand, was liked in both Europe and America, even though he never achieved the literary fame of Cooper. "Very quiet, yet so kind and mild, so true and unaffected," said philosopher Francis Lieber, "that one cannot help liking, nay, cherishing him." This isn't how someone would likely describe Cooper, a virulent social and political critic.

But Cooper could write, when he chose to. His tales of the American forest, the vast, brooding presence that gave birth to his country, are his best-known writings today, especially that magnificent novel *The Last of the Mohicans*. We tend to forget, though, that Cooper is the progenitor of modern maritime literature, the sea novel in particular. In 1823 he published *The Pilot*, in 1827 came *The Red Rover*, and in 1830 *The Water-Witch*.

People had written about the sea before, of course, as far back as the dawn of history. The Odyssey, the biblical account of the Flood, and Jonah's interlude with the whale are just a few of the better examples. But with Cooper the genre emerged in the modern world: the sea, a feral, untamable element that became man's test and proving ground, his liberation, his prison, his highway and even his destiny, found a place in modern writing. At his best, Cooper was better at it than Mackenzie, drawing on his own few years as a midshipman to breathe authenticity into his words. He was, as one critic has said, a writer who was a frustrated sailor. Mackenzie was his mirror image, a sailor who was a frustrated writer. And the two took exactly opposite views when it came to the Battle of Lake Erie.

In those days the greatest strength of the American navy—and its greatest weakness—lay in the pride of its captains. They were knights-errant. There were no battle fleets; there were never fleet actions, and scarcely even squadrons. Ships operated alone, and since a ship obeyed the will of her captain, individual captains emerged as the ocean's lone rangers, taking on enemies in near-single combat. John Paul Jones in *Bonhomme Richard* against His Majesty's Frigate *Serapis;* Thomas Truxtun of *Constellation* and his duels with *L'Insurgente* and *La Vengeance;* Isaac Hull and his *Constitution,* going up against *Guerrière;* these victories were great shining moments, proving the navy's mettle, and though they were cause for American pride, they had no strategic importance worth mentioning.

Even Lake Erie revealed this same weakness. There Oliver Hazard Perry had commanded a squadron, but he had had that same lone-wolf honor and pride that other American captains shared. So, too, did his second-in-command, Commander Jesse D. Elliot. Immediately after the battle, in victory's glow, Perry had commended Elliot, along with others, in his official dispatches. But later he changed his tune, criticizing Elliot for keeping his own ship out of enemy range for too long, while Perry and the rest of the squadron engaged. That was an insult to Elliot, and a squabble broke out between the two men. It was the same sort of outburst that was always happening among the navy's egotistical officers who were used to having their way at sea. And this one nearly got out of hand. In 1818 Perry demanded that Elliot face a court-martial, and Elliot called for a duel in return. Neither of these took place, but the blood was very bad.

Whatever the merits of each man's case, Lake Erie passed for a great naval battle in the annals of American arms, and so naturally people wanted to read and write about it. Enter James Fenimore Cooper. In 1839 the former midshipman wrote a history of the United States Navy, and, quite naturally, he devoted several pages to this most famous of actions.

It was a good enough work. Even Mackenzie thought so. But in the view of the Perrys—and Mackenzie was one of their in-laws—the account of the battle was unfair to the American captain. Oliver Hazard Perry was a great naval hero, to his family and to the nation at large, but not to Cooper, who took a dispassionate view of the subject, giving attention to Elliot's side of the argument. The Perrys, quite naturally, didn't very much like it.

Neither did Mackenzie. He wrote a review of Cooper's new history shortly after it appeared, criticizing his account of Lake Erie. That started a new naval battle, this one on paper, that would continue for years. A lot of it was quite public, with the two men sniping at each other in print. One of Mackenzie's strongest salvos was his biography of Oliver Hazard Perry, which denounced, quite naturally, Elliot's actions. It was an attack that Cooper refused to take lying down. He wasn't a man to pull punches—a social and political gadfly, he was always bringing libel suits against people who he felt misrepresented his views—and when it came to Lake Erie, he really let his enemy have it. "Mr. A. S. Mackenzie is a writer of no authority in matter of fact," he sneered at one point. "He has brought criminating charges against others that are not only untrue, but of which he had the clearest evidence of their own untruth."

Cooper could say what he wanted about Mackenzie the writer, but Mackenzie was also a mariner, and a good one at that. The navy recognized this, giving him a commander's commission in 1841. And then he got a command, one for which he seems to have been rather junior. He had skippered a warship before when he was just a lieutenant, the schooner *Dolphin* on the South American station.

But the ship he took charge of in the autumn of 1841 was in a totally different class. She was the steam frigate *Missouri*.

The most famous *Missouri*, of course, is the *Iowa*-class battleship of a hundred years later; the *Iowa* were probably the most awesome big-gun ships ever to sail the seas. In her way, Mackenzie's *Missouri* was the great-grandparent of that later warship, for she, too, was powered by steam and had global range, at least with help from the wind. She was one of the navy's first steam-driven vessels; and as such she was different. She had sails, too, of course, but with boilers roaring and engines engaged, her timbers scarcely trembling, she handled differently from every other ship in which Mackenzie had served. She was a dangerous and odd new breed, and a big one as well. She and her sister ship, *Mississippi*, were the longest naval vessels the world had seen until then, longer even than American ships of the line, yet with the graceful profiles of frigates; but those profiles were broken by side paddle wheels and large funnels. They were good ships. Matthew C. Perry, who had helped oversee their construction, would take *Mississippi* with him on his mission to open Japan to the West later on in the 1850s. *Missouri* fell into the care of Mackenzie.

He had her for only a few months. Something went wrong. It may have been due to the strange way she handled or to Mackenzie's unfamiliarity with steam. But whatever the cause, he ran her aground in the Potomac while taking her up to Washington. His wife loyally blamed the pilot who'd come aboard to help him navigate the river, and maybe the pilot really did something wrong. *Missouri*, after all, was new to him, too. But a commanding officer is responsible for every last thing that takes place on his ship. Total responsibility: that is the flip side of a captain's unparalleled power. *Missouri* was a new type of ship, and an expensive one, too. Someone had to pay for the mistake. The captain had to be that someone. Five months after being assigned to the new steam frigate, Mackenzie was relieved of command.

If the problem had lain with *Missouri*'s new means of propulsion, then it is easy to see how Mackenzie might come to fear, perhaps unconsciously, the threat that new technology posed to his years of hard-earned knowledge, an age-old way of seamanship. The Jacksonian era was a profoundly unsettling time. And though the navy was conservative, dragging its feet, it couldn't drag them forever. Instead the navy itself would be dragged—if necessary kicking and screaming—into the future.

It wasn't just the technology. The navy was being forced to change in a great many things, and some of the most profound changes were taking place the same year Mackenzie ran *Missouri* aground. And they, too, were unsettling to an officer corps long settled in its ways.

Ever since February 1815—for almost exactly the whole of Mackenzie's career—the service had been under the rule of the Board of Navy Commissioners, a three-officer body that was charged with administering naval affairs. It reported to and advised the secretary of the navy; but, over time, complaints popped up that since secretaries came and went, the real power lay in the board, and that decision by committee slowed naval progress. By 1841 criticism was rampant, not only from the few citizens who actually cared, but from the secretary's office, and even from some farsighted officers. "The organization of the navy Board is bad," wrote one lieutenant that season. "The seeds of disease were implanted in its system from the beginning." It had failed in all sorts of ways, especially in design and procurement. It had "turned out upon the navy a nest of tubs and sent them to sea as men-of-war."

Abel P. Upshur, President Tyler's superbly competent naval secretary, agreed heartily. "I have had but a short experience in this department," he wrote in 1841, a few months after taking charge of the navy, "but a short experience is enough to display its defects, even to the most superficial observation. It is, in truth, not organized at all." So he set about modernizing the system. The very next year, in the summer of 1842, he prevailed upon Congress to abolish the board and establish five bureaus, with the head of each one to report directly to Upshur. It was the most sweeping naval reorganization between the War of 1812 and Fort Sumter. And though it was badly needed, it shook up the men of the navy, making officers' futures uncertain. In the past, promotions were slow and service was rough, but there was a plodding predictability in the process. Now things were happening, in administration, in design, in ordnance, in propulsion. Engineers and their vaunted steam power were getting more and more crucial. The navy was finally beginning to shift, to change. And change can be frightening.

Things changed for Mackenzie, too, and at almost exactly the same time as the administrative upheavals. One day he commanded *Missouri*, one of the navy's most advanced ships, and one of its most powerful. The next, he'd been relieved. And in light of the shake-up in organization, it had to be profoundly disturbing. Grounding a ship is no small thing. Watching one's skills grow outmoded is also traumatic. A lot of things were hitting Mackenzie within a very short time span. Any number of suppressed forces must have been circling in his unconscious mind, and perhaps his conscious thoughts, too.

But Mackenzie's career hadn't ended; it had merely changed course. Maybe it was even a change for the better. He'd served in large ships, but he was at home in smaller, sail-powered vessels. And his brother-in-law Matthew C. Perry, working hard to promote his naval apprenticeship system, had just the place for him: command of the brig-of-war *Somers*.

She was smaller by far, in every conceivable way, than *Missouri*. She had half the length and half the beam, and much less weight of broadside. Her complement was smaller, too. She was no step up from *Missouri;* at best she was a giant step sideways. In assuming command of her, Mackenzie might well have seen the straws in the wind. But she was now his, and by the spring of 1842 she was ready for a shakedown cruise.

It was no intercontinental, transoceanic voyage, although she was designed and built to be fully capable of those. No; her first time out, she would merely sail south to Puerto Rico and then back, though a journey of even this length was nothing to be laughed at. The island was as far from New York as the Grand Banks were, and the Grand Banks were fully a third of the way to Europe. She'd be gone for a few weeks, and Mackenzie would have the chance to find out what kind of a ship she was, and what kind of people he had.

To crew her, he had his pick of the apprentices who were serving aboard *North Carolina,* the large receiving ship in New York's navy yard. Matthew C. Perry was anxious to get them out onto the ocean, and as *Somers*'s new skipper, Mackenzie obliged him. The little brig's nominal complement was something under a hundred, but by the time she sailed for the Caribbean, she had nearly twice that many aboard. Good specimens, too, most of them, at least on the surface, though they were largely untrained. Mackenzie had handpicked them all for size and strength and agility, as well as for brains and spirit.

Still, she was new, with a young and raw crew, and rough spots were bound to develop. That, after all, is the point of a shakedown, to bring those rough spots to light and then work on them. There were the usual matters, common to every cruise, small aberrations that led to occasional floggings. Mackenzie had ordered that the boys be treated somewhat gently, but the older ones were a different story. Twenty-one-year-old Daniel McKinley, for one, felt the cat on his back, the knotted thongs drawing strips of blood. Then there were the more serious things: on the outbound half of the voyage, a boy fell overboard. It had been inevitable, given the high-wire balancing act that sailors were always performing on the masts and the yards and the rigging. Still, it was a nuisance at best, and deadly at worst. When it happened this time, two boats put out to rescue the youngster amid a flurry of hasty commands to put down the helm and heave-to. But soon the routine was restored.

Perhaps this day-in, day-out normality was what led the purser's steward, young James W. Wales, to get himself into trouble. A youngster, Wales had never been to sea before, and had likely never traveled too far from home, wherever home had been for him. Now he found himself in an exotic Caribbean locale, and it must have gone to his head. Whatever the trouble—it was probably something such as dereliction of duty, or women, or fighting, or spirits, or a combination thereof—Mackenzie had to dress the boy down. He had the natural makings of a schoolmaster, keeping alcohol off his ship and tending to spare the rod. He probably didn't enjoy disciplining Wales, any more than Wales enjoyed getting disciplined. But the youngster probably remembered the lesson; perhaps he even resented it. That would have explained some things that happened much later.

Despite the unpleasantness, the ship and her crew survived and returned to New York in early summer. Mackenzie spent the following weeks evaluating his people's performances, deciding which of them had done well enough to earn further training with him. His standards were tough; of the hundred and sixty he'd taken to Puerto Rico, he returned nearly half to *North Carolina*, replacing many of them. That was the nature of life during the era of Andrew Jackson, years before anyone had heard of Charles Darwin. Opportunity should be open to all, but some people had what it took and others did not. There was no use dwelling on failures, or on the world's injustice.

This didn't apply to the crew alone. Mackenzie took the same view of his officers, at least to a certain degree. The wardroom he now lined up for *Somers* boasted more than one of his relatives, but in several cases he knew the men he chose, either personally or by reputation, as good sailors. One was Lieutenant Matthew C. Perry, Jr., who would be serving as acting master. The other was Oliver H. Perry II, captain's clerk, whom Mackenzie promoted to acting midshipman. Other than Lieutenant Perry, Mackenzie had only one other commissioned officer aboard: Guert Gansevoort, member of an old New Amsterdam family and first cousin to Herman Melville. Unlike Perry, however, Gansevoort was a sailor of long service, having been in the navy for nearly two decades, inching his way slowly up the ranks of the peacetime service. Other officers included midshipmen Egbert Thompson and Charles W. Hays, and Acting Midshipmen John H. Tillotson and Adrian Deslonde. Deslonde was a relative, too, an in-law to Mackenzie's brother. Mackenzie had no chaplain; he had no schoolmaster. He did have a passed assistant surgeon, Richard W. Leecock, although he wasn't a line officer. So the wardroom, too, was young, just like the crew.

This was Mackenzie's lineup when, in late August, Philip Spencer reported aboard.

The record of their first meeting is scant, and comes mainly from Mackenzie. That is the problem with most of the facts that we have from this moment on: there were no disinterested witnesses. But Mackenzie's account of his first meeting with Spencer seems innocuous enough. He appeared to know nothing of what had brought the young acting midshipman aboard his command, and he offered the youth his hand, as he would have to any officer and gentleman. Only later did he learn that Spencer had a black cloud hanging over his head.

One thing that Mackenzie almost certainly didn't know was that Spencer had arranged to smuggle liquor aboard. One night, while *Somers* lay alongside the newly launched frigate *Savannah*, Gunner's Mate Henry King saw something unseemly. Spencer had the watch;

at night and in port during peacetime, it was good training for an acting midshipman. It was also a good time for him to abuse his trust. King saw it happen. Two sailors, Elisha Small and Chief Bo'sun's Mate Samuel Cromwell, surreptitiously brought liquor aboard from *Savannah*. Spencer said nothing—and neither did King, whose business it emphatically wasn't. Later events would suggest that the liquor was Spencer's, especially when seen in light of his liking for alcohol.

If Mackenzie had learned of the incident, he would have dealt with it instantly. He didn't deal with it, so he must not have known. Still, he eventually found out about Spencer's prior conduct, and it bothered him. He had orders by now to take his ship on an extended training cruise to Africa, to seek out *Vandalia* and deliver dispatches to her, a voyage that was bound to take months. He didn't want troublemakers aboard. That was why he'd taken such pains to hand-pick his crew. And so he didn't want Spencer.

Just a day or two earlier, he had gotten a couple of new additions to his wardroom. One was Midshipman Henry Rogers, whom Mackenzie knew as a highly competent mariner and a young man of honor, the son of John Rogers, the famous commodore. He was now overstocked, with seven officers and officers-in-training. He wanted to get rid of a couple, with Spencer being one of them.

And Spencer wanted to go. True to form, he was still restless. He still couldn't buckle down. Mackenzie had heard that he wanted to be detached from the ship, and that suited the captain just fine. He told Gansevoort, his first lieutenant, to let Spencer know that if he wished to apply for a transfer, Mackenzie would second it earnestly.

Spencer promptly applied for a transfer to *Grampus,* a schooner, and Mackenzie approved the request. But it wasn't all up to Mackenzie. Normally the Navy Department would have to approve as well before the transfer could happen. But *Somers*'s refit was through, and she was almost finished taking on stores. Her complement was complete. She would sail within hours. There was no way that Mackenzie and Spencer could get word to Washington, much less have time to hear back, before she weighed anchor. So the request went to Commodore Perry instead.

Perry refused. Either he felt too strongly for Mackenzie to move him, or Mackenzie didn't feel strongly enough to try to press the point. The commodore was probably under some pressure to get the boy out to sea, away from New York, where his next screwup would attract little attention. But whatever the reason, Spencer would stay with *Somers*. With him would stay a crew of a hundred and twenty, nearly a hundred of them below the age of eighteen.

At last the day arrived. Tuesday, September 13. One can imagine the moment, the ship, with Mackenzie on deck watching over every detail, the shrill note of the bo'sun's whistle, the controlled chaos of scores of sailors and sailors-in-training running and climbing and hauling, the creak of the capstan as the anchor came up. The sails were set in the freshening winds, and *Somers* freed herself of the shore, beginning to make her way down the river, toward the narrows, and finally into the open sea. It looked routine, though it was anything but. Sailing a ship was the most difficult job in the preindustrial world, and even into the early industrial days. Operating an exquisitely complex and massive machine, coordinating and choreographing the work of more than a hundred people, doing all this in the face of a cruel and heartless nature, with nobody to help if something went wrong, was demanding in the extreme. The ship and her progress were beautiful, a blend of art and science. But the opportunities for disaster were constant.

On this cruise, the greatest dangers would lie within—within *Somers,* and within the hearts and minds of her crew and her officers, especially those of Mackenzie and Spencer.

The journey into darkness had started.

PART FOUR

Cruise

A WARSHIP IS UNDER ATTACK from the moment it first leaves harbor. So are all other ships, even in times of peace. The sea is a hostile, inhospitable place, and it assaults every vessel any number of ways.

The wind is one enemy. As soon as *Somers* weighed anchor, she had to start wrestling with it. It was her engine, of course, her ticket to Africa and back. She could feel the tug of the air as she made for the Verrazano Narrows, the gateway into the Atlantic from the haven of New York. But the wind could be fickle. It could blow too hard, or not hard enough, or in the wrong direction, and any of these three could be deadly. Too hard and lines could give way, or sails could split and shred themselves to tatters in seconds. A breeze from the wrong quarter could prod her onto a lee shore, grounding or wrecking her; or it might keep her from making landfall when she was desperately short of supplies. A calm could manage that, too. A ship's provisions are limited, and a stroke of bad luck or bad winds could leave her at sea with her crew dying slowly of thirst.

Then there is the water, not water for drinking, but the water below and the water above. The sea on which *Somers* sailed could be calm and as flat as a table, but the North Atlantic is usually something quite different. The waves could be high, especially in autumn or winter. They could hit her head-on, over and over again, in a mindless, furious effort to bury her under mountains of solid green water; or they could come at her from quarter or beam, capsizing her quickly. Even when the water was less volatile it could be a great nuisance. It rusted ships' metals; it was host to teredo worms and other small creatures that feasted on wood, even copper. Something was always eating at *Somers*. And the sea contained salt, lots of it, and salt is highly corrosive. Before too long, everything on board the brig would show signs of the chemical battle.

The rain didn't have salt, but it, too, could cause problems. A squall could blind the vessel, masking dangers that might be lying in wait for her—shoals, perhaps, or a derelict. While these last two dangers were slight on the open sea where *Somers* was bound, they were much greater as she skirted the land. But the greatest danger of all came when the winds and the waters colluded. Fierce gales could blow sheets of salt spray horizontally, stinging exposed skin like sandpaper, while high surges could stand the ship on her beam-ends. A sudden shift in the winds could take her aback and dismast her; or she might find herself broaching to, swimming sideways into the waves. She would start taking on water faster than her pumps could handle. She would become waterlogged, grow sluggish, and finally founder and sink. Even a naturally buoyant, all-wooden vessel has limits.

All ships, of course, *Somers* included, had weapons to meet these onslaughts. The most important was the seamanship of her captain and officers—their ability to assess, avoid, and take countermeasures against the dangers that the elements held. Given the right understanding, the right orders, *Somers* could become very nearly a living thing, reacting almost consciously to whatever water and air were doing, and sometimes even seizing the initiative. Sailing is, after all, a matter of harnessing nature, not simply beating it down. *Somers* could never defeat the Atlantic, but she could certainly use it, as long as Mackenzie knew his job, which he did. But Mackenzie's knowledge wasn't enough. He was the brain and the will, but to make the ship work like a thing alive he needed muscles that would obey the orders he gave, far more muscles than his own body possessed.

This was *Somers*'s next weapon, the manpower that she boasted. She had a hundred and twenty souls aboard, all of them the tools of the captain's decisions, mechanistically turning his will into action without pause for reflection. But in normal conditions only a small number of the crew were necessary to sail her. The main reason for the others was to fight the ship, to service the guns in combat. But combat—even including the drills—took up only a very small portion of time, even during an actual war. The rest of the time these men provided the pool of labor that was needed to fight the more mundane battles, the wear and tear, the slow leakage, the corrosion, all the little wars of attrition that the sea was incessantly waging against *Somers*. Sanding, scraping, painting and varnishing, trimming sail, constantly adjusting the standing rigging, manipulating the running rigging in order to catch the wind; there was almost no end to it.

And even when everything had been done, every item put in its place, every sail properly set or furled, every yard correctly braced, every rope neatly coiled, then still things remained—of necessity. Idle hands are dangerous, and busywork was a must in order to prevent goofing off, or skylarking, as it was known in the navy. One endless task, sometimes assigned as a punishment, was picking oakum. It involved breaking down an old rope into its fibers, which could be used for caulking the ship. Another was holystoning the decks, scrubbing them down with blocks of sandstone so that they were spotlessly white. This kept the sailors down on their knees a lot; hence the nickname holystone. Whether picking oakum, scrubbing the decks, or performing other mundane tasks, the sailors could be sure of one thing: they would have little rest this cruise. In that respect, at least, *Somers's* voyage was nothing unusual.

The crew seemed to accept it all in good humor, by most accounts, and the first part of the outward voyage was a happy one, with nearly all hands in high spirits. Gradually the old routines asserted themselves; the starboard and port (or larboard as it was still known in those days) watches sorted themselves out and began to work the ship in regular, monotonous sequence, changing every four hours, when eight bells sounded. In the evening came the dog watches of two hours each, instead of the usual four, during which the starboard and larboard watches changed their sequence of watch-standing from the previous twenty-four hours. Thus a sailor who came on duty for a four-hour watch at noon on one day would find himself coming off a four-hour watch at that same time the following day. All of this was old hat to the officers, and to the few experienced hands; soon the apprentices learned the system.

Even the course was likely routine. The ship had to ride with the winds, whose patterns changed little. The Gulf Stream, along with the prevailing westerlies, would have tended to sweep the ship north and east from America's coast in the general direction of Europe. *Somers* could have made directly for Africa, but that would have been less efficient. It would have meant sailing closer to the wind, which would have called for more tacking, and thus a longer, zigzag journey. Better to use the winds as much as she could, instead of wasting energy fighting them. The dispatches she bore for *Vandalia* were merely pretext; the cruise itself was her mission, the training of the boys her object. Let the journey take time, then. She would sail with the wind; in time she would swing to the south to land at a natural waypoint to Africa, the islands of Madeira.

Not much shattered the steady routine. Of course little dramas occurred; *Somers* was not a large vessel, and she had too many people aboard. Nobody had any real freedom, and there was no personal space at all. In such close quarters, tempers can sometimes flare, and the temptation to skylark can be strong. On other ships rum was the answer, a way of keeping the sailors complacent. But before the cruise had begun, Mackenzie had hinted strongly to Gansevoort that he didn't want spirits aboard a training vessel, and Gansevoort had taken the hint. Apart from some wardroom brandy, *Somers* was dry. So breaches of discipline were going to happen, at least as often as they did aboard other ships. When they did, confinement wasn't an option. The ship lacked the space. And pain was a powerful teacher, which the navy well knew.

Discipline on a warship was crucial. Even little *Somers*, in the great scheme of things, was one of the more potent concentrations of firepower on the face of the globe. What she lacked in raw striking power, she made up for in mobility. Improperly handled or used, she could become a serious threat—a threat to the men aboard her, a threat to navigation, a threat to America's peaceful relations with other countries, a threat to merchant shipping, even a threat to her own nation. The navy, and indirectly the sovereignty of the United States, had given Mackenzie command of this vessel, the nearly unrestrained power of sailing and fighting her. In exchange for that power, he had the sole responsibility of making quite sure that she did as her orders required. That meant that he had to have the power to see that his men executed his every command, without delay or incompetence. The only way to do this was to use discipline, stern and unyielding.

He had to delegate *something*, of course. He couldn't stay awake and run the ship "24/7," as a later generation would say. He had to rely on his officers; he had to know that they could handle things while he slept, that they could at least understand the night orders he always wrote for them before he retired in the evening. But even that meant that his power over them was complete. If *Somers* grounded or foundered while he was asleep, or if some other accident happened, he was just as responsible as if he had been on the quarterdeck giving commands. He might even be more to blame, for when danger threatened, his place was on that quarterdeck. No incompetence in his officers could excuse his failures; any failures aboard *Somers* were his by definition. The only way to prevent, to curtail, such failures, was through discipline. So, at least, the conventional wisdom said.

Perhaps it was even correct. Nearly a decade after *Somers*'s cruise, the navy gave in to the wave of reform that was sweeping the nation, abolishing the practice of flogging. And the instant that happened, discipline went to hell. The 1850s saw the service's nadir, in terms of morale at least. Rarely has it fared so badly. But of all the things with which Mackenzie would have to contend, this wasn't one of them. He had the cat aboard.

The cat-o'-nine-tails was a whip with nine knotted thongs, designed for use on an offender's bare back. It was a brutal device, so brutal that the navy barred captains from imposing a sentence of more than a dozen lashes for any single offense. But even one lash was strong medicine. The thongs would sail whistling through the air, and then they hit the epidermis, popping easily through it, instantly raising ugly welts. Indications were similar to a second-degree burn. In seconds some bloody serum began to ooze from the wounds. The harder strokes abraded the dermis as well as the epidermis, drawing forth more serum and causing some permanent scarring. Of more pressing concern than the scar tissue problem was the threat of secondary infection. This probably wasn't deliberate. After all, the seaman was valuable, and productivity was the ultimate goal. But no antisepsis was available. (Rum would serve, if applied topically, just as internal administration would have some mild anesthetic properties—that and laudanum.) Anyway, no one knew much of the need for disinfection.

Flogging also brought more immediate dangers, especially if the strokes were too hard. When laceration of the basal layer occurred, some real bleeding would start—not just the bloody, watery serum that leaks from an abraded epidermis, but pure, glistening blood, mingling with the sweat of numb pain. A major concern at that point was blood loss, but shock was the greatest threat of all; it could cause circulatory collapse. Modern primary treatment is to recline the patient, elevating the legs to get the blood pressure up and increase the oxygen flow to the brain, but that wasn't practicable when the man was lashed to a grating that held him upright with his arms outspread. Prompt medical attention could still save him even at so late a point; but as blood pressure vanished, the heart would start to fibrillate; then the brain would begin starving, the vessels dilating, the blood unable to make the climb to the skull. Unconsciousness would soon be followed by death. Yes, the cat could be quite brutal, but if used correctly it was also effective.

Mackenzie had other punishments, too. He could make an offender kiss the gunner's daughter, for instance, bending him over one of the guns while the bo'sun's mate took a cane to his backside. Gauntlets were another option, as was stringing a man up in the standing rigging. Some of the worst punishments, such as keelhauling and flogging around the fleet, rarely or never took place in the American navy; but the other punishments were enough to get the job done.

One of the favorites aboard *Somers* was the relatively tame whip called the colt, also known as the starter. This was a short, thick rope, which stung a lot less than the cat. It was used through the shirt, and not on bare skin, which reduced the sting further. But it was painful enough, and it got a good workout on *Somers*.

The flogging of American citizens, the casual whipping of teenagers—all of this shocks the conscience of a later generation. It shocked the consciences of people back then as well. The parallels between seamen and slaves were striking, and the same currents of reform that were stirring the one were also stirring the other. But here was *Somers*, barely a dozen miles at sea, then a hundred, then more like a thousand, out of view of the land-bound reformers, and far beyond their control. The captain, the officers, took a dim view of the humanity of the crew. For all practical purposes, *Somers* might have been sailing a hundred, five hundred, years earlier. Officers were one thing with their pretensions to a caste of nobility that the United States had never seen; common seamen were something else. Discipline would be enforced on them the old-fashioned way.

Oddly enough the sailors accepted it. If the treatment they got was similar to the treatment of slaves, so, too, were their responses like those of slaves. During danger or battle they put their hearts into their labor; but on other occasions many of them tended to do as little work as they could, since it usually brought them no immediate benefit. And when they crossed an invisible line they had to pay for the trespass. They could have rebelled, of course. They outnumbered the officers greatly. A captain at sea may have the authority of the government behind him, but it was a long, long way behind. The sailors had the bigger battalions, but something kept them in line. It was likely the knowledge that discipline, constant discipline, was the only way to make sure that the ship performed as a single, seamless entity, and that was the only way to ensure that in moments when danger threatened—be it in the guise of an enemy warship or the sea itself—*Somers* would win her battle. Thus the colts and the floggings were just another part of the ship's routine, along with the standing of watches, the picking of oakum, the occasional skylarking, and everything else.

But even during the calm outbound voyage, something was starting to interfere with this ancient routine very slightly, almost imperceptibly at first. Soon people were beginning to sense it. Something was wrong. And it began as an assault on the invisible wall that separated the seamen and officers.

Somers was a world unto herself: mobile, self-sustaining to a large degree, and utterly cut off from the rest of humanity for as long as she was at sea. But this world was a tiny one. Its farthest inland reaches were a mere ten, perhaps twenty, feet from the waters. But within those confines her geography, though overpopulated, was very diverse.

Her uppermost deck was the scene of much of the action. Some would call it the main deck; it might also be called the weather deck, or the gun deck, for it was home to all ten of her thirty-two-pound carronades. They lined the sides of the ship, half to starboard and half to larboard. But more often it was called the spar deck, for from it led a network of hundreds of ropes, reaching up to the masts and the spars that soared overhead. There were sheets; there were braces; there were ratlines and halyards and backstays. Mismanagement of a single rope, slackening or belaying at the wrong time, could spell disaster for a man or even the ship. These lines could be under huge strain. If one parted, it could lash the air like a monstrous whip, slicing to ribbons any flesh that got in its way. If a line went at the wrong moment, *Somers* could spill her wind or fall off; in a gale she might heel hard over and capsize. The lines were both vital and deadly.

The yards and masts to which they led were vital and deadly, too. The foremast and mainmast, stepped deep in the bowels of the ship, respectively stretched ninety and a hundred and thirty feet above the spar deck, into the realms of the winds that let *Somers* go where she pleased. As she pitched and rolled even mildly on the swells of the North Atlantic, the tops of the masts, and the mastheads, leapt and reeled through the sky with a far greater and wilder motion than the rest of the ship, dizzying the heads of the topmen. Even old hands could get seasick aloft. But they knew both the ropes and the sails— the jibs, the staysails, the courses, and all the others. The sails' canvas was tough, catching and using the winds, though really stiff breezes could play with the sails in turn. One moment a sail could be full, pulling hard in a screaming gale; the next it would part in the center and be ripped into pieces, instantly flapping away crazily into the storm like some vast, insane bird. Manning the tops, farming the winds for their power, living in a spiderweb of canvas and hemp, was a job for the few and the best that the ship had to offer.

On the spar deck below, life was a little less wild. A deck below that it was more mundane still. This was the berth deck, where the men lived and slept. It was a dim and stifling place. Like every other square inch of *Somers,* it was designed for efficient space usage, not for comfort, and certainly not for luxury. When hammocks were slung, each man had claim to an area not much greater than that of a coffin, a sagging and swinging coffin surrounded above and below, to left and to right, by dozens of other sagging and swinging coffins. When the hammocks were struck away there was a little more space, but not much. Between the galley and the storerooms and the lockers or sea chests—the latter being the one sacrosanct bit of personal space that a sailor could have—there simply wasn't much room. Aft of the berth deck, just beyond the mainmast, was steerage, the small cabin that was home to all the midshipmen. Maybe sixty square feet in size, it was living room, bedroom, and dining room for all of these junior officers. Behind lay the wardroom, smaller still, and at least as crowded and cramped. The ship's few officers could just barely wedge themselves into the place. The ship's population was simply too large. Aft of the wardroom, reachable only by a hatch from the spar deck, was the minuscule captain's cabin. A prison cell would have seemed roomy compared to that cabin, but it was the best housing to be found in the ship, except, perhaps, for the spar deck in pleasant weather.

Below the berth deck was the netherworld of the holds and the bilges, the nearly airless and lightless region where most of the ship's stores were stowed. Everything had to be packed with utmost care. The powder had to stay dry, the fresh water free from contamination by salt. The thirty-two-pounder shot had to be placed very wisely; a few feet too far forward or aft and it could wreck *Somers*'s natural trim, making her wallow through the waves like a pig. And if any stores shifted in heavy seas or high winds, the ship could go straight to the bottom.

Duty down in the bowels of the ship, amid the stink and the dark, was something that nobody envied. Life on the spar deck was easier, and more varied, too. Forward was the forecastle, or fo'c'sle, although in *Somers* this was a misnomer; there was no raised deck, no "castle," either forward or aft. *Somers* was flush-decked, the topmost spar deck running the whole length of the ship. But the fo'c'sle was a favorite place for sailors to skylark, for farther aft were the officers. Between the two masts were the galley stovepipe, the hatch to the berth deck, and the ship's boats as well. To either side rested the guns; aft of the mainmast were hatches to steerage, wardroom, and captain's cabin; the roundhouses, the binnacles, the wheel; and the quarterdeck.

A quarterdeck is a place of mystical, nearly religious, significance aboard a sailing ship. Even today, *Ticonderoga*-class Aegis missile cruisers, *Nimitz*-class carriers, and nearly all other warships still have a symbolic quarterdeck. In the old days it was home to shrines and icons; the practice of saluting the ensign when boarding or departing a ship bears close relation to genuflecting to the quarterdeck's crucifix. By the time the American navy was born, the Anglo-American world had no quarterdeck altars; but they still had captains, and captains strode their quarterdecks the way God dwelled on Sinai. This was the spot from which radiated all power aboard. A captain needed space, space from which to observe, space in which to think. On any ship, especially on a brig the size of *Somers,* space is at a premium. Even the captain has little room. So authority and tradition give him not actual but virtual space, an invisible wall all around him. When Captain Mackenzie was on the weather side of the quarterdeck, speaking to no one, looking at no one, absorbed in thought, his privacy, his space, was absolutely inviolable.

Mackenzie was privileged to have even this small bit of privacy, for nobody else had any. Tops, spar deck, berth deck, hold—there was simply no room for it. If two or three men wanted to talk, only others' courtesy could let them discuss things "alone." There was, however, one other such wall as surrounded Mackenzie—the wall between crew and officers. Unlike Mackenzie's, this was a corporate, not a personal, wall. It divided two groups from each other. Physical fraternization between seamen and officers was impossible to avoid. Even the bulkhead between berth deck and the after cabins was quite flimsy. So the only way to prevent fraternization was through an exercise of the will. And his failure to do so was the first sign that Philip Spencer was moving toward trouble.

Some modern theories hold that juvenile delinquents tend to seek out fellow troublemakers. Spencer's adolescent years were behind him, but just barely, and if what his shipmates said is true, then his words and his actions support these theories. *Somers* had a small group of old hands, at least old by teen standards, seamen in their twenties and thirties who knew the ropes and who could help train the youngsters. Spencer, as a midshipman, shouldn't have had much to do with them when he was off duty, but he did, especially when it came to Samuel Cromwell, a seaman of the starboard watch.

Bewhiskered, recently married, in his mid-thirties, Cromwell was one of the oldest aboard, almost as old as Mackenzie. He had joined *Somers* in mid-August, not quite a month before she had sailed, but early enough to help smuggle some liquor aboard. He was an experienced hand; and he had once been to sea in a slave ship, which may help explain why he was *Somers*'s chief bo'sun's mate. The job included keeping people in line and doing the flogging. That was a shame, because he had a terrible temper.

Somers may have been a happy ship on the outbound voyage, but Cromwell didn't share in the feeling. He was jealous of his personal space, for one thing, or what passed for it. When Thomas Dickerson, the carpenter's mate, once tried to store a few pieces of wood in the bo'sun's storeroom, Cromwell got surly, even when Dickerson told him that the wood was Lieutenant Gansevoort's. That should have been enough, but Cromwell groused that he didn't care whose wood it was. Nevertheless, Dickerson had his orders, and he put the wood in the storeroom. When he came back out, Cromwell was still there, waiting for him. "Your time's damn short," he said. "I'll pay you for this before long."

This wasn't his only run-in with the carpenters. An apprentice was once pulling some pieces of wood from the forepeak storage area, and one of them fell onto Cromwell's foot. This time he didn't use threats. Instead he simply picked up one of the pieces and threw it at the apprentice, who dodged it. Cromwell picked up another, but then someone started yelling for him on deck, to the relief of the apprentice, no doubt.

Irritability happens sometimes on a cruise. But Cromwell's was constant. He was rough on the apprentices in the voyage's first weeks. He had little to do with them except when he had to punish them. When he got to hit them, he hit them hard—so hard, in fact, that Mackenzie had to tell him to take it easy on them and not whip them as if they were full-grown men. He would hurl curses at them as well—"the most outrageous and blasphemous language," according to Gansevoort, who, in two decades at sea, had had plenty of opportunity to hear filthy words.

Then, rather abruptly, Cromwell calmed down. Apparently one of the reasons was his growing friendship with Spencer, who began seeking him out just a few days into the cruise. At first the contacts were few, but within a month that had changed.

Why Spencer should seek out Cromwell, or why Cromwell should ally himself with Spencer, is anyone's guess. While the men had no grog, the officers had access to brandy. That could have been a motive for Cromwell, especially if Spencer was keeping the liquor that Cromwell had smuggled aboard. But what could Cromwell offer Spencer? He was a store of nautical knowledge; he was one of the few men before the mast, in fact, who understood how to navigate. That made him someone useful to know. But whatever the reasons, Spencer and Cromwell started to fraternize.

One of the first signs was money. A few days out of New York, Spencer gave Cromwell fifteen dollars, in big bills, a large sum in those days. This wasn't the first time that money had changed hands. The night before *Somers* sailed, the midshipman had also given cash to Elisha Small, who had helped Cromwell with the smuggling. Small, too, was an experienced hand; he had sailed very often before, sometimes in slavers. He even bragged of having killed a man once, probably a slave fresh from Africa. And, like Cromwell, he knew how to navigate. These two, in fact, were the only ones other than officers who comprehended this crucial skill. And Spencer paid both of them money.

But money was more or less useless at sea, and Spencer had to find other ways to do whatever it was he was trying to do. He seemed to spend most of his efforts on Cromwell. Sure enough, some of those efforts went into alcohol, brandy he got from the wardroom and passed on to the bo'sun's mate. This, alone, made Spencer valuable in the older man's eyes.

Spencer had another commodity: tobacco, both for chewing and smoking. Spencer drew a great deal of tobacco and cigars from the ship's meager stores. From his hands they found their way not just to Cromwell but to several apprentices. He gave tobacco by the pound to the boys; he gave cigars by the handful to Cromwell. With the officers and the other midshipmen he was cool and aloof, but he gave every sign of trying to win the crew's favor, sometimes even tossing coins on the deck for the boys to scramble after. But sometimes he showed some impatience, especially with the youngest hands. He was once talking with Cromwell when the bo'sun's mate was in one of his moods. Cromwell was dressing down an apprentice who had done a poor job with something or other, no doubt enjoying the boy's discomfort. That was when Spencer made a strange comment. "The sooner we get shot of these little devils the better," he told Cromwell, "for they eat bread and are of no use."

This was one of any number of times that Spencer and Cromwell talked. People noticed them all the time, discussing things quietly, intently. Once someone overheard Spencer ask Cromwell how *Somers* would do as a pirate ship. Cromwell was favorable. She would need some modifications, he pointed out, such as "clearing the decks of the boats," but she might do, for she was quite a fast ship. Another time, during the dog watch, Spencer was on the fo'c'sle with Cromwell—a lot of these talks took place on the fo'c'sle—when an apprentice overheard the midshipman ask if Cromwell could disguise the brig, disguise her thoroughly enough to bring her into New York without anyone being the wiser. "Yes," replied Cromwell, and Spencer asked how. At that moment an officer began to come forward. Cromwell gave an absurd answer. "By shipping the bowsprit aft," he said—something roughly akin to putting the headlights on the back of a car—and then moved away forward, abruptly ending the talk.

All of this could have been idle chat. Spencer's station, after all, was forward, so he had reason to be there. He wasn't supposed to fraternize, but he was young, and an uneventful cruise can be boring enough to make someone seek a distraction, even if regulations forbid it. There was all of the tobacco and alcohol changing hands. This, too, could be nothing more than bad judgment by a young man trying hard to fit in. Everything Spencer did in the cruise's first weeks could be dismissed as more or less innocent, if it weren't for a couple of points. The first is that the night before *Somers* set sail, a seaman took a ship's steward aside and told him something surprising. The steward wouldn't be aboard for this cruise, and the seaman apparently wanted to unburden himself. "There will be mutiny on board this time," he told his erstwhile shipmate. "Be glad you are not going out."

This was just one statement, a statement that didn't come to light until weeks after the cruise. Far more serious was what began aboard *Somers* on the second leg of her voyage. As the ship approached Africa, a darkness began to settle about her, almost palpable in its weight. Nearly everyone aboard could feel it. The change took place, all agreed, in early October, when *Somers* reached Funchal, in the bejeweled islands of Madeira.

Madeira: one of the outriders of maritime Europe. Along with the Azores and the Canaries, it was among the first places that the Age of Exploration's sailors discovered. Verdant and mountainous, the island seemed almost tropical, though it lay too far north to qualify for that label. Yet Madeira and its island group remained a favorite port of call for centuries; they lay near the northeast trades, a natural stop for outward-bound Europeans on their way toward Good Hope or the Horn. The New World seafarers who rode the west wind also found it a useful way station for watering and provisioning when they were heading for southern locales. A few months before *Somers's* arrival, the frigate *United States* called there. One of the frigate's crew recalled it as an Eden-like garden, albeit a mountainous one, where the snow-capped Pico Ruivo loomed over valleys full of grapevines and fragrant lemon and orange trees. He spoke especially of the hedges of daisies and roses, the latter growing wild everywhere.

After a hard sea voyage—and every nineteenth-century sea voyage was hard—Madeira must have seemed a drowsy paradise, not merely sensual, but liberating in an emotional, spiritual way. "While walking the deck of a clear evening," the *United States's* crewman had written,

> I stopped, and, leaning listlessly over the hammock netting, the sound of the vesper bells could be heard distinctly stealing o'er the still waters of the bay; and, assisted by imagination, could be heard the deep and solemn tones of the organ and the chanting of the nuns at their devotions while all else was hushed in sleep, and which certainly tended to create a feeling of solemn awe in the minds of those who kept their solitary watch on the decks of the stately vessels which lay at anchor on the bosom of the peaceful waters, but who little dream that in a few short hours they are destined to dare the storm. . . .

Sixty years earlier, His Majesty's Armed Transport *Bounty* put in at nearby Tenerife in the Canaries, where *Somers* would call after leaving Madeira. While *Somers*'s voyage was a quarter way done, *Bounty*'s had been only beginning, for she had been on the way to Tahiti, on the opposite side of the planet, a voyage to dwarf that of *Somers*. But *Somers* resembled *Bounty* in more ways than one. The vessels were roughly the same size, flush-decked and crowded; neither had space for a complement of marines. *Bounty*'s travels were far longer, but most of *Somers*'s crew was new to the sea, so the three weeks just past no doubt seemed more like months to them. Near the midpoint of each of the cruises was an island filled with delights, Madeira for *Somers*, Tahiti for *Bounty*. The two ships shared a further trait: their terrible troubles began when they came to their respective Edens, and climaxed a month or so after they left. And in each case the trouble centered around a junior officer of good birth. Fletcher Christian, late acting lieutenant, had been twenty-four; Philip Spencer, acting midshipman, was eighteen.

Maybe none of this is coincidence. A ship, after all, is a perfect place for unrest. Lack of space, lack of privacy, terrible food, constant damp and motion, broken sleep, and personality clashes that can't be solved simply by walking away, not when a hundred feet or so is as far as someone can walk—all of these can grate on the nerves. Add to that the discipline, the lack of freedom of action, the wholly undemocratic way of doing things on a warship, and the psychological pressures increase. History's great maritime powers, among them Athens, the Netherlands, England, and the United States, have always tended to be more libertarian than their land-oriented counterparts, but at sea their ships are anything but democratic. The United States, in particular, was a land of growing democracy in the mid-nineteenth century, and Philip Spencer, as a young white male with a father of influence, was at the cutting edge of privilege. Being on the receiving end of naval authority was something new and unpleasant to him. Mackenzie was no William Bligh; still, the discipline chafed.

Then came Madeira. As *Somers* bobbed in the Bay of Funchal, the island must have been tantalizing, with its chants and its bells drifting to Spencer on citrus- and rose-scented breezes, bringing to mind his earlier short stay in the tropics. It lay just beyond reach; and so it reminded him of the things that he didn't have, and that the cruise was not over. Fletcher Christian would have understood well.

Somers's call at Madeira meant still more discipline rather than less. For three weeks the brig's crew had lived a life of routine, of evolutions, of running the guns in and out. Now those routines ended, at least for the moment, but new ones replaced them, as boats went to and from shore, bringing aboard provisions. As Madeira held out its promise of idyll, the bawling commands of the officers must have seemed like salt in a wound.

Whatever the cause, from the time *Somers* arrived at Funchal, morale went sharply downhill. Lieutenant Gansevoort later tried to describe it. After *Somers* arrived at Madeira, he stressed, "I observed a change—a neglect to obey small orders, sullenness, a change in the manner of a ship's company." It was the sort of change, he explained, "which is easily observed by one who understands the character of seamen on board of a vessel." His fellow officers, and a lot of the crew, picked up on it, too. And Spencer began acting more strangely, together with Cromwell and others.

He had talked ill of Mackenzie before. Soon after leaving New York, he had dismissed the captain as a "damned old granny" during a rare discussion with his fellow midshipmen, and more often he called Mackenzie a "humbug." But after Madeira his complaints came more often. Mackenzie required his midshipmen to keep journals, since this was a training cruise, but Spencer was slack about doing it. John Tillotson, one of the other midshipmen, once spoke to Spencer about it. "Damn the journal," Spencer replied. There was no love lost between the two boys (Tillotson was sixteen, and Spencer often acted that young); one time Spencer was slow to relieve Tillotson as the watch was changing. Spencer hit Tillotson; Tillotson hit back. But damning the journal went beyond trading punches. Flying in the face, as it did, of the captain's own orders, it was more insubordinate.

Cromwell, too, spoke more openly against Mackenzie. He was a slacker, apparently, at least some of the time. ("Damn it," he once swore in front of a boy when Mackenzie had issued an order, "there's no use in doing it; he only wants to make more work for the crew.") At Funchal he was involved in the ship's provisioning, and he wasn't happy about it. Gansevoort later described him as "sullen and disrespectful," lampooning the lieutenant's orders instead of following them. After the brief early October days at Madeira, *Somers* weighed anchor, setting out for Santa Cruz in the Canaries, and Cromwell, stationed forward, fouled up some of the rigging. The problem was so obvious that Mackenzie himself went forward to see what was going on, asking the sailor how it had happened. The captain's direct attention should have been enough to straighten things out, but once he had gone back aft, Cromwell got surly again. Proclaiming that he didn't "care a damn about the rigging," he told the men forward that Mackenzie was trying to get "too much work out of the crew." He went so far to wish the "commander and the brig farther in hell than they were out." Before the cruise ended his wish would come true.

The rigging really bothered Cromwell. Once, when *Somers* was at sea, and he was helping get the jib in, the lacing—the rope that held the sail to the stay—jammed on him, and he lost all patience. "God damn the jib and the lacing," he cursed, "and the damn fool that invented it." The inventor was Captain Mackenzie, and Cromwell well knew it.

It was all still just talk, and sailors had to be given a little allowance for griping. But some types of talk are especially dangerous, and Cromwell and Spencer were going too far. They were starting to skirt the sharp lines set down in the Articles of War.

The Articles had an ancient lineage by 1842. Their genesis reached back to Roman days. Neither the transition from classical to medieval and modern times nor the advance from oar to sail had done much to change the nature of what lived in them. John Adams, a lawyer from a quintessential American seaport, once noted how much the British Articles of War owed to their much older Roman counterparts. "There was extant, I observed," he recounted in his twilight years, "one system of Articles of War which had carried two empires to the head of mankind. The Roman and the British; for the Articles of War are only a literal translation of the Roman." Adams kept this in mind as he began to draft rules of discipline for the infant American navy in 1775. "It would be vain," he explained, "for us to seek our own invention or the records of warlike nations for a more complete system of military discipline." Thus he copied the British Articles, which had come into being, in the form Adams knew, more than a century earlier. When Adams became president, he signed into law a permanent version of the Articles that Congress enacted in 1800, as naval war bloomed between France and America.

The thirteenth article was the one that Spencer and Cromwell were skirting. "If any person," it recited in part, "shall utter any seditious . . . words" or "shall treat with contempt his superior . . . he shall be punished at the discretion of a court martial." There was no question that Spencer and Cromwell knew of this law; the practice on all naval vessels was to read all of the Articles aloud once every few Sundays, so that even illiterate sailors couldn't plead ignorance. But Articles or no Articles, Spencer and Cromwell were to say even more dangerous things as the voyage continued.

That a midshipman and a chief bo'sun's mate, of all people, were indulging themselves in this kind of talk was disturbing. A midshipman, even an acting midshipman, was a junior officer, or at the very least an officer-in-training. He was to hold himself apart from the crew, showing loyalty to his captain. Blowing off steam was all right for a sailor; it wasn't all right for a midshipman. A bo'sun's mate, too, was supposed to be loyal, for he was responsible for enforcing good order and discipline before the mast. Other than bo'sun's mates, ships' captains had only marines to make sure that the crew stayed in line. It wasn't that marines were more orderly; they weren't. In fact marines broke the rules more often than sailors did. But marines were a different breed. They were more purely military in function; they were in uniform and went armed all the time, which made them an insular little group, even by a ship's standards, isolated and different from anyone else. Naturally, then, the sailors disliked them, and the marines hated the sailors back. If either camp rose up and threatened the ship, the captain could rely on the other group to handle the problem fast.

The trouble in this case was that with a single exception, *Somers* had no marines. She had no room for them. Other than the bo'sun's mates and her handful of officers, *Somers* had no enforcer except for the master-at-arms, marine sergeant Michael H. Garty. It was Garty who was the first to hear truly sinister talk from Spencer.

At age twenty-eight, Garty was one of the older men aboard. Irish by birth, he was in New York in 1841 when he joined the marines, and then he was chosen as *Somers*'s master-at-arms, earning the rank of sergeant. He had no complement to command; he had nobody on board to help him keep the crew under control except for a few bo'sun's mates, who didn't answer to him. Now and then he instructed the apprentices in the use of small arms, both muskets and pistols. If *Somers* had gone into action, he might have stationed some of the crew in the tops with orders to try to take out the enemy officers or possibly the enemy powder boys who kept the main guns supplied. That was marines' work; lacking marines, he would have to make do. But this was a mere training cruise, and the chance of battle was slight. Before the cruise even started, Mackenzie had impressed upon Garty the need to go easy on the apprentices, the same advice that Cromwell had spurned. Mackenzie further told

Garty he wanted to hear as few reports of disciplinary problems as possible; the master-at-arms should give crew members every chance to mend their ways. Perhaps that accounted for Garty's lack of alarm when, between Madeira and Tenerife, Spencer told him some remarkable things.

It happened one day as Garty sat on the spar deck forehatch, forward above the crew quarters. For once the midshipman seemed interested in learning about one of his shipmates, asking Garty about his career. He especially wanted to know if Garty had been promoted to sergeant specifically to allow him to serve as master-at-arms. Spencer was right, replied Garty; that was so. Wasn't it true, Spencer asked next, that Garty would be demoted if he returned to shore duty? No, said Garty. "Not unless I committed a crime."

Spencer apparently changed the subject, commenting on how fine a vessel the little brig was. Garty agreed politely. And then Spencer casually said that he could take her with a half-dozen men.

This was like walking up to a police officer standing outside a bank and mentioning how easy it would be to rob it. But Garty's reaction was muted, probably because Spencer was so offhand, as if he were engaged in an intellectual exercise to pass the time. And, after all, he was an officer, not some rough sailor. But Garty did take issue with him, saying that even a dozen and a half men would be too few. Spencer, though, seemed convinced he could do it. The first thing he'd do, he explained, would be to "secure" the captain and officers; next he would arm himself and his men; then he would turn the crew out on deck. As soon as they saw that Spencer and his half-dozen had control of the ship, the sailors would promptly give up. Everything would go fast and smoothly—provided that Spencer knew beforehand where the keys to the arms chest were.

Garty had charge of those keys, as Spencer was well aware.

The sergeant challenged the plan. Once the crew had turned out, he argued, it could rush Spencer and his people, tossing them overboard and losing no more than six men in the process. Spencer "must think us a very poor crew," he told the midshipman, to believe that he "could take us with six men."

"Oh, no," disagreed Spencer, but he made no counterarguments. Instead he won the debate by walking away. But he would cross Garty's path again. On a ship the size of *Somers,* that was inevitable.

As day followed day, *Somers* dropped down the latitudes, morale and Polaris both sinking lower, and tension perceptibly climbing. This was routine, boring duty. America wasn't at war and neither were Europe's Great Powers. The epic sea battles of Nelson's and Napoleon's age had been done for a generation, and war at sea would not regain that high a pitch for three generations to come. The job of the little American squadrons was to show the flag abroad, policing the waters and protecting commerce from pirates and greedy regional princes. So *Somers* dutifully put in at various ports as she deftly sailed south. From Madeira she traveled to Tenerife in the Canaries, arriving in mid-October and standing off Santa Cruz for a time. A fortnight later she made Porto Praia in the Cape Verde Islands. Despite their name there was nothing much green about them, for they were Atlantic extensions of the Sahara. She was now approaching the breeding ground of slavery, the nursery of tempest and hurricane, the hot, dry region in which the most terrible storms on earth had their faintest beginnings. Still she sailed south, farther into the furnace, well into the tropics, heading for Liberia.

The calls were good for the ship, or so Mackenzie might think, breaking routines, or at least changing them. The ship had new needs when she came close to land. Soundings had to be taken, tide charts consulted, proper anchorages found. But at heart it was still more routine, the same as the rest of the cruise. *Somers* might, with some luck, intercept a slaver or two; she was, after all, approaching the African coast, and soon she would be a hundred miles or so off

Guinea, a perennial source of slaves. But that was all she could hope for. Even piracy was fading these days, except in the brain of Acting Midshipman Spencer.

He still kept to himself a lot. Now and then someone observed him drawing. A few people saw what looked like an ink-and-lead likeness of a brig, roughly resembling *Somers,* but flying the black flag of a pirate ship. (The famed Jolly Roger was largely an invention. When pirates bothered to use a flag, other than when they flew false colors, they usually opted for black.) At other times he turned outward, but in disturbing ways. Sometimes, for instance, he asked shipmates what they knew of the Isle of Pines. This was, or had been, a pirate lair off Cuba's southwest coast. Known also today as the Isla de la Juventud or Isle of Youth, it sits astride the choke point between Cuba and the Yucatán, one of only two passages into and out of the Gulf of Mexico. As such it was a fine strategic location for anyone wanting to take control of the Gulf. It had a good, though shallow, harbor, useful to small pirate vessels while keeping out larger ships. It was exactly the sort of harbor, in fact, for which *Somers* had been designed. Spencer apparently learned of the island from Cromwell, who described it as "a very beautiful place." Young Matthew C. Perry, purser Horace M. Heiskill, and Leecock, the *Somers's* surgeon, all saw Spencer in the wardroom one day going over West Indies charts, trying to pin down the island's location and talking out loud about it. Leecock knew the place's piratical heritage. He asked Spencer if he had any acquaintances there—whether joking or in a serious way we don't know today—but his question was answered with silence. Spencer simply kept looking over the charts, apparently wholly absorbed.

Along with this interest in piratical matters, Spencer sometimes talked of commanding a ship of his own, and not at some distant date when he might be promoted, but in the very near future. He brought it up with Alexander McKee one day when the sailor was out on the forescuttle. Spencer asked him if he knew how to tailor.

Yes, McKee answered, and Spencer asked if McKee would like to sail with him to a warm place where warm clothes wouldn't be needed. McKee seemed agreeable, and Spencer gave him a wad of tobacco. Garty was another who heard this sort of talk. Apprentices got wind of it, too: while giving a fifteen-year-old "third class boy" a piece of tobacco, Spencer asked if he would like to sail with him. "I would like it very well," replied the apprentice. Spencer even promised to rate him seaman. He made similar overtures to nineteen-year-old William Neville one night while showing him the ins and outs of lunar observation. These comments seem like a joke; but the repetition suggests something more serious.

Whether or not he was joking about having a ship of his own, one thing was clear. Spencer despised *Somers's* current commander. His name-calling during the earlier part of the cruise was just the beginning. The longer the ship stayed at sea, the worse things got, and soon Spencer was having run-ins with Captain Mackenzie.

Reproof and disciplinary action are common enough at sea, and according to most accounts, Mackenzie chastised Spencer no more than he did the other midshipmen, and possibly less. But these same accounts suggest that Spencer richly deserved whatever chastisement he got, for he took his duties too lightly. Sometimes reproach came for small failures; once, during gunnery practice, Mackenzie had to tell Spencer to shout his orders more loudly, so the men in his gun division could hear him over the din. Other times his offenses were worse, such as when he let the fo'c'sle lookouts fall asleep, and Mackenzie gave him a talking to. A sleeping lookout is a dangerous thing; without him the ship can be blind, both to the elements and to the enemy. Sleeping on duty was a grave enough matter for the Articles of War to address, mandating death as the usual penalty.

Spencer did nothing to hide his anger, even from the crew, before whom he should have at least been impassive, if not absolutely supportive of his commander. Once, after Mackenzie upbraided him for something or other, he took refuge in the steerage. "The Captain has been reprimanding me," he seethed to the cabin steward, "but he shan't do it much longer." And sometimes the threats were even more open. One day in early November, Spencer was forward chatting with Cromwell and Small; both Spencer and Cromwell were on duty. Mackenzie was on deck, sitting on the roundhouse; Midshipman Henry Rogers was on deck giving orders. "Let go some brace!" he called out at one point, but the three kept talking and laughing. Again Rogers gave the command, and then still again. The chatter continued. Rogers finally had to go forward to take care of things himself.

Now Mackenzie ordered Spencer to lay aft. Spencer went, no doubt aware that he was in trouble. It wasn't a flogging; it was merely another reprimand. But when he came forward again, he was cursing Mackenzie for all he was worth.

James Wales, purser's steward, had seen the whole thing. "Spencer, what's the matter?" he asked the midshipman.

"The commander says that I don't pay attention to my duty," fumed Spencer, "and urges me to pay better attention hereafter." He began cursing again horribly. "God damn him," he burst out, "I should like to catch him on that roundhouse some of these dark nights and plunge him overboard; it will be a pleasure to me." He gritted his teeth in anger. "I'll be God damned if I don't do it." Several seamen who heard him just smiled. Among them were Cromwell and Small.

Sometimes Spencer moved beyond words and into open defiance. At Cape Mesurado in Liberia, Mackenzie wanted him to take command of a boat bound for shore. Spencer wasn't in uniform; Mackenzie told him to put it on. Spencer ignored the order, boarded the boat, and shoved off. Mackenzie either overlooked Spencer's refusal, or else he didn't realize what had happened, probably the latter, but he did hail the boat to ask if Spencer had the American ensign aboard. Spencer replied that he didn't, but by this time he was tired of Mackenzie. "Go to hell, you damned old humbug!" he muttered loudly enough for the boat's crew to hear. "I won't come back for it."

The Liberian coast brought out the worst in others as well. One was twenty-one-year-old landsman Daniel McKinley. It was McKinley, oddly enough, who had supposedly talked of trouble aboard the night before *Somers* sailed. He, like Spencer, had been punished more than once on this cruise, as well as having been flogged on the previous one, and he was in a bad frame of mind. He once abused and swore at a shipmate; that got him in trouble. Mackenzie gave the crew liberty when *Somers* called at Santa Cruz, but McKinley stayed ashore too long, and Mackenzie had him flogged again for this new transgression. It infuriated McKinley, who told a shipmate that he wouldn't "forget Commander Mackenzie for what he had done."

Later, when *Somers* reached Cape Mesurado, McKinley again went ashore. This time he purchased an African dirk, a large, sharp knife, one with little use other than killing, although a sailor might find something to do with it. A few other crewmen bought similar knives; later McKinley sold his to Charles Wilson, another angry crewman. Like Cromwell, Small, and others, Wilson had been spotted sometimes talking with Spencer; like McKinley, he had been punished, and he was taking it hard. At least one sailor heard him threaten revenge on Mackenzie. Now he had found a knife, and crewmen sometimes saw him honing it to a razorlike edge. Once, when a fourteen-year-old apprentice had helped himself to the dirk for some task or other, Wilson told him to put it down. That knife, he explained, "had to do a great deal of slaughtering some of these days." But not yet; Wilson said that it needed further sharpening first.

Cape Mesurado was *Somers*'s last contact with land before she returned to the New World. When he called at the Cape, Mackenzie learned that *Vandalia*, for which he carried dispatches, had already sailed for St. Thomas in the Caribbean. So on November 11 he decided to do the same. But *Somers* wasn't alone. For weeks she had cruised waters that spawned the slavers, and she fit in quite well. Her size and her speed, and the rake of her masts, were a lot like those of a "Guineaman," one of those ships from the Guinea coast with their cargoes of captive Africans. As she pointed her nose to the west, another vessel was watching.

She was an English cruiser, no doubt on anti-slavery duty. The English took that duty much more seriously than did the Americans, despite the congressional ban on the trade; Secretary of the Navy Upshur was, after all, a southerner. Given the prevailing winds, the English ship probably had the weather gage, but *Somers* was running. Mackenzie didn't know who was following him, but he prepared the brig for battle. Clearing for action was always good practice. Gansevoort ordered Master-at-Arms Garty to break out muskets and pistols—*Somers* carried a couple of dozen each, in addition to all the battle-axes and pikes that were scattered about the spar deck. In the end, no battle took place, but the small arms' appearance set Spencer thinking again.

A couple of afternoons later, on a fine, clear day, Garty was on his way forward. Spencer was standing there, to one side of the hatch, and he spoke up as Garty passed by. "Master-at-Arms," he asked, "are all the arms loaded?"

The question must have seemed odd, coming out of the blue. Spencer wasn't even on duty. But Garty answered him. "All but six or seven muskets," he said. Spencer then asked why everything wasn't kept loaded. Garty had a system for keeping track of the loaded weapons, which he now described to Spencer. When stored in the arms chest, some of the muskets pointed in one direction, while others pointed the opposite way. The ones pointing aft were loaded. "If they were all loaded and pointed aft," he explained, "they would not fit in the arms chest." Then Spencer asked if the weapons were primed. No, replied Garty; none of them was. A couple of days afterward, Spencer repeated the questions.

The midshipman seemed disturbed, and most of his attention was on authority—his resentment of the authority that others had over him, combined with a desire to exercise some of his own, by violence if necessary. So far his infractions were minor. But as *Somers* sailed deeper and deeper into the Atlantic, his talk, and then his actions, began to spin out of control.

For all of its openness, the fo'c'sle was one of the more private places aboard. The berth deck was usually crowded and active, and even the hold was often occupied. The fo'c'sle was partly hidden by the booms from the quarterdeck, where captain and officers kept watch over *Somers*. A midshipman could be there without raising too much suspicion, especially if that was his station. It was more innocent-looking than if a seaman were hanging around aft with nothing to do. The fo'c'sle had only one drawback: it lay on the main path to the head, the frontmost part of the ship, where the crew answered calls of nature. This meant that men and boys were constantly coming and going through the fo'c'sle area.

One afternoon, as their lessons down on the berth deck ended, two apprentices made for the head. They saw Spencer and Cromwell on the forescuttle; Spencer was writing down something on a piece of old, yellow, and dirty paper. They were talking in low, earnest tones as the boys walked past, and one of the youngsters, Edward English, heard Spencer say "Yes, yes." The other, William Inglis, saw Spencer write something down and show it to Cromwell. "Yes, sir," the seaman replied.

Inglis continued to watch the pair from the head. Spencer would glance at a group of apprentices who were on the larboard side— English and Inglis were to starboard—and then write something else down, showing Cromwell what he had written. This happened three or four times. Inglis got the impression that Spencer was jotting down names. As the apprentice walked past the two, he looked back over his shoulder. The characters on the paper were cryptic, unintelligible, though Inglis could read and write.

When Spencer saw what Inglis was doing, he got up and shook his fist at him. "Damn you," he told Inglis, "if you don't go away I will take you to the mast." Faced with the threat of a flogging, Inglis and English both fled.

Others saw Spencer and Cromwell together on the forescuttle, sometimes with the mysterious paper, sometimes without, sometimes by day, sometimes by night. That wasn't all. As *Somers* sailed farther into the waste of ocean that stretched out before her, Spencer's odd behavior increased. Before they arrived off Liberia, the midshipman had asked young William Clark if he had a knife. When Clark told him no, Spencer promised to get him one. Now, with Africa a week and a half behind, Spencer came to Clark in the night. "Here's a knife for you," he said, handing him a brass-hilted blade. Clark claimed that he had already gotten one. "Never mind," answered Spencer. *"Take this and keep it sharp and ready."*

At first glance, there is something Tom Sawyer–like in all of these things, the sort that Mark Twain labeled "dark, deep-laid plans." Tom had an active imagination, seeing exotic caravans ripe for plunder where there were only children's Sunday school picnics, sending secret signs to victims of sham-piratical plots, and indulging in other boys' games. But Spencer was too old for the role of Tom Sawyer, and this gave his behavior a sick, sinister twist, especially on a ship full of weapons in which he took a great deal of interest. And though Tom Sawyer liked his tobacco, he never got drunk. Weapons and alcohol are a bad combination, and sometimes the crew spotted Spencer staggering on deck, and giving brandy to sailors. As November began to draw to a close, he developed another interest: the ship's chronometer.

The easy part about navigation, in the days before marvels such as GPS, Loran, and gyroscopes, was measuring latitude. By using a quadrant or sextant to shoot the stars, or measure the sun's meridian altitude, a mariner could know just how far he was to the equator's north or south. He could thus know if he was on the same latitude as a particular charted location, for instance, the Isle of Pines. But longitude, the east–west measurement, was much harder. It required a chronometer, a highly accurate clock that wouldn't be fooled by the ship's incessant pitching and rolling. By comparing high noon with the known time of the ship's home port, a navigator could know how far east or west of that port he was. Chronometers were standard equipment for warships by the time *Somers* came along, but some were better than others.

About the 25th of November, Spencer decided to learn just how accurate *Somers's* timepiece was. He approached Henry Rogers, the senior midshipman, who was sitting in steerage. Young Oliver Hazard Perry was there when it happened. Spencer asked Rogers if *Somers's* chronometer was a good one. Rogers didn't know for sure; he said that he supposed that it was a very good one. Spencer pressed further, asking if Rogers knew the rate at which it gained or lost time. (Even a few seconds' error a week could cause big navigational problems.) Rogers, again, wasn't very much help, so Spencer dropped the subject.

It was arguably the most innocent thing that Spencer had said or done yet. Learning about navigation, about *Somers's* own particular foibles, was an honest and laudable project, and a natural one for a midshipman who was intent on improving himself. But in light of what had been happening, it was strange. And perhaps hearing Rogers say that he thought the timepiece a good one egged him on further. Maybe it helped bring about what happened later that night.

James Wales, the purser's steward, had been in trouble with Mackenzie before, when *Somers* was on her shakedown cruise to Puerto Rico. Maybe Spencer had heard of the episode. That may have been why, about seven o'clock on the evening of Friday,

November 25, he came forward and started a conversation with Wales, who was standing on deck. At first he made small talk about the weather; then he asked Wales to climb onto the foremast booms—a forbidden place to sit, but one that would give them some privacy—for he had to discuss something very important. Wales was agreeable, so up they went. Some other crewmen could see the two talking, but their words were hard to make out.

Once on the booms, Spencer and Wales began a conversation that would run for nearly two hours. His first words were startling. "Are you afraid of death?" he asked Wales. "Do you fear a dead man? And dare you kill a person?"

Wales, quite surprised, paused before answering. He thought that Spencer might be joking around, but as he looked at the midshipman he could tell that Spencer seemed utterly serious. There was an intensity about him as he spoke. Wales's answer was faintly humorous; he confessed that he wasn't "particularly anxious to die quite yet," but he had no fear of a dead man. Then he, too, grew serious. If a man were to insult him enough, he said, "I could muster sufficient courage to kill him if necessary."

"I don't doubt your courage at all," replied Spencer. "I know it. But," he asked Wales, "can you keep a secret? And will you keep one?" He had something to tell Wales, something that would put his own life at risk, and the lives of others as well. Wales had to be willing to keep this secret. "If so," Spencer demanded, "take the oath." So Wales took it, solemnly swearing never to speak of what Spencer was preparing to tell him. Then Spencer continued.

He had a plan, he told Wales, a plan to take *Somers*. He was in league with about twenty others to make her a pirate ship. It would mean killing all of the officers, but the plan was in place, the men's stations assigned, and everything written down safely in code. He had the paper concealed in his neckerchief; he told Wales to feel it. Wales touched the kerchief, could feel the crumple of paper inside it. Spencer then explained more fully.

The coup would come in the mid-watch, the hours just after midnight when human circadian rhythms are at their lowest ebb and darkness conceals movement. The night would be one when Henry Rogers, the senior midshipman, had the watch with Spencer, as *Somers* was nearing St. Thomas. Some of Spencer's confederates would stage a sham fight on the fo'c'sle; Spencer would pretend to call them down and ask Rogers for help. When Rogers came forward, Spencer's group would grab him and throw him overboard. That would give them the spar deck.

Spencer told a horrified Wales that he could get hold of the arms chest keys very quickly. His men, once armed, would take stations at the hatches, to stop anyone from coming above. Spencer, meanwhile, would go below, into Mackenzie's cabin, and murder the captain himself. From there he would go to the wardroom with some of his men and kill the sleeping officers.

The next step, Spencer went on, would be to slew around the two aftermost guns so that they pointed forward, covering the whole of the spar deck. Presumably he would load them with grape or canister, if it was available, though he didn't say as much. With that accomplished he would have, in effect, two massive shotguns that could sweep the deck clean with a single blast each. With those guns in place he could let the crew come up from below.

At this point Spencer and his people would be in total control. From the crew they could pick the people they wanted to keep. The others they would throw overboard. The youngest boys, the "small fry," as the midshipman called them, would go. They ate a lot, and they would be useless, so he would make them walk the plank. Then he would clear the deck of its boats and any spars and spare rigging. This done, *Somers* would head for the Isle of Pines, or possibly Cape St. Antonio or some similar place. There Spencer's group would find someone who knew about piracy, and *Somers*'s new career could begin. Her victims' equipment would see to her needs, and any women on board them would see to the needs of the crew. Males, though, would go straight to the bottom, said Spencer, since "dead men tell no tales."

At some other time, in some other circumstances, all of it would have been melodramatic, but not in the night on a ship a thousand miles from the nearest land; not coming from Spencer. Wales would not sleep a wink for the rest of the evening. At this point he was practically speechless.

Now Spencer summoned up Small. The seaman stood on the rail rather than climbing onto the booms, but that was close enough, and the two began conversing in Spanish. Wales didn't know exactly what they were saying, but he saw that Small was surprised, even astonished. "Oh, you need not be under any apprehension on his account," Spencer told Small in English. "I have sounded him pretty well and find he is one of us." That relieved Small, who remarked that he was "very glad to hear it." Small then had to leave, but not before Spencer told him that he wanted to talk with him later, during the mid-watch, and that he wanted Small to "see that foretopman" in the meantime, naming no names.

Once again, the purser's steward was alone with the midshipman. Spencer asked Wales what he thought, and he offered to make Wales his third officer. Wales remained silent. Spencer enticed him further, mentioning that Mackenzie had a lot of money on board. Wales decided to lie. He told Spencer that he favored the plan.

By now nearly two hours had passed, and the moon was shining down. Wales had his duties to see to, so he got down from the booms. Spencer told him that they would talk again the next day. But he followed Wales a short way, warning him again not to breathe a word of what he had just heard. If he did, Spencer told him, Wales's life "would not be worth a straw." If Spencer didn't kill him, one of his people would. With that the ghastly meeting was over. But for Wales a long night was only beginning.

He had to tell the captain what Spencer had just revealed, apparently dismissing the solemn oath he had taken without any qualms whatsoever. He might not have known it, but Spencer and Rogers were scheduled to share a mid-watch just four nights from now, when *Somers* would be a few days from St. Thomas. That would likely have been the night for the plan to go down. But whether Wales knew this or not, he sensed that speed was crucial. He started to make his way aft.

He had gotten almost to the companionway, the hatch and the stairs that would take him below, when he spotted Small farther forward. The seaman seemed to be shadowing him, watching him closely. With Spencer's warning fresh in his mind, Wales decided he had better be careful.

As he moved through the ship, he was always aware of Small's presence. He finally went below to the berth deck; maybe from there he could at least get to the wardroom and warn Lieutenant Gansevoort. But to do that he would have to go through steerage, to which Spencer had already retired. The lights were out, and most of the occupants sleeping. Spencer's hammock was slung directly in front of the door to the wardroom. As Wales approached the steerage door, Spencer raised his head. "What the devil are you about, cruising around there?" he called out. The hour was late; why hadn't Wales turned in?

Wales didn't answer. Instead he pretended to be opening the small purser's storeroom, and then he went back forward. The berth deck would have been dark, with people sleeping all around him. Some of them, if Spencer were telling the truth, would have killed him, had they been able to read his thoughts. Nearly an hour passed. Then Wales went aft again. Now he could see that the wardroom lights, too, were out; the officers were asleep. But Spencer was still awake, so Wales gave up for the moment. He tossed and turned the rest of the night, waiting for the dawn.

Wales was probably right to worry, if his story is true. Apparently his efforts to pass himself off as Spencer's ally fell flat. Small seemed to suspect him, and that night, unknown to Wales until later, another meeting took place. Nineteen-year-old Peter Tyson was lying between two guns on the spar deck, trying to get some sleep, when McKinley and Wilson stopped nearby. Wilson was carrying an ax and a sharpening stone. Tyson heard the men talking as they approached, unaware that he was listening. He caught a fragment of conversation: ". . . just told me that we had spies, and that we had better be careful." Tyson feigned sleep, listening to the discussion. Wilson said that he wasn't afraid; he had been in too many scrapes before for that. "Would you join them?" asked McKinley. Wilson seemed agreeable. "I would not mind joining them," he replied.

"I don't know," said McKinley. "I would rather go in a regular slaving expedition, for there you have $35 a month and prize money. . . ." He got back to the main point. "When we get to St. Thomas we will be fitted out."

Tyson pretended to wake up, asking McKinley why he was talking about slavers. Startled, McKinley stammered, "I was talking about a slaver that went from St. Thomas in regular man-of-war style, and returned, and had taken three vessels." They were pirates, he said, regular pirates.

The warning of spies came from Small, perhaps, or maybe from Spencer. Certainly the latter seemed alert while Wales was skulking about. The next morning, when the purser's steward tried again to warn Lieutenant Gansevoort, he was still being watched. About 7:00 A.M., after his sleepless night, he went into the wardroom and sat down next to Horace Heiskill, the purser. In a low voice he quickly filled in Heiskill on what had been happening to him. He explained that he was afraid to be seen with Gansevoort. This was dicey business; for all that Wales knew, Heiskill could have been one of Spencer's men. But Heiskill said that he would speak to Gansevoort himself, as soon as the lieutenant came below. He told Wales to follow Gansevoort down and open the purser's storeroom door, which would help screen the wardroom from steerage.

Wales went above and found Gansevoort, telling him that Heiskill had asked to see him below. As Wales was speaking to the lieutenant, he could see Small, McKinley, and Wilson, together with Cromwell, hovering around watching him. But Gansevoort went below without incident. Now Wales summoned his courage and went to find Spencer, to have the talk that the midshipman had wanted, leaving Heiskill to confer with Gansevoort alone.

When Gansevoort got to the wardroom, Heiskill asked him if he knew of a plot to take *Somers* and kill the captain and officers. Gansevoort said that he wasn't aware of any such thing. It must have sounded fantastic. But then Heiskill started to tell him about what had happened to Wales. As the story unfolded, Gansevoort's outlook instantly changed, and he cut Heiskill off in his haste to get to Mackenzie. He found the captain below in his cabin. Quickly he passed on what he had heard. Now, for the first time during the cruise, Mackenzie learned the worst piece of news a captain could hear, that he had a mutiny brewing aboard.

He handled the revelation coolly, Gansevoort thought. The lieutenant's conviction was clear, but the idea of something as outrageous as this was one that Mackenzie had trouble accepting immediately. Later he said that it had occurred to him that Spencer had been reading too many pirate stories, that he must be playing games with Wales. But he couldn't have helped noticing the crew's low morale, and maybe his reprimands of the midshipman crossed his mind at this point. Then, too, there was all of the trouble with Spencer before he even boarded the ship. Finally, of course, mutiny was such a dangerous thing that any prudent commander simply had to look into the possibility, even if it seemed slight. So Mackenzie told Gansevoort to keep Spencer under surveillance for the rest of the day without calling attention to the fact, and to try to keep an eye on the crew.

Gansevoort set out on his job of spying on Spencer, who gave him the slip at dinnertime, but others were noticing him, too. One apprentice saw the acting midshipman staring out to sea from the rigging above the spar deck, muttering to himself "The die will soon be cast." About halfway through the afternoon watch—2:00 P.M. or so—Gansevoort spotted him in the foretop, high aloft on the forward mast, sitting with his head sunk onto his chest, lost in thought. He didn't hear Gansevoort until the lieutenant had pulled himself up into the top and was standing beside him. At that point Spencer seemed surprised and confused, and he began asking questions about the rigging, mainly about the shrouds, which helped hold the masts in place. Gansevoort carefully answered them. Then he asked Spencer why he had missed dinner; Spencer replied that he hadn't been hungry. Gansevoort departed, but an hour later he found Spencer still in the top. Benjamin Green, a foretopman, was now with him, giving him a tattoo.

Gansevoort hailed the top, telling Green to come down on deck. Spencer stuck his head over the rail, and though he said nothing, Gansevoort could tell he wanted Green to stay where he was. But Gansevoort, as a lieutenant, was used to being obeyed. He told Spencer to send Green down, along with anyone else who might be aloft. Green came on deck; Spencer stayed in the top. Gansevoort turned his attention to the men on the deck, mustering them and ordering the hammocks stowed.

Then he turned and saw Spencer, and his blood ran cold.

The midshipman had come down from the top, and was sitting on the Jacob's ladder, the rope ladder that led to the spar deck. As Gansevoort turned his eyes toward him, he could see Spencer staring straight at him—a long, direct stare, which lasted more than a minute. From his description it resembled the stare of a dog or a wolf that is angry and ready to fight, and Gansevoort's own hackles went up. Spencer's countenance, he said later, wore "the most infernal expression I have ever seen upon a human face. It satisfied me at once of the man's guilt."

Mackenzie, meanwhile, had been piecing things together. Throughout the day he had heard about what Spencer had been up to: he had found out about his constant, cryptic writing; about his fascination with the Isle of Pines; about his sudden interest in *Somers*'s chronometer. The evidence was all circumstantial or hearsay, but there seemed to be a whole lot of it. Then Gansevoort found Mackenzie and told him what he had seen, recommending that Mackenzie do something, perhaps confine the midshipman.

Mackenzie replied that he didn't want to act harshly. But he did say that Gansevoort should maintain a sharp lookout, and that he would decide what to do by nightfall. Later he asked Gansevoort what he would do had he been commanding the vessel. Gansevoort wasn't commanding the vessel, so he had no trouble giving advice, especially now that Mackenzie had requested it. He spoke in no uncertain terms. "I would bring that young man aft," he stated, "and iron him and keep him on the quarterdeck."

Night falls fast in the tropics, and already it was late afternoon, almost evening. The night could be dangerous. Mackenzie would have to decide very soon.

From the moment he heard his lieutenant's report about Spencer, Mackenzie had to have known that no matter what happened next, his life had taken a terrible, irreparable turn for the worse. The same was probably true of his officers, and it might even turn out to be true for the crew. But for him it was inescapably certain.

In a strange sense, a captain's power rests on the consent of the governed. A crew must *accept* a captain's authority for that authority to exist. Mackenzie was one man out of more than a hundred. The crew outnumbered the officers ten to one. If the consent of the governed were being withdrawn, as a wave draws back from the shore, he was very nearly defenseless. The boys were young, strong, driven by hormones, lacking the inhibitions of mature adults. They could do whatever they wanted out here. They might have to pay a price later; then again, they might not. Most of *Bounty*'s mutineers had never been apprehended.

If Spencer was talking mutiny, if he was recruiting confederates, then everyone's life was at risk. No. More than that. *Somers* herself was at risk. She was a major capital asset of the United States government. Her loss would be a major blow. But even worse was the fact that *Somers* was a very powerful weapon, a weapon that criminals could turn on innocent lives and property. She was faster than most merchant craft, and more lethal by far. They wouldn't be able to run from her, and they wouldn't be able to fight. And no American frigate would be able to catch her. She could kill and plunder almost at whim. Mackenzie couldn't allow that to happen, even if it cost him his life.

But what if Spencer had been joking? What if this was simply some misunderstanding, a warped sense of humor, a product of scuttlebutt, a vendetta among boisterous youngsters to get a midshipman in trouble? Spencer's father was a powerful man, one of the country's key figures. He was an associate of Abel P. Upshur, Mackenzie's own superior. If Mackenzie was wrong, and Spencer innocent, it could easily wreck the captain's career. Even if Spencer *was* actually plotting a mutiny, the father might be vindictive. He, and the public, might ask what Mackenzie had done to cause this kind of rebellion aboard his vessel. From the moment he arrested the midshipman, Mackenzie's future would be under a cloud, a cloud that might well come to loom over the career of every officer aboard. Their professional lives would be marred. They would all be damaged goods. Even exoneration by a board of inquiry could never completely remove the stain. A top-heavy navy would be happy to have an excuse to thin the junior officers' ranks. Mackenzie was courting professional suicide, for his shipmates and, most especially, for himself.

But what was the alternative? If Spencer was serious, then giving the boy a talking to wouldn't accomplish anything. It might even force Spencer's hand, and those of the other mutineers—assuming that there *were* other mutineers. Mackenzie had no way of knowing how strong Spencer's backing was, or how stable he was, for that matter. All he knew was that he was as isolated out here in the heart of the Atlantic as if the United States no longer existed, at the mercy of his young crew. No; Mackenzie had to take the initiative, had to stop Spencer from doing the same. It would put Mackenzie's career in jeopardy, but standing by idly and risking a full-scale insurrection would be far worse than that. Officers were called upon to give their lives for their country; thus lesser sacrifices, such as careers, were just as legitimate.

Mackenzie had made his decision. Now he had to act on it. Before the sun went down. Before the mutineers, if they existed, rose up from the shadows.

PART FIVE

Crisis

"I LEARN, Mr. Spencer, that you aspire to the command of the *Somers*."

The ship was at quarters, and the men were at their stations. Mackenzie had received the reports of his officers, and then he had told Gansevoort to call them all aft, except for Mr. Hays, who remained on the fo'c'sle. The others came to the quarterdeck, lining up on the starboard side. Heiskill was there, too, summoned up from his post in the wardroom, and Leecock, the surgeon, was on deck as well. Matthew C. Perry, Jr., the acting master, had the wheel, a few feet away from the officers. By now everyone knew that something was going on, something very unusual. The group watched as Mackenzie walked up to Spencer; then they heard the captain's fantastic words.

Spencer heard them, too, and he had to know, when he did, that he had been nailed. But he gave no sign of nerves. "Oh, no sir," he answered, smiling and maintaining an air of deference.

The outright denial did nothing to put off Mackenzie. "Did you tell Mr. Wales, sir," he asked the acting midshipman, "that you had a project to kill the commander, the officers, and a considerable portion of the crew of this vessel, and convert her into a pirate?"

Spencer's reply was the age-old response of every schoolboy who has been caught in the act. "I may have told him so, sir," he responded, "but it was in joke."

"You admit then that you told him so?" asked Mackenzie again. It was less question than statement.

"Yes, sir," Spencer repeated, "but in joke."

By now everyone on the quarterdeck knew what was going on, or at least they knew what Mackenzie and Spencer were saying. The captain's accusations of mutinous plotting probably took some time to sink in. The conversation went on for ten or fifteen minutes, Mackenzie continuing to ask Spencer what he had been doing, and Spencer continuing to say "No—it's all a joke." But Mackenzie was getting tired of hearing that answer. "This, sir, is joking on a forbidden subject," he told Spencer. "This joke may cost you your life."

It was a strange and ominous statement, given that Spencer hadn't actually done much of anything yet. Maybe Mackenzie was trying to scare him, but if so, it didn't seem to be working. Spencer was still very calm, even bland, as if he had nothing to fear in the world.

Mackenzie tried once more. "Do you deny having had frequent conversations with Small and Cromwell?"

This seemed to confuse Spencer, but he stuck with his schoolboy's excuse. "No," he said still again, "it was all a joke."

Mackenzie was getting nowhere, so he changed his approach. "I understand you have been carrying a paper in your neck handkerchief," he said. "What are the contents of it?"

"It is a paper containing my day's work," said Spencer, "and I have destroyed it."

"That is a singular place to carry a day's work," Mackenzie remarked. "Why should you carry it there?"

"It is a convenient one," Spencer imperturbably said.

A captain doesn't lose arguments aboard his own ship. Mackenzie didn't need to keep debating young Spencer when he could simply use his authority. "Be pleased to remove your neck handkerchief," he told the midshipman.

Spencer took the neckerchief off and gave it to Gansevoort, who searched it and came up with nothing. The dead end seemed to frustrate Mackenzie, and he stepped up his assault. "You must have been aware that you could only have compassed your designs by passing over my dead body, and after that, the bodies of all the officers," he told Spencer. "You had given yourself, sir, a great deal to do; it will be necessary to confine you, sir."

There was nowhere on the ship to take Spencer, no out-of-the-way nook that would hold him. Mackenzie had only one decent option. "Step aft there, sir," he said, and then turned to Gansevoort. "Arrest Mr. Spencer, and put him in double irons."

The first step in the arrest was ritual, yet more than ritual. Spencer, as a member of the officer class, had a sword, both symbol and weapon. As a prisoner he could have neither, so Gansevoort took it away from him. Then the lieutenant summoned the armorer, calling for hand and leg chains. Once the hand irons were on, Gansevoort asked the midshipman if he was still armed. No, Spencer told him, but since he supposed that Gansevoort wouldn't believe him, he suggested that the lieutenant search him. Gansevoort took the suggestion, but he found nothing but an old pipe and a few scraps of paper, none of which was the mysterious list. Then he had Spencer chained down to the deck, at its aftermost part on the starboard near one of the two arms chests, which Master-at-Arms Garty carried below. It was the only place. It was in plain sight, and close to the quarterdeck, where the officer of the watch would usually be, and as far as possible from the seamen's usual haunts. Only the helmsmen and the men of the afterguard would be in the vicinity.

Spencer's arrest wasn't the end; it was, instead, the beginning. He had been quite clear, whether joking or not, that others were in on his plot. If Mackenzie had reason enough to arrest the midshipman, then he also had reason enough to assume that he had others aboard who might mutiny. If that was true, then he had to take countermeasures against them. It was a necessary precaution. Arresting Spencer was only the opening salvo.

As evening came on and the men were dismissed from quarters, then, Mackenzie got busy. He gave Gansevoort his orders: the officer of the deck was to be armed with cutlass and pistols. So, too, was the fo'c'sle officer, whose station was deep in the realms of the seamen. Regarding Spencer, Mackenzie's orders were clear. He was to be kept comfortable and his needs seen to, but if he attempted escape, or if he tried to communicate with the crew, the officers were to "blow out his brains." Gansevoort told Spencer the orders, to make very sure that he knew that his life was at stake.

Mackenzie, meanwhile, got together with his petty officers, warning them that they might be facing a mutiny. This was risky business. As senior but noncommissioned sailors, petty officers tended to be loyal to the established regime, but if a midshipman could go wrong, then so could nearly anyone else. Mackenzie had no way of knowing whether one or more of these petty officers was in on Spencer's plan. The poison was already spreading; even the suspicion of mutiny was enough to set a warship against itself, releasing a wave of distrust. Nevertheless, Mackenzie had to trust someone. He told the petty officers to be on the lookout for anything sinister, and to prevent small assemblies of men on deck.

If Mackenzie could get a sense of who might be in on the plot, and how many—assuming that a plot really existed—then he would be in a better position. There were Cromwell and Small, of course; Small, in particular, was acting strangely, having to be called above from the berth deck when the ship went to quarters. But Mackenzie had to have more information. The paper that Spencer had mentioned would be a great help. Maybe he hadn't destroyed it. Maybe it was hidden somewhere. A warship, even a little brig, has plenty of places in which to hide things, but there is always a risk that someone will stumble across them. Lockers, though, were different. An officer's locker came closer than anything else on board to being his personal space, sacrosanct, nearly inviolable. It was the logical place to start looking. Mackenzie told Gansevoort to do it.

Gansevoort went below into steerage, where he found Midshipman Rogers. Together the two searched the locker, while some other officers watched. They took out nearly every last thing. Rogers found a small looking glass case, which contained a still smaller drawer. Within the drawer he discovered a razor case. It felt very light, and he opened it up. Inside were two papers, wrapped up in a third sheet of brown oil paper.

Gansevoort took the two sheets and unfolded them. They contained columns of words in Greek, the sign of a traditional, classical education, the same sort of schooling that Spencer had gotten during his earlier years. The lieutenant showed them to Mackenzie; this was just what the captain had wanted. But because of the Greek, Mackenzie needed a translator.

More people knew Greek in those days, and Latin as well. Not many years earlier, when Alexander Pope turned out a new English text of the *Iliad,* a debate sprang up about whether he had translated it properly. In one small New England town, a newspaper tried to settle the question by printing a part of the poem—in the original Classical Greek—together with Pope's rendition. It wasn't a joke. The publisher knew that his readers could handle it. Spencer might have thought that he was being clever by writing in Greek, but he should have realized that one or more of the ship's other officers likely would be able to break his childish code. Henry Rogers, the senior midshipman, took care of it.

One of the papers held three lists of names, headed respectively "Certain," "Doubtful," and "To be kept, willing or unwilling" (or as it came to be called by the officers, "nolens volens"). This third list was the longest, containing a total of eighteen names, among them Thomas Dickerson, who had had run-ins with Cromwell, and Richard Leecock, the ship's surgeon. The "Doubtful" column was ten names long, some of them marked with Xs. At the top of this list, each with an X beside it, were the names of Charles Wilson and Alexander McKee. Benjamin Green's name, too, appeared here, lacking an X. Down at the page's bottom, a note explained the markings. "Those doubtful marked X," it read, "will probably be induced to join before the project is carried into execution. The remainder of the doubtful will probably join when the thing is done; if not they must be forced." Another line followed. "If anyone, not marked down, wish to join after it is done, we will pick out the best, and dispose of the rest."

The "we," perhaps, referred to those whose names appeared under "Certain." This was the shortest list of the three, holding only four names. Spencer's headed it, followed by the names "E. Andrews," "D. M'Kinley"—and James W. Wales, the same Wales who had given Spencer away.

Had Wales been totally honest with Heiskill and Gansevoort? Had he been willing at first? Or had he simply done a great job of acting the previous night on the boom? Or was it that morning, when talking to Heiskill, when he had played a role? Or had Spencer merely been hearing what he wanted to hear when he had talked to Wales? It was a puzzle, and it wasn't the only one. The paper, in fact, held more questions than answers. One of them revolved around Andrews. He was clearly a key player, being listed among the certain. The problem was that he didn't exist, not aboard *Somers,* not, at least, under that name. But Cromwell's name appeared nowhere.

The second paper was just as mysterious and even less helpful. It assigned people to various parts of the ship, presumably during the coup. McKee would handle the wheel, and by implication the helmsman. Spencer, Small, and Wilson were assigned to Mackenzie's cabin, and to steerage as well. Spencer was to take the wardroom all by himself, even though he would have found several men there. Small's name showed up twice on this page, but not at all on the first one.

It was all quite confusing, and maybe a little demented. What Spencer had written seemed too haphazard for a cold-blooded, well-planned plot; but nothing says that all plots must be well planned, and these pages couldn't possibly be innocent writing. If Spencer was not merely joking—and Mackenzie was right, this wasn't the sort of thing that people normally joke about—then his plans, to judge from his papers, seemed sketchy. Still, Spencer seemed to have plans, and sure enough, the plans smacked of mutiny. These pages were the first physical evidence that he was angry, perhaps disturbed or even unbalanced, and that he might have been going to act on those feelings.

Having an unbalanced officer aboard was nearly as bad as having one who was mutinous. In fact it was probably worse in this case, given that the two weren't mutually exclusive. But Mackenzie had other things to do besides figuring out Spencer's problems. He now had further evidence, strongly suggestive though by no means conclusive, that Spencer had been plotting a mutiny. But far more frightening was the fact that it also suggested that he had substantial support. Even a few well-organized men could cause chaos aboard, and there were more than a few names here. He had to take this seriously. His next challenge was how to use this intelligence.

The best thing to do was to talk to the men—or rather, the boys—especially the ones on the list. So that night, and the following morning, that is what some of the officers did, especially Gansevoort and Acting Master Perry. They each questioned several sailors. Few admitted to knowing much, even when they had been seen having mysterious dealings with Spencer. When Gansevoort approached Benjamin Green, who had been with the midshipman for much of the day, Green denied knowing a thing. That was almost impossible for Gansevoort to swallow. "You have been very thick with Mr. Spencer lately," he told the young sailor, "and I know damned well you do know something." But Green stuck to his story of ignorance. Nobody else had heard anything either; nobody claimed to be in on the plot. But this was only to be expected. The Articles of War made mutinous talk, even without any mutinous acts, a hanging offense. If anyone was involved, therefore, he had good reasons not to admit it.

Gansevoort, Acting Master Perry, and others, however, felt that some of the sailors were lying. For one thing, the men answered the questions strangely, making the officers suspicious. Then there was the crew's collective demeanor. It had been sinking since the brig sailed from Madeira, and by now it was really low. The sailors were sullen, drifting away from their stations and into little clusters of boys and men, talking quietly among themselves, falling silent when approached by an officer. Sometimes the officers had to repeat their orders twice or even three times before the crew would turn to. Once, Perry saw Wilson using a file on a battle-ax, honing it to a razorlike sharpness, and the sailor was insubordinate around Midshipman Hays. Now and then someone would mutter that Mackenzie shouldn't have put Spencer in irons. Wilson, McKee, and McKinley, all of them on Spencer's Greek list, now and then met at the mainmast to talk. McKee sometimes told people that he wished Spencer's plan had succeeded, that life as a pirate would have been better than living ashore. But at least the sailor was smart enough not to make such remarks to an officer.

Not everyone could have been in on the plot, of course. Had that been the case, then all of the stealth and muttering would have been totally pointless. The crew could have dealt with the officers any time that it wanted. Acting Master Perry guessed that as many as two thirds of the crew were involved, though that seems a very high number. But most of the officers felt that something was wrong, and that Spencer's arrest had done nothing to make it better. It might even have made things worse.

Whatever the numbers involved, some people had little idea what was happening even after the midshipman's confinement. Most of the younger boys thought that he was in irons because he had fought with Egbert Thompson, one of the other midshipmen. McKee might have started this rumor, possibly to increase the confusion and thus to protect himself. But Cromwell and Small took a different approach. Immediately after Spencer's arrest, a couple of nineteen-year-old apprentices, Peter Tyson and Joseph Sears, found the two older men forward, heatedly talking about something. Cromwell in particular seemed furtive and angry, casting his eyes back and forth, keeping a sharp lookout around himself, since one or two boys were hovering nearby. Sears asked the men the reason for Spencer's arrest. "For a supposed mutiny," Cromwell replied. When Sears asked what a mutiny was, Small jumped in with the answer. "It was a plan to kill the captain and officers and take the vessel," he said. He then started musing aloud. "Who could be Mr. Spencer's aides in the supposed mutiny?"

Cromwell asked the same question, adding that Spencer "could not do it alone." Small answered back that he didn't know who else was involved. As for Spencer, Small continued, the captain thought—and Small concurred—that there wasn't any mutiny happening, "that the young man was half crazy, half out of his head."

The two men were probably very afraid, with a good bit of anger thrown in. They were both violent men—at least Cromwell was—and they knew of the violence the navy could show when somebody went over the line. Mackenzie himself could see their nerves the morning after Spencer's arrest. The ship had survived the night without incident, although the officers hadn't slept much. Mackenzie had apparently decided to hold as much as he could to *Somers's* normal routines, probably as a means of showing that he and the navy were in control. So at ten o'clock in the morning he called the crew to quarters, taking the opportunity to inspect both Cromwell and Small. Cromwell's body language still revealed anger. Spotlessly clean, fully upright, he stood braced as if ready for action, grasping his battle-ax tightly. He was pale, though, and staring straight ahead fixedly with what Mackenzie later described as "a determined and dangerous air." But where Cromwell was like a coiled spring, Small was loose and fidgeting. "His appearance was ghastly," as Mackenzie described it. "He shifted his weight from side to side, and his battle-ax passed from one hand to the other; his eyes wandered irresolutely, but never toward mine."

After quarters came church, and although nothing untoward took place, the crew seemed especially attentive, uttering the responses with more emphasis than it usually did. The sailors obviously knew that something was up, and the pitch of life aboard ship was higher than normal. As for Cromwell and Small, they kept coming to people's attention. That morning Gansevoort talked to Henry King and Thomas Dickerson. The latter, whose name appeared on the "nolens volens" list, had had run-ins with Cromwell. He had reasons to hate the man, and under Gansevoort's questioning, he called attention to Cromwell. "That big fellow forward is more dangerous than the rest," he told the lieutenant. "He ought to be confined." So far, despite Cromwell's frequent and angry outbursts, he was not under any special suspicion, and Dickerson's accusation was vague. Gansevoort had to ask whom he meant. "Cromwell, the Boatswain's Mate," he replied. King concurred, and Dickerson told Gansevoort the story of the confrontation over the wood in the bo'sun's storeroom. The two talked to Gansevoort on several occasions, and they took every chance that they could to warn him about Cromwell. King even once claimed that the man was stowing arms in a storeroom, though Gansevoort found nothing odd when he searched it. It was King, too, who told the lieutenant that he thought all of the older boys were in on the plot, a claim that was hard to prove or disprove. The charge sowed suspicions, and tensions increased.

Cromwell, meanwhile, was being obstructionist. He was supposed to go aloft in the morning watch and examine the rigging, but this Sunday found him on deck instead. Gansevoort finally had to order him up, but even then Cromwell refused, Gansevoort apparently not realizing it. Besides this insubordination, other bad things were happening. Sixteen-year-old Jonas Humbert had found Wilson's African dirk and was using it for some petty task when Wilson came by and took it away, telling the boy that it could cut his throat quickly. Spencer was only a few feet away, and now Wilson, still holding the blade, said loudly enough for the midshipman to hear, that he "would like to put it into Mr. Spencer's hands."

There was other interaction as well. Spencer had spent the night on deck, and that morning Gansevoort had freed him so that he would be able to wash. But William Inglis, the seventeen-year-old apprentice who had seen some strange things before, now spotted the midshipman exchanging signals with Wilson, or at least he thought that he did. The description he gave later on is reminiscent of baseball signals: Wilson put his hands to his chin, striking it and the side of his face, with Spencer answering in much the same way. And Inglis saw Wilson standing beneath the mainmast, not too far from the stern, talking with McKee and McKinley.

Maybe people's imaginations were starting to get out of hand. But whether they were or not, nearly everyone seemed to agree that something was wrong. Trouble, even disaster, seemed to hang in the air; and that afternoon, less than twenty-four hours after Philip Spencer's arrest, a near-disaster is exactly what happened.

Somers had made about one hundred fifty miles since the previous evening, drawing to within fifteen hundred miles of St. Thomas. She had the wind on her quarter, blowing from a point between her beam and her stern. She was thus doing what was called "sailing large," and it happened to be her best point of sailing, the direction from which she could make her most efficient use of the breeze. But in the afternoon, that breeze started to wane. To keep up *Somers*'s good pace, Mackenzie ordered the crew to set skysails and royal studdingsails. The royals were some of the highest sails on the masts; only the skysails were higher, flying more than a hundred feet over the spar deck. The studdingsails rode to either side of the royals, reaching out beyond the sides of the ship. Because they were so far up, their leverage on the masts was tremendous. Even with the lightening winds, the extra canvas that Mackenzie now spread kept *Somers* booming along in excess of seven knots.

With the wind on her quarter—in fact, with the wind blowing from almost anywhere except dead astern—*Somers* needed to turn her sails at an angle to make the best use of it. In maritime language this is called "bracing the yards up," or more simply "bracing up." From each end of each yard led lines known as braces; by pulling the brace that led to one end of a yard while letting the other go slack, the crew could brace up the yard, or brace it back, or brace it in, restoring it to a ninety-degree angle to the hull. The thing to look out for was too much strain on the braces. The wind and the sails were already putting lots of pressure onto the masts, and on the smaller and slenderer topmasts and topgallant masts. If over-taut braces added pressure to what was already there, serious problems could happen.

At about six bells in the afternoon watch, or three o'clock, Mackenzie was on the weather side of the quarterdeck, the captain's position of privilege. Hays was on the quarterdeck, too, as officer of the watch, and young Oliver Hazard Perry was on the fo'c'sle. Ward M. Gagely, a fifteen-year-old apprentice, had just helped set the main skysail; he was aloft on the mainmast's royal yard, a hundred feet straight over the quarterdeck, completely surrounded by rope, canvas, and the air that sang through the rigging. Well forward on the spar deck sat Small, sewing his clothes, with Cromwell standing nearby. Everything seemed as routine as could possibly be, given the trouble with Spencer. Then, suddenly, everything began to go wrong.

The brace on the weather side of the main royal had gotten too much play in it, and it needed tightening up. Hays noticed the problem. "Haul through the slack of the weather-royal brace!" he bellowed. "Leave the lee one slack!"

Small and one or two others went to the brace and started to pull. It didn't need much adjustment, and too much could be dangerous. But Small gave not one, but several strong pulls of the brace, far too many for safety, throwing his whole weight into the job.

Everyone saw what was happening, and Hays saw it, too. "Belay!" he called out. The other men at the brace quit pulling, but Small kept on going, jerking the line tighter and tighter. Now Mackenzie was yelling, too. "Belay! Belay!" Even the other men at the brace were telling Small to quit pulling. Finally Small cut it out, and he wandered away from the brace.

The royal yard was now under terrific strain, and so was the topgallant mast that held it. But the strain lasted for barely thirty seconds: a half-minute after Small quit pulling, the topgallant mast, the royal yards and booms, and the attached rigging and sails pulled loose from the topmast completely. A few seconds later, everything fell crazily over, dangling by a rat's nest of lines, with wreckage strewn over the quarterdeck. And young Gagely fell with it.

For an instant Mackenzie was sure that Gagely had been thrown overboard. He looked up, seeing nothing but nightmare; then he caught sight of the boy. Miraculously he had managed to stay aloft somehow, avoiding the hundred-foot plunge to the water, or worse still to the deck. As the mast and royal yard started to go, he had grabbed hold of the shrouds, the standing rigging that helped to support the masts. Then he fell onto the topgallant sail. Mackenzie saw Gagely's shadow as the boy climbed up to the topgallant yard, which was still somehow in place, although everything above it was gone. The youngster's narrow escape hadn't fazed him, and he looked around to see what had to be done to start clearing away the wreckage.

The loss of the main topgallant mast, along with its sails and rigging, threw everything into a frenzy. *Somers* started to handle differently, and the wreckage swung dangerously over the brig. There was a lot to be done, and fast, or things would get worse. Gansevoort had been in the wardroom when he heard the shouting. He looked up through the skylight, saw the topgallant mast going, and came above right away, where Mackenzie ordered him to take charge. The lieutenant quickly ordered the men aloft; Cromwell, Small, Wilson, and others swarmed up the rigging. Officers and crew both noticed that these three, and some others, didn't seem to be doing too much, despite their fast climb to the masthead. They seemed totally unconcerned, in fact, and some found it strange that Cromwell should be up there at all, for the masthead wasn't his station, and the same was true of Wilson.

Nothing like this had happened before on the cruise. Mackenzie had set royal studdingsails, and the skysails, too, in stronger winds than these, with no mishap at all. Now, a day after Spencer's arrest, Small, an experienced sailor, blatantly ignoring orders, had done just the thing that would cause exactly this sort of commotion, with sails, rigging, and spars dangling over just the part of the ship where Spencer was chained and from which Mackenzie commanded. And suddenly it seemed to Mackenzie that none of it was an accident.

During *Somers*'s shakedown voyage, when an apprentice fell from aloft, the crew had gotten to see the drill for recovering a sailor who had gone overboard. The officer of the watch had standing orders on how to respond when someone went into the water, a choreographed set of steps to follow. The helm was to be put down, the ship hove-to, while the life buoy would be let go and the boat cleared away. Heaving-to involved shortening sail, no small thing to do on the spur of the moment. In sum, losing a man overboard, even in normal conditions, would spawn controlled chaos all over the ship. And if someone—Gagely, for instance—fell into the sea as a result of a mast being carried away, the chaos would be anything but controlled. It would be a perfect occasion for mutineers to capture the ship.

But Gagely, whose name was on Spencer's list, had contrived to hang on, and the complex dance of rudder and sails hadn't happened. Things were very confused, all right, but Mackenzie and Gansevoort were both present on deck, and together with Perry and Hays they had things more or less in hand. The captain was angry.

Acting Midshipman Oliver Perry had been forward, where the after-braces were belayed, and he should have put a stop to what Small had been doing. Mackenzie was so angry, in fact, that he sent forward for the midshipman. "Mr. Perry," he snapped, "this is all your fault." That was very strong language, since everything that goes wrong on a warship is by definition the captain's fault. But the outburst passed quickly. Lieutenant Matthew Perry went below for a while; Gansevoort followed him down, telling him to arm himself with a cutlass and pistols, and then to get back on deck. The first lieutenant was clearly worried that the mutineers would try something soon.

Gansevoort was especially concerned about Cromwell. The man's behavior, coupled with the warnings that the lieutenant had heard from the crew, convinced him that the chief bo'sun's mate was bad news. Cromwell was one of the primary reasons why Gansevoort had told Perry to arm himself. Mackenzie had noticed things, too, and during all the repair work, he told Gansevoort that he was going to place Cromwell under arrest. Gansevoort was preparing to hail the masthead and summon the sailor down, but Mackenzie told him to wait until he came down on his own. In the meantime Gansevoort armed other officers, warning them to be on the lookout and to stop anyone from hindering Cromwell's arrest when it came.

When Cromwell finally got down from aloft, Gansevoort drew a pistol on him. The two headed aft, where Mackenzie told Cromwell to sit on the deck. The captain explained his suspicions, and that because of them he was placing Cromwell under arrest. "Yes sir, but I don't know anything about this," said Cromwell, all innocence. "I assure you I don't know anything about it." Mackenzie asked if he had talked with Spencer the previous night on the boom. "It was not me, sir," Cromwell replied. "It was Small."

It wasn't good enough to free Cromwell, but it did get Small in trouble, as if the latter needed anything else to land him in irons. When Gansevoort led Small aft as well, Small, at least, admitted to talking with Spencer and Wales.

With two more people under arrest, the excitement came to an end for a while. The repair work went fairly smoothly. But it took hours to finish, for the damage was pretty extensive. The topgallant mast itself was gone, but *Somers* carried a spare, which the crew would have to sway up and attach to the main topmast. While the sailors were getting it ready, Mackenzie and Gansevoort had everything brought down from aloft, so that the crew could untangle and sort everything out. Apart from some goofing off, nothing went wrong with the process. But now evening was coming on, the sun getting low on the horizon ahead of the ship. The shadows were lengthening; then everything turned to shadow, except for small yellow pools surrounding the lanterns, and perhaps the faint light of the binnacle. At last most repairs were completed, and it was time to sway up the mast.

Spencer had been signaling Wilson again, if his contortions really were signals. But that had been before nightfall. Now the only thing an observer could see was vague shades, the shapes of crew members lounging around on the fo'c'sle. Swaying up a topgallant mast was pretty serious work, requiring a lot of hands at the ropes to help pull it aloft. William Collins, originally gunner's mate but now serving as bo'sun's mate in place of Samuel Cromwell, was in charge of this part of the process. At a crucial moment, with the mast halfway up, he looked around and saw that some of the hands had wandered away from the ropes.

Immediately Collins went forward to where the sailors were standing and lying around. "What did you leave the mast rope for?" he called out. "Go aft and man it again." Nobody answered. Nobody moved. Again Collins told them to do it, and then still again. He might as well have been talking to nothing. His orders went completely unheeded.

By this time Midshipman Rogers had noticed the problem. Finding Collins, who had just come back aft, he asked the new bo'sun's mate where all of the men had gone. They were all forward, answered Collins, and he couldn't get them to lay aft.

Rogers moved forward, drawing a pistol. He found Oliver B. Browning, another bo'sun's mate. Browning was equipped with a starter, and Rogers told him to head up to the fo'c'sle and use it. The pair moved forward; Rogers saw the men skulking around, some of them talking in low tones. He ordered them to get busy, telling Browning to get his starter going. Browning started swinging away, striking two or three of the crew.

Instantly everything changed—for the worse. Men and boys were suddenly scrambling out of the way of the starter; then they were rushing aft, in a tramping stampede. Nobody aboard had ever seen anything like it.

Back on the quarterdeck Mackenzie and Gansevoort heard all the odd stamping. "What noise is that?" Gansevoort called out. He looked forward, into the darkness, and saw two large groups of sailors, one on each side of the deck, come rushing straight toward him. "God, I believe they are coming!" he yelled to Mackenzie, and drew his own pistol. It was one of Samuel Colt's new revolvers, the idea for which Colt had gotten from watching a ship's wheel spin. With that, Gansevoort could take out a lot of the crowd headed toward him, but by no means all. Mackenzie replied that his own weapons were down in his cabin, diving below to get hold of them. Gansevoort leaped up onto the trunk, running forward to meet the two throngs. He yelled at them not to come aft. He picked out one shadowy form, the tallest that he could see, and took aim; it might have been Wilson, but he couldn't be sure in the night. He continued to bellow his warning that he would blow out the brains of the first man to set foot on the quarterdeck. Now he could hear Rogers shouting at him. "It's me, sir!" the midshipman was shouting. "I am sending the men aft!"

By now Mackenzie was back on deck with his own pistols in hand. Gansevoort turned and could see him; then he called out again to the slowing mob of sailors, telling them not to try anything. The ship was in a dangerous state, he warned, and unusual actions might get someone's head blown off before anyone knew what was happening. His orders and threats, backed up by the pistols, finally did the job. The crew returned to the ropes, and the topgallant mast was swayed up.

It was a very near thing. Some of the officers had almost expected a rescue attempt in the dark, and now one seemed to have happened, despite, or maybe because of, the arrest of Cromwell and Small. Mackenzie's decision to put the ringleaders in irons hadn't averted the danger. At the very least the boys were sullen and slow, endangering the welfare of *Somers;* at worst they were mutinous, and only Gansevoort's fast actions had prevented the officers' deaths. The night was only beginning, and more nights would soon follow.

It was almost the 28th of November. Spencer had been under arrest for a day. *Somers* was almost a thousand miles from the nearest land, more than a week away.

The next hundred hours passed in a fuzzy and broken pattern: constant stress, occasional sleep, suspicious events, and the unchanging tedious sailing routines. After Spencer's confinement, Mackenzie had put his officers in one-in-three watches, four hours on duty, then eight hours off. Following the crew's rush aft, he changed the schedule to watch and watch, four hours on duty, then four hours off, then four hours back on, twenty-four hours a day. To add to the strain, Mackenzie armed all of his officers, not merely the ones standing watch. Now each of them carried the weight of a cutlass and pistols, along with a cartridge box. Gansevoort gave his Colt to Mackenzie. With it and some luck the commander might gun down a half-dozen men before they could get him. Around and around the officers went, patrolling the spar deck and berth deck, frequently looking aloft. They were a haunted, hunted group. Sleep was the enemy, an enemy in league with the boys. Those boys, and their older instructors, had to be watched every minute. Mackenzie gave strict orders to his younger officer complement to make sure that the crew didn't get hold of the officers' weapons. To all of the officers he gave clear instructions regarding Acting Midshipman Spencer: if they saw him trying to communicate with the crew, they were to stop him and those to whom he was trying to talk, by any means necessary. If the prisoners tried to escape, the officers were to shoot them.

Both Spencer and the crew were problems. Mackenzie showed his errant midshipman, together with Cromwell and Small, every reasonable courtesy. Each morning they were freed in order to wash themselves, and then they were shaved and fed. Spencer had books to read, although no paper to write on. He maintained a confident attitude. Once or twice someone caught him trying to get to the battle-axes in the rack near the arms chest that remained on the deck, after which the officers moved them.

The crew bore watching, too. Some of the men, such as McKee and Wilson, seemed to want to get close to Spencer. Acting Master Matthew C. Perry, Jr., believed that the arrests had pushed people toward the edge: now that the plot was known, they were getting afraid for their necks. Going through with it might seem safer than hanging back, for hanging back might now lead to hanging. Breaches of discipline started happening more often. Henry Waltham, an African-American steward who had been friendly with Spencer, was caught stealing brandy, perhaps to try to smuggle up to the prisoners. Mackenzie ordered him flogged on the morning after the apparent rescue attempt. An apprentice, Charles Lambert, was another who felt the cat that day for stealing a hat from young Gagely. But it was Waltham whose name was on Spencer's list.

Mackenzie probably had this in mind when, after the floggings, he made an address to the crew.

The officers had tried to maintain an air of normality, but after what happened the night before, and the wild flying rumors, that was growing impossible. The thing to do, Mackenzie decided, was to be honest with the sailors, to remind them that he had the law on his side, that mutiny was a grave, a heinous, offense. So that is just what he did, telling the boys why Spencer and Cromwell and Small were in irons. He kept his tone reasonable, reminding the crew of its duty. He didn't mention the cipher list: his goal wasn't punishment, but to make the threat dissipate, to try to get his ship home in one piece. Naming names wouldn't help, and anyway, keeping the find a secret gave him a slight advantage.

According to Mackenzie, his speech had a strong effect, filling some of the sailors with horror, moving several others to tears. Gansevoort's account was more taciturn. He described an air of astonishment rather than horror, although he may have seen a boy or two crying. Regardless of the reactions, however, the speech let everyone know what was up. The reason for the arrests and the discipline was now clear to all. But if Mackenzie had hoped that his address would help him restore order, he turned out to be badly mistaken.

He must have thought, for a time at least, that he had things under control. That morning a sail showed on the horizon. She was a Frenchman, a small merchant craft, and Mackenzie closed and boarded her, in a routine search for slaves or possibly pirates. If he had been worried that he was in trouble, the logical thing to do would have been to ask for some help. But he decided against it. One of the things that weighed in the balance was the black eye the country would get from asking for foreign assistance. Still, the code of the sea is to render aid freely, and Mackenzie had only to ask. He didn't. By the end of the day he was probably wishing he had.

Gansevoort, meanwhile, kept talking with Spencer. The two had a number of interviews, Gansevoort trying to gain information,

Spencer reluctant to give it. He did say some things that show pretty clearly that he had some personality disorder. He confessed to the first lieutenant that this wasn't the first time he had plotted and spoken of mutiny. He had done it when he served in *Potomac,* and on *John Adams,* too, though he had never gone as far as he had aboard *Somers.* It seemed, in his words, to be "a mania" with him.

But it wasn't all in his mind. Obsessive thoughts are one thing. Acting out the obsessions is something else entirely. Spencer had gone too far, unleashing forces that the officers couldn't contain merely by placing him under arrest. Ironing the three prisoners had made things worse, and Mackenzie's speech hadn't improved matters at all. If that wasn't yet clear, the night of the 28th would be further proof.

The previous day, the problem had been with the topgallant mast, almost certainly because Small had deliberately mishandled a brace. Nobody claimed that what happened now, twenty-four hours later, was also due to malice, but it was a strange coincidence.

The boom was a long and heavy column of wood that stretched aft from the mainmast, sticking out over the stern. It provided a means of controlling the trysail, a large triangular sail that was rigged fore-and-aft. Aboard a brig such as *Somers,* a trysail sometimes bore the more ominous name of *spencer,* and it was this trysail or spencer that was about to cause the next uproar. Once the boom, and thus the sail, were set at the proper angle, they were held in place by a tackle.

On the night of the 28th, *Somers* was rolling heavily, just the right sort of motion to put strain on the tackle. That was when the tackle gave way. The boom began swinging side to side crazily, sweeping across the aftermost part of the deck. As long as the prisoners kept their heads down they were safe, but anyone standing up too high could easily have been clubbed in the head by the massive piece of wood, possibly getting knocked overboard and probably suffering serious harm. Given the boom's location, the victims, if

any, would likely be officers—the officer of the watch, the first lieutenant, or the captain himself.

Somehow everyone dodged the boom, but *Somers* was now sailing strangely as the wind started to play with the trysail. Hays himself jumped to the weather sheet, a rope attached to the sail, to get
the boom under control. "Some of you lay aft!" he sang out to the
crew, without stopping to remember the prisoners or the wild rush
aft the previous evening. A moment later the same scenario was
spookily replaying itself, as at least fifteen crewmen came running
straight at him.

Hays instantly saw what was happening. He spotted two or three
people he thought to be trustworthy and called out their names,
telling the others to go forward again. Nobody obeyed. Hays gave
the order again, moving forward to meet the crowd. By now
Mackenzie had come up from his cabin, armed, no doubt, with
Gansevoort's revolver. Hays tried again. "This is a time when you
must not disobey orders," he cried, "a time when you might lose your
lives for it." Challenged that way, and facing Mackenzie's Colt pistol, the crew gave in and did Hays's bidding.

Weeks later, Mackenzie would write that "The night was the
season of danger." For all of the melodramatic phrasing, the fact was
perfectly true. It hid what the sailors were doing, letting them talk
and move much more freely than they could in the daylight. For the
time being *Somers* had a tropical moon that provided some help in
the night. But after the call at St. Thomas, the ship would head
north-northwest toward New York, a distance nearly half that from
the Caribbean to the African coast. Climbing the latitudes, sailing
further into the autumn, she would likely find gloomy and thunder-
ous weather. The nights there would be darker and colder, with
higher and heavier seas. But that was more than a week away. The
immediate problem was making it to St. Thomas, and by now some
were asking whether that could be done. The question soon got

much more urgent, for on the 29th the dangers held by the night began to spill over into the daylight hours.

In the morning Mackenzie had Waltham flogged again. This time the steward had tried to steal brandy to give to McKinley, and McKinley, who was under suspicion, reported him for doing so, perhaps to allay that suspicion. Later that day Wales saw Charles Wilson reach for a handspike from under the launch, where he had apparently hidden it earlier. Wales was afraid that Wilson was going to brain him with it, so he drew his pistol and the sailor backed off.

Meanwhile the officers grew more exhausted, catching an hour or two of sleep when they could. Gansevoort kept up his efforts to get the prisoners to come clean. He finally revealed to Spencer that he had found the midshipman's mysterious cipher, pressing him to answer some questions about it. The name "E. Andrews" was puzzling. Did it or didn't it refer to Samuel Cromwell? If not, was the name something that Spencer had simply invented, or was there really an Andrews on board, still at large, still dangerous? He asked Spencer for answers, and for help in translating the papers.

Spencer agreed to help Gansevoort, asking for the originals, but Gansevoort used copies instead. Spencer boasted that this was a cipher that he had invented in college, a cipher that nobody but he could unravel. If he really believed what he said, then Gansevoort must have surprised him, since Rogers had deciphered it earlier. Gansevoort showed his hand during a discussion about Cromwell, asking whether or not he were "E. Andrews." Spencer, who seemed anxious to exonerate Cromwell, claimed that the name referred to Elisha Small.

"How is that," Gansevoort asked him, "when you have Small's name twice on the list?" He pointed out the two spots.

Spencer seemed startled. "Ah!" he exclaimed. "I did not know I had written it that way."

This wasn't much help, and now night was returning again. As the sun dropped toward the horizon, darkness spread up from the sea. The waters lost their gleam and turned the color of gunmetal; the last of the light retreated up the masts and the sails, the shadows crawling up from below. The crew was still surly and muttering. Michael Garty, the master-at-arms, knew something bad was happening. He had been ill for days, possibly with malaria or some other bug that he had picked up in Africa. But he was still on the alert and being as much help as he could. This night he was watching Wilson from his hammock. The young sailor seemed restless, frequently glancing around the darkened berth deck. Garty had felt that something was very wrong; as the master-at-arms lay in his hammock he had a cutlass next to him under the blanket, and he was ready to use it if Wilson tried anything funny. When the change of watch was called, at midnight and then at 4:00 A.M., Garty got up as well, ready to deal with possible trouble.

Wilson was trouble, all right. His liking for blunt and sharp objects, especially the latter, was just too strong for anyone's good. Gunner's Mate Henry King had tried to warn Gansevoort about it. "Has Wilson drawn two or three knives from the store room lately?" he had asked the lieutenant earlier. No, replied Gansevoort, not that he knew of. "I heard that he had several knives in his sail-bag," King had continued, "and I think it would be a good plan to overhaul it." Wilson had had that bag aft near the prisoners, the gunner's mate had insisted, and he had hidden knives up in the rigging. Gansevoort had taken King's advice, but all he had found was the lethal African dirk.

Now, in the dark, Wilson was acting strangely. At sundown King had found handspikes and heavers—heavy chunks of metal—hidden in the stern of *Somers*'s launch, where someone could get to them fast. He stowed them away, but later that night he found that someone had returned them to the launch. Around midnight he spotted Wilson go to the launch as if looking for something. And

Wilson wasn't the only one who was acting in a peculiar way. When the watch changed at midnight, Green and McKinley missed muster, failing to report for duty. They were already suspect, both for their behavior and for being on Spencer's list, and this infraction made them stand out even more. McKinley came stumbling up on deck fifteen minutes late. He had had a deal with McKee, he tried to explain; the two had agreed to call each other when the change of the watch was called. But this time McKee hadn't done it; instead he was claiming that the petty officers hadn't let him go below, since they were forbidding any strange movement. Green came up with a similar excuse.

Mackenzie, irritated by tension and lack of sleep, lost patience when Green told him this. He sent the landsman forward, making him serve as lookout for the rest of the watch, under a midshipman's close supervision. The strain was wearing on the commander, and it only got worse when, as the next change of the watch came around, more sailors missed muster.

The sun returned at last. *Somers* had survived another long night on the water, but by now people were asking themselves whether it would be the last. The officers were already wondering whether they could handle more prisoners. Too many might compromise the ship's operation. But given Wilson's attraction to blades, and the others' nocturnal wanderings, Mackenzie made more arrests anyway; by the end of the morning McKinley, McKee, Wilson, and Green all found themselves in irons, lining the after sides of the spar deck.

Mackenzie wasn't being vindictive. His irritability of the previous night seemed to have vanished, but it was replaced by signs of indecision, a fatal flaw in a captain. It showed how tired he was. When he summoned Green to the quarterdeck, he complimented him on his general behavior. It had been good, Mackenzie told Green, up until the last several days. But now things were different. For a time the captain seemed torn, undecided about possible confinement, but at last he decided. "I will put you in irons for the present." With that, and the other arrests that day, the number of prisoners rose to seven.

Conditions were getting desperate. The officers were having trouble controlling things as it was. The arrests may have put the prisoners themselves out of action—although some people claimed that Spencer was signaling sailors—but it seemed to be agitating everyone else. Mackenzie couldn't arrest his whole crew, and by putting still more people in irons, he might further alienate the mutineers who were still at large. He had to think of another solution, and he had to do it fast. *Somers* was still nearly a week from St. Thomas, and the menace was growing too quickly.

While a nineteenth-century warship's captain was a man of tremendous power, that power did have its limits. And one of the limits that Captain Mackenzie constantly faced was the bewildering tangle of statutes and regulations and rules that governed naval discipline.

There were the Articles of War, for one thing, which officers had nicknamed "Rocks and Shoals" because they were tricky and could wreck a captain's career. The navy also had other rules, though sorting them out could drive someone to despair. There was the Black Book, a compilation of regulations that Congress had approved decades before *Somers* was built; the Blue Book, which it hadn't, but which the navy used anyway; the amendment to the Blue Book, which repealed all Blue Book regulations that flew in the face of the Black Book and its congressional sanction; the much newer Red Book, which the navy itself, to say nothing of Congress, had never fully approved; and a brand-new set of hundreds of regulations that James Kirke Paulding, a recent secretary of the navy, had seemingly pulled out of thin air. Figuring out what all the rules meant was a very serious headache. Even figuring out what the rules *were* was no easy task. Despite all the confusion, however, one thing was clear: everyone, ships' captains included, was subject to the Articles of War.

Not that the Articles didn't have problems. Among other things they had gaps that the regulations failed to address. As a result, naval discipline was a confused and chaotic process, as well as an arbitrary and sometimes brutal one.

Article 13, for instance, expressly made mutiny—whether simply making mutinous statements or engaging in actual mutinous conduct—a capital crime. If the mutiny was actual, and not confined merely to words, death was the only permissible penalty. But that same article required a general court-martial before conviction and punishment, and a court-martial required at least five officers to hear the charges. What was more, a general court-martial could only be convened by order of certain officials, including the president, the secretary of the navy, the commander-in-chief of a fleet (the Old Navy didn't have fleets), or the commander of a squadron. A ship's captain lacked the power to order one, even if he had the requisite number of officers. In other words, even if Spencer and others really had plotted and talked of mutiny—which very probably met the Article 13 definition—then legally, under the Articles of War at least, Mackenzie could do nothing about it except put them under arrest and bring them back to port.

Mackenzie faced another problem. He could hold a captain's mast, a fairly informal proceeding for dealing with petty offenses. This was a regular thing aboard warships, and it was how he had punished Waltham and all the others who had gotten out of line in less serious ways than Spencer. But Article 30 limited the punishments that he could inflict by his own authority. Twelve lashes with the cat-o'-nine-tails was the most he could impose on an enlisted man for any single offense. When he punished an officer, confinement and suspension from duty were very nearly his only legal choices. In the eyes of the Articles of War, then, Mackenzie had already done all he was able to do with regard to Midshipman Spencer, and nearly as much with regard to the others.

But by dawn of November's last day, Mackenzie was thinking about taking things further. There are indications, in fact, that he had been having such thoughts for a day or two before that.

According to criminal law theorists, society punishes offenders for a number of different reasons. One possible purpose of punishment is to rehabilitate the offender, to teach him to be more productive in the future, or at least to teach him not to commit more crimes. Another, more savage reason to punish is to give free rein to the spirit of revenge, to seek retribution.

Somewhere between these two extremes lies the concept of deterrence. By punishing an offender in various ways, the system can dissuade him, or even outright prevent him, from committing more crimes. Some call this specific deterrence or incapacitation. By making an example of him, it can teach others that crime doesn't pay, deterring them from breaking the law. This is often called general deterrence.

The most effective type of incapacitation is capital punishment. For all of its shortcomings, one thing is certainly true of the death penalty: once someone, whether guilty or innocent, has been put to death by the state, that person will never commit any more crimes, at least not in this world. And if that person is key to a criminal enterprise, then once he is dead, the enterprise cannot go forward, thus deterring his partners in crime.

Other than Mackenzie's loyal officers, only Spencer, Cromwell, and Small knew how to navigate. Only since Spencer's arrest had the crew actually tried to take over *Somers*, if that is what had really been happening. Thus Spencer, Cromwell, and Small, alive and in chains, were still dangerous, maybe even more dangerous than if they hadn't been in confinement. But eliminate these three people, and perhaps the mutiny's force would be spent. All that the boys could seize then was a vessel they wouldn't be able to use.

But if something didn't change soon, the boys were going to win. The officers had been four days with almost no sleep. They were getting jumpy, making mistakes. When Gansevoort had arrested Cromwell, his pistol had accidentally gone off. When the boom tackle parted, Hays had thoughtlessly called the crew aft, provoking a second stampede. The nearest land was several more days away. Mackenzie didn't think that the officers could hold on. Something had to give soon, or the boys would succeed and the officers would die. Such were Mackenzie's thoughts, or at least so he claimed later.

He lacked the authority to execute prisoners, at least under the Articles of War. He had to know that. But what did the Articles of War mean out here? What good were they, if obeying the law got everyone killed? Innocent lives were at stake, and he was convinced of Spencer's guilt, and Small's and Cromwell's too. But if he hanged them he would face a court of inquiry, and quite likely a general court-martial.

It was much the same sort of analysis as Mackenzie had probably gone through before he arrested Spencer. But now it was undoubtedly a life-or-death judgment. In retrospect it seems as if a great many people aboard thought that someone had to die before *Somers* made landfall. Many people swore to it later, crew and officers both.

But an execution would still fly in the face of the Articles of War. And, what was more, Mackenzie was tired, his judgment impaired. He could be wrong. If the specific deterrence effect is the strongest argument in favor of capital punishment, the strongest argument against it is that sometimes society makes mistakes and executes innocent people. And when someone is tired and under powerful stress, mistakes are all too common.

He had to be certain. He had to take steps to protect the prisoners, to protect the ship, and to protect himself, too.

In the end he chose to seek the advice of his officers. This was a rare enough thing in the Old Navy, and all the rarer for the fact that he sought it in writing. The captain, and the captain alone, bore the responsibility for what took place on his ship. Asking advice, while it could be useful, could also look like a weak captain's attempt to spread the blame around if things were to turn out wrong. But Mackenzie obviously felt that he needed consensus, or at least another opinion. So on the morning of the 30th of November, even before he made the four newest arrests, he wrote a remarkable letter to all of his officers except for the junior midshipmen.

> GENTLEMEN: The time has arrived when I am desirous of availing myself of your counsel in the responsible position which, as commander of this vessel, I find myself placed. You are aware of the circumstances which have resulted in the confinement of Midshipman Philip Spencer, Boatswain's Mate Samuel Cromwell, and Seaman E. Small, as prisoners, and I purposely abstain from entering into any details of them, necessarily ignorant of the exact extent of disaffection among a crew which has so long and so systematically and assiduously been tampered with by an *officer.* Knowing that suspicions of the gravest nature attach to persons still at large, and whom the difficulty of taking care of the prisoners we already have, makes me more reluctant than I should otherwise be to apprehend, I have determined to address myself to you, and to ask your united counsel as to the best course to be now pursued, and I call upon you to take into deliberate and dispassionate consideration the present condition of the vessel, and the contingencies of every nature that the future may embrace, throughout the remainder of our cruise, and enlighten me with your opinion as to the best course to be pursued.
>
> I am very respectfully, gentlemen, your most obedient
>
> ALEX. SLIDELL MACKENZIE,
>
> Commander

When he had written the message, Mackenzie found Gansevoort on the quarterdeck and handed it to him there, and Gansevoort and the other officers went below to the wardroom to discuss what to do. Before long they started to send for various people, including some whose names appeared on Spencer's list and others whom Gansevoort suspected, mixed in with some of the petty officers.

The group met before noon and stayed in the wardroom the rest of the day, with Purser Heiskill taking notes. This was no court, or if it was, it was like no court the American legal system would have recognized. Still, the group referred to itself as a "Council"—not a council of war but merely a council—and referred to Heiskill's notes as "minutes," which recounted the "testimony" of "witnesses," who spoke after taking an oath that the officers gave them. After giving his sworn statement, each witness corrected and signed his "deposition," with the illiterates among them making their marks. The officers were doing their best, but they were no lawyers. This council may have been a good practical step for Mackenzie to take, but as a legal proceeding it had serious flaws. Inquisitorial rather than adversarial, it was totally *ex parte;* the prisoners were neither represented nor present. As for the Fifth and Sixth Amendments, they might as well not have existed, not that even a general court-martial would have paid much attention to them in those days.

The council worked hard, not stopping for food, though occasionally duties called members away. The hours wore on as witnesses came and went; Van Velzor, Warner, Gedney . . . Garty, Dickerson, Browning. By the time the first dogwatch was called at four in the afternoon, the council had heard from eight or nine witnesses, and most of their stories sounded the same. Nearly everyone condemned Spencer and Cromwell, and most added Small to the mix. A lot of finger-pointing went on. People often claimed that Waltham was in on the plan, and a few included the other stewards as well. More than fifteen names came up in the statements, although nobody admitted to any wrongdoing—the bad guys were always somebody else—and nobody supplied any hard evidence. A mutiny seemed to be hovering around, just out of reach. But nobody said that everything was all right. To the contrary: nearly everyone said that something was terribly wrong.

Another thing that most witnesses stated quite clearly was that they were scared to be on the same ship with Spencer and Cromwell. Maybe the officers prompted or led them, but time after time these statements popped up. Browning, the bo'sun's mate who was good with the colt, spoke particularly of Cromwell. "I would not like to be on board the brig if he was at large," he declared. Others hedged more, dwelling perhaps on the tribulations to come on the final leg of the cruise. "I think they are safe from here to St. Thomas," one crewman said, "but from there home I think there is great danger, on account of the bad weather on the coast and squalls." He did have a point about the certain change in the weather, but his was still the minority view. Most of the others wished for fast action; the tropics, too, could spawn squalls and gales. "If we get into hard weather, I think it will be hard to look out for the prisoners," a quartermaster opined. "I think if Cromwell, Small, and Spencer were disposed of"—by which he meant *killed*— "our lives would be much safer." Others feared those who were still at large. "If [Charles] Golderman and [Eugene] Sullivan could get a party among the crew now," Gunner's Mate Henry King swore, "they would release the prisoners and take the vessel."

Most of the witnesses had the same answer, at least according to Heiskill's minutes: kill Spencer, Cromwell, and Small. George Warner, who had occasionally fallen under suspicion himself, was one of the most vehement. Even before the council convened, he had told Green, now under arrest, that Cromwell was very bad news. "The damned son of a bitch ought to be hung," he had said. Now, under oath, he repeated himself. Spencer was the main figure, he said, and he was using Small and Cromwell as cat's-paws. But the latter was the worst of the three. "Cromwell deserves to be hung," he told the group of officers. "He is the most desperate person in the ship; if I had my way of it I would hang him."

Most people who suggested a killing, however, didn't single anyone out. Instead they spoke of all three. Again and again came the recommendation. Browning: "I believe Cromwell, Small, and Spencer ought to be made way with (that is, killed); I think the vessel would then be more safe." Collins: "Wishes Cromwell, Small, and Spencer were out of the ship. . . . She would be more safe." Dickerson: "I think if Cromwell, Small, and Spencer were made way with, it would put a stop to, and I think by that means the vessel *will* be safe."

About the time when the second dogwatch was called, Mackenzie broke up the council. He had more pressing concerns, for the night was approaching again. He divided the officers into watch and watch, stationing them all over the deck. Then the night happened, blooming like some dark flower. Every half-hour the bells sounded their knell; every four hours the watches were called, the sleep-deprived officers on guard for the assault they were certain would come before daybreak. Exhaustion battled adrenaline as *Somers* groped through the void, sailing from November into December. Then, far behind, the sky paled, grayed, and lightened. Somehow—incredibly—nothing had happened.

The council reconvened in the morning watch, about 9:00 A.M., but this second meeting was to be shorter. After hearing a few more witnesses, the officers discussed what to do. The first, overriding question was whether the ship could get to St. Thomas, or even some other port. While the minutes don't mention this point, everyone apparently thought it very unlikely. They were all worn out; sleep was circling the edges of consciousness like wolves circling a dying campfire. But even assuming that *Somers* could get to a port in the Lesser Antilles, what then? The tropics were one thing, but the North Atlantic in late autumn would be something else again. The commonsense thing to do would be to ask for assistance from local authorities, to offload the prisoners. But that would have made the United States appear weak at a time when national pride was important. Even so, given *Somers*'s condition, Mackenzie might have gotten no blame for asking for foreign help.

But all this was of secondary importance. The immediate issue wasn't whether to ask for help, but whether the officers could even make port, any port, before the boys took over the ship. The answer they reached was a very emphatic *no.*

The next question, then, was what they should do about it. This question answered itself; there could be only one possible answer, in fact, given the premises. Death. A multiple hanging, in order to prevent still more death.

Gansevoort gave Mackenzie the news orally while the officers wrote a letter, a formal reply to Mackenzie's formal request of the previous day, condemning Spencer, Cromwell, and Small. "After as dispassionate and deliberate a consideration of the case as the exigencies of time would admit," it read, "we have come to a cool, decided, and unanimous opinion, that they have been guilty of a full and determined intention to commit a mutiny on board of this vessel of a most atrocious nature." Onward the letter went, taking note of the latest batch of arrests and the possibility that other mutineers were still at large and in league with the prisoners. "We are convinced that it would be impossible to carry them to the United States," it continued. "The safety of the public property, the lives of ourselves, and of those committed to our charge, require that (giving them sufficient time to prepare) they should be put to death, in a manner best calculated as an example to make a beneficial impression upon the disaffected."

Mackenzie was in agreement. There was no point in delay. He started his preparations.

He had to be careful. This was the moment of the greatest possible danger. Once those involved and still at large realized what was happening, they would either have to hope that they would never be found out, or else they would have to take the ship immediately, before the navigators were dead and their own options at an end. He would have to keep iron control.

He would need extra help. He told Gansevoort to summon all of the petty officers to the quarterdeck. The lieutenant doubted their loyalty, but Mackenzie had to take chances. He had Gansevoort issue the arms, and then he gave them a brief address. "My lads," he told them, the familiarity belying emotion, "you are to look at me, to obey my orders, and to see my orders obeyed. Go forward." They went. Meanwhile Mackenzie stationed his officers around the vessel again, giving them the same sort of instructions that they had received before. If a rescue attempt took place, he commanded, the officers were to shoot the prisoners and rescuers both. Next the captain had ropes, or whips, run from the main yardarms. Hanging made the most sense; it was surer than something like keelhauling, more simple than drowning, less dangerous than having loaded muskets on deck for use in a firing squad. It was also a traditional way for the navy to execute men, and the navy, after all, was a service that honored tradition.

While the crew was being called to quarters to witness punishment, Mackenzie went below to his cabin and changed into full-dress uniform. When he came back above, one person, seeing that uniform, assumed he was planning to board and inspect some other vessel. But there was no other vessel. *Somers* was completely alone.

Mackenzie went to the condemned prisoners one by one: first Spencer, then Cromwell, then Small. He told them that they were to die in ten minutes. Each took the news differently. Spencer went down to his knees for a few moments, apparently overcome. He said that he needed more time to get ready, that he wasn't fit to die. "I know you are not," responded Mackenzie, "but I cannot help it." He then moved on to Cromwell, who was reading a magazine. When the sailor heard his doom pronounced, he, too, dropped to the deck.

"I am innocent," he cried out. "Lord of the universe, look down upon me!" Then came Small. Some saw him smile, as if what he heard were too incredible to be true; others claimed to see him in tears.

Mackenzie came back to Spencer, calling for Bibles and prayer books. He asked the midshipman if he had any messages to send to his friends. "None that they would care to receive," replied Spencer, by all accounts composed. He entered into a protracted talk with the captain. Mackenzie had told young Oliver Hazard Perry and Thompson to let him know when ten minutes had passed, but when they approached him at the end of that time, he uttered a curt "Very well" and continued talking with Spencer.

"This will kill my poor mother," Spencer was saying. "I fear this may injure my father." Wouldn't it have been harder on them, asked Mackenzie, if the plot had succeeded? Spencer paused for a moment. "I do not know what would have become of me had I succeeded." He went on, in partial explanation of what had been happening, repeating things he had already mentioned to Gansevoort. "I had the same project on board the *John Adams* and *Potomac*," he confessed. "It seemed to be a mania with me." That could be no excuse for Mackenzie. "Do you not think," he asked Spencer, "that this is a mania which should be discouraged in the navy?"

"I do, most certainly," Spencer responded. Then came the attempt to bargain. "But have you not formed an exaggerated estimate of the extent of this conspiracy?"

"No," said Mackenzie. The youngster's efforts had succeeded too well, he explained. Spencer tried once more. "But are you not going too far—are you not fast?" he queried the captain. "Does the law entirely justify you?"

Mackenzie cited the findings of the officers' council and the petty officers' opinions. He had reached his decision. Like any good captain, he was not going back on it now.

Spencer seemed to recognize that, and his resistance came to an end. He did ask how it was to be done, and Mackenzie told him by hanging. Spencer asked to be shot instead; Mackenzie denied the request.

Spencer's gaze was now beginning to focus somewhere beyond *Somers,* as he prepared for his journey there. "I am a believer," he told the commander. "Do you think that repentance at this late hour can be accepted?" Mackenzie, who couldn't stop what was going to happen, reminded his acting midshipman of the crucified thief whom Christ promised salvation. With that, young Spencer took a prayer book and knelt on the deck for a while. Afterward he asked again if God would accept his repentance, and Mackenzie reassured him.

God was one thing; Mackenzie was another. "I beg your forgiveness," Spencer addressed him, "for what I have meditated against you." Mackenzie held out his hand, adding his forgiveness to God's, but then curiosity got the better of him. It was an age when people were seen as totally responsible for their actions. Mackenzie would neither have understood nor agreed with the idea of a personality disorder even if anyone had been able to explain what one was in 1842. As he saw it, there had to have been some reason. Spencer had wanted to kill him; thus he himself had to have been the cause of the youngster's desire to kill. So he asked his would-be murderer why he had hatched this plot to take his commander's life. Was it something Mackenzie had done?

"It was only a fancy," Spencer said vaguely, trying to put into rational words something that he himself knew, but could not understand or describe. "Perhaps there might have been something in your manner which offended me." But Mackenzie hadn't been on *John Adams;* he hadn't been on *Potomac.*

There was no point in pressing him further. By now nearly an hour had passed, far more than the original ten minutes, and at some point things had to proceed. Mackenzie had been jotting down notes of the whole conversation. A reader can see the captain's, as well as Spencer's, stress in them. "Objected to manner of death; requested to be shot. Could not make any distinction between him and those whom he had seduced. . . . Asked that his face might be covered. Granted. . . . many crimes. Dies praying to God to bless and preserve . . . be the death of my poor mother. Do you not think she would have felt worse if, instead of dying, you had succeeded in your undertaking? Horrors here. Cut off by Cromwell, passing to gallows."

The prisoners were now starting to move forward to where the ropes waited, but Spencer had a final statement to make after reading over Mackenzie's notes. "These are about the last words I am going to say, and I trust they will be believed," he announced.

"What is that?" answered Mackenzie.

"Cromwell is innocent."

Mackenzie moved away for a moment, and then came back toward Spencer, telling him something quietly. Then Gansevoort approached him, too, guiding him forward.

Cromwell was unrepentant. Or rather, he continued to maintain that he had nothing for which to repent, at least when it came to mutiny. "I die innocent to the last," he said, when Gansevoort asked him if he had any messages to send to his family. That, coupled with Spencer's last statement, apparently did make the captain think twice about what he was doing. He asked Gansevoort what he thought. The lieutenant answered that he believed that Cromwell was guilty, and to make very sure, he took a quick poll of the petty officers. Dickerson, whom Cromwell had abused a few times, was openly callous. "He ought to have thought of that before." It was very cruel treatment of a man who was minutes from death.

But Cromwell wasn't going to go without a show of defiance. Once he was in position under the main yardarm, with the rope encircling his neck, Gansevoort approached to tell him goodbye. Cromwell now asked his forgiveness, but he once again said he was innocent. He grabbed Gansevoort's hand. It was more than a handshake. It was a violent, desperate grasp. Gansevoort suddenly feared that Cromwell planned to jump overboard, to drag the lieutenant down with him, and the petty officers holding on to the prisoner seemed to think the same thing. For a few insane seconds Gansevoort tried to think how he would get back aboard; then, suddenly, Cromwell let go, and the moment had passed.

Spencer was still penitent as he moved toward his fate. He had already bidden Gansevoort goodbye, asking his pardon. Now he asked Mackenzie if he could speak with Wales, the boy who had squealed on him, and Wales came up to him. "Mr. Wales," Spencer said, "I sincerely hope that you will forgive me for tampering with your fidelity." Wales assured him that he did; this time the handshake was genuine. The two never spoke again.

Small, too, seemed remorseful. When Gansevoort and Mackenzie were standing nearby, he asked the lieutenant to bid him goodbye and forgive him, and Gansevoort did so. Mackenzie watched the exchange, and then he spoke up. "Small," he entreated, "what have *I* done to you that you won't bid me goodbye?"

He seemed to be overlooking the fact that he had ordered Small's death, but Small overlooked it as well. "I did not know that you would bid a poor bugger like me goodbye, sir," he explained. The gross obscenity was understandable under the circumstances, and not all that unusual on board ship. Mackenzie took no notice of it, and the two men shook hands. Now it was Mackenzie who asked forgiveness of Small. He told the seaman that he had to go through with the execution; both the honor of the flag and the safety of the crew demanded it. "Yes, sir, and I honor you for it," replied Small. *"God bless that flag!"*

Then came the last meeting of Spencer and Small. While Spencer had maintained Cromwell's innocence, those two never spoke from the time Mackenzie told them that they were going to die, even though they both had the chance. But Spencer did seek out Small, whose innocence he never asserted.

"Small, I hope you will forgive me," he said simply.

But that was asking too much, it seemed. "Mr. Spencer," Small answered, "how can you ask me that when you have brought me to this?"

Mackenzie stepped in. "Don't go out of the world with any hard feelings at your heart," he told Small. "Forgive him."

"Since you request it, sir, I forgive him."

At last the three prisoners were all in position. The minutes were waning. "Tell my wife I die an innocent man," said Cromwell. "Tell Lieutenant Morris I die an innocent man." Morris was a former shipmate; he couldn't help Cromwell now.

"You may have heard that I am a coward," Spencer called out to Gansevoort, "and *you* may think that I'm not a brave man. You can judge for yourself whether I die like a coward or a brave man."

Now Small, too, had something to say; he asked permission to address the crew. Mackenzie granted it.

Small's voice rang over the deck. "Messmates and shipmates!" he cried. "I am no pirate. I never murdered anybody." Immediately Mackenzie doubted the wisdom of letting Small speak. He turned to Gansevoort to ask what he thought, but by now Small had continued. "I only said I *would*. Now see what words will do. Take warning by me."

Something terrible was about to happen, to the prisoners, to the crew, to the officers. Spencer and Cromwell and Small were to die. When a charge was fired from a gun, their shipmates, holding on to the ropes that reached up to the yardarm and down around the three necks, would run up the deck, hoisting the three struggling bodies into the air. Spencer had asked and received permission to give the signal to fire. But Small didn't flinch at the future. The final words of his address seemed almost an absolution. "Now, brother shipmates," he called, "give me a quick death; run me up smartly; do not let there be any interval between word and firing." He spoke his last words. "I am ready, Mr. Spencer."

The gun was primed and ready, live coals on hand to ignite the powder charge. The crew stood holding the whips of rope. Waltham was at the head of one of the lines, holding its end, and for a horrible instant Midshipman Rogers feared that he wouldn't pull. If he didn't, then no one would.

The three men stood silent, their faces all shrouded. The rest of *Somers* was silent, too, except for the usual sounds of a ship underway, the creaking of timber, the wind in the rigging, the music of water as it parted under the bow. Everyone waited for the boom of the gun. Mackenzie stood on the trunk aft of the mainmast, waiting along with everyone else. Time was suspended; it seemed to stretch out.

Now Bo'sun's Mate Browning approached and saluted Mackenzie. "Mr. Spencer says he cannot give the word," he reported. "He wishes the commander to give the word himself."

There was absolutely no time lag.

"*Stand by,*" snapped Mackenzie. "*Fire!*"

The bark of the gun.

"*Whip!*" shouted Gansevoort.

The tramp of men running.

The prisoners swung up toward the yardarm. Since they hadn't dropped from a height, there was no question of mercifully broken necks. Death would come rather slowly, by asphyxiation. Nobody who witnessed the deaths, the bodies that had to have wildly twisted and jerked, bothered to pass on any grisly details in the interviews and reports that were to come.

The whips were belayed to hold the bodies aloft until enough time had passed. But Mackenzie also had to make sure of something else, and this was the moment to do it. Still standing on the trunk, he summoned the crew aft. He gave a little lecture on the fate of dishonest men. He had one sailor, Collins, tell a story he had heard from Cromwell regarding his lust for gold, as if to prove that Cromwell was guilty. The point was obvious in a frightening, sickening way. Cromwell had been dishonest; now Cromwell's body hung twitching above the gathered crew as the captain gave this lecture. Things couldn't have been much more macabre.

But the crew got the point. Frightened, subdued, disabused; whatever the show's particular impact on the individual sailors, and whatever the problem had been, the hangings straightened everything out, and very, very quickly. Everyone could see that Mackenzie really meant business. Gansevoort suggested, at the end of Mackenzie's address, that the captain order three cheers for the ship: the enthusiasm in the sailors' voices, or else the lack of it, would speak volumes about whether the executions had done the job. Mackenzie called for the cheers; they were exceptionally loud and hearty, seeming to break the spell that had held the ship in its grip since Madeira.

Mackenzie finally ordered the crew dismissed. It was an hour or so after noon, and dinner was waiting below. He himself went aft to speak to the four remaining prisoners. At least one of them, and probably all, had expected that they were to be next. But now Mackenzie told them that they were to return to New York in irons.

After Mackenzie had left them, McKinley asked Gansevoort if the captain thought them guilty of mutiny.

"No," answered Gansevoort. "I assure you if he did he would have strung you up."

Mackenzie was back in command.

The bodies stayed aloft for an hour. After that long they were certainly dead. Then they were lowered to the deck and prepared by the crew for interment.

Spencer, as a midshipman, was placed in a coffin that the carpenter's mate built from two mess chests. He, like Mackenzie, was in full-dress uniform, lacking only his sword, for his offense denied him that honor. The two other bodies were sewn into hammocks that were weighted with shot.

Arrangements weren't complete until nightfall. A little tension remained, a slight fear of the darkness, but not much, for the whole crew's demeanor had improved dramatically. Now the lanterns gleamed brightly, candles pouring a soft illumination onto the spar deck. The remains lay amidships—Spencer's the farthest aft, then Cromwell's, then Small's, in order of rank.

The service began, coming, of course, from the Book of Common Prayer, the prayer book of America's all-but-official Episcopal Church. The crew stood at quarters as Captain Mackenzie, who had removed his executioner's hat, now took on the role of priest. The candlelight played on the pages as he spoke the stately phrases, the language reminiscent of Shakespeare, suggesting, quite apart from their content, a permanence greater than that of the ocean itself. "I am the resurrection, and the life," he began with the words from the Gospel of St. John. "He that believeth in me, though he were dead, yet shall he live: and whosoever liveth and believeth in me shall never die." Onward he read, the crew making the responses as the service directed, the voices calm and assured. At last Mackenzie came to the final words of the service, one of the stronger, more beautiful prayers in a book whose prayers are nearly all strong and beautiful.

> We therefore commit his Body to the deep, to be turned into corruption, looking for the Resurrection of the Body when the Sea shall give up her Dead, and the life of the world to come, through our Lord Jesus Christ, who at his coming shall change our vile Body, that it may be like his glorious Body, according to the mighty working whereby he is able to subdue all things to himself.

Then it was done; the bodies slid into the waters, the same waters that had covered the earth since the Spirit of God had moved across them in the opening lines of Genesis.

There was still one more prayer to be said, a prayer that Mackenzie added after everything else was finished.

> O eternal Lord God, who alone spreadest out the heavens, and rulest the raging of the sea; who hast compassed the waters with bounds, until day and night come to an end; be pleased to receive into thy Almighty and most gracious protection, the persons of thy servants, and the ship in which we serve. Preserve us from the dangers of the sea and from the violence of enemies, that we may be a safeguard unto the United States of America, and a security for such as pass on the seas upon their lawful occasions; that the inhabitants of our land may in peace and quietness serve thee, our God; and that we may return in safety to enjoy the blessings of the land with the fruit of our labor, and with a thankful remembrance of thy mercies, to praise and glorify thy holy name, through Jesus Christ, our Lord.

The service was over. The crew was dismissed. *Somers* sailed on toward St. Thomas.

Between hanging and funeral, a squall struck the brig, bringing high winds and rains. The crew covered the bodies, already laid out, with tarpaulins. Once the weather had cleared, things continued.

One writer, in a fanciful moment, imagined the squall as the final assault of the forces of darkness on the small, troubled vessel, noting that once it had passed, discipline and morale were restored. This last statement was true. The change was nearly miraculous. Now that Spencer, Cromwell, and Small were dead, their skills no longer available to any potential mutineers, and now that Mackenzie showed what he could and would do to people who stirred up trouble, everyone fell into line, and fast. This was no game. It never had been. This was for real, and now everyone knew it.

But the idea that the dark spirits had fled the ship with the passing of the squall is mistaken. The trouble was over for only three people, the three whose bodies were now sinking thousands of feet into watery graves. For those who remained aboard, the troubles were only beginning. The darkness was by no means finished with *Somers*, with her crew, with her officers, and least of all with her captain.

PART SIX

Inquiry

WINTER WAS CREEPING UP on New York. The leaves had long since turned from green to golden and red to brown, whipped away by the autumn winds. In the country the fields had grown fruitful and fat, and the farmers had brought in the harvest. The days were getting short; in less than a week the longest night of the year would commence. Coldness echoed and rolled from the north, down the valley, in the air that swept over the face of the Hudson, and in its wide, deep currents. The stream's waves met the Atlantic in the harbor below Manhattan, fighting it for a short while, then conceding the battle and flowing resignedly into it. The slight chop of the rivers—the East as well as the Hudson—pounded in weak futility against the shores and anchored ships, including the brig-of-war *Somers*.

She lay quietly in New York Navy Yard; too quietly, in fact. Since her arrival on the night of December 14, almost no one departed or boarded her. After a cruise of three months, almost to the day, with barely a hundred hours of that time spent in port—any port—she should have disgorged her crew of trainees pretty quickly. Instead she seemed almost a ghost ship, aloof, quarantined, wrapped in an inscrutable mystery. The city had seen her come in, or had at least heard that she had. As the days passed, curiosity grew and the mystery deepened. Lieutenant Gansevoort's brother finally rowed out toward the brig, only to be ordered away. A warning of that sort from a warship, with its grinning rows of gunports, had teeth in it. The boat pulled back toward land. And still *Somers* held her peace.

She seemed, in a way, like a creature of the deep ocean that had struggled to come to the shore. Now, having very nearly reached land, she seemed worn out, used up, unable to cover the last few yards of water that stood between her and destruction. A few men and boys came and went: that was all. And they bore the signs of stress and exhaustion that told of a far worse struggle than any mere training cruise could account for.

The journey north had been rough. The executions had settled the crew down, at least to every appearance. But the captain and officers couldn't take any chances. They had kept standing extra watches, armed with their pistols and swords. The danger seemed to be over, and the change in morale was like the difference between night and day. Still, Mackenzie and his wardroom were outnumbered by a group of apprentices that could easily have become a mob, turned into a headless beast, without any warning, much as Spencer had planned. And there was yet the matter of prisoners. McKee, McKinley, Wilson, and Green had remained ironed to the spar deck among the aftermost guns.

Three days after the executions, *Somers* had stolen into St. Thomas in the dead of night. Mackenzie had thought himself in control enough not to ask port officials for help. He had never wanted to give the impression that his navy or nation were weak. But *Somers*'s stay had been brief; a few hours after she let go her anchor, she raised it again, this time on a more northerly heading which would bring her back to New York.

With each passing day the calm, sunny tropics had fallen farther and farther behind. Soon the waning year's North Atlantic, with its storms and its swells, was rising to meet the racing brig. Six days out of St. Thomas, the temperature had suddenly plunged thirty degrees as *Somers* sailed into winter. The spar deck was cold—the whole ship was cold—and the officers had ordered Charles Wilson to sew large body bags out of the studdingsail covers for himself and the other three prisoners. They were roomy and warm—too warm, in fact, according to McKinley, who complained once or twice that he was being smothered, though the bag kept him safe from the spray and the cold.

But the prisoners hadn't been alone in their suffering. Mackenzie and his officers had had to keep watching their own backs as they worked the ship, following the same tiring routines that had governed them since the night of Spencer's arrest. They weren't taking chances. They did switch from a watch-and-watch schedule to a slightly less draining one-in-three watch, which allowed them more regular sleep and meals. They ordered the crew not to skylark, and to avoid gathering in their odd little groups. The only real difference was the comforting fact that the crew had stopped showing signs of wanting to make trouble. The image of those three dying bodies swinging from the main yard would take a long time for the boys to forget.

At last, nine days after departing St. Thomas, *Somers* had raised New York, and the nightmare voyage had ended. Everyone was exhausted, beaten down by hard work, exposure, and stress. Master-at-Arms Garty, who had fallen sick even before Spencer's arrest, was almost too ill and weak even to make it ashore; soon after *Somers* came to her moorings he was carried off to the hospital. As Mackenzie and his officers headed toward the commandant's office to report their arrival, they staggered as if they were drunk, and they were, with exhaustion and the weird feel of motionless land unyielding beneath them. A few days later, Lieutenant Gansevoort finally got to see his family, who were shocked at how he looked. "He had a violent cold, coughing constantly," wrote his mother. "He walked like an infirm man of seventy; his eyes were red and swollen, & his whole face very much bloated." That wasn't all. "His back and sides were so sore, from the strap & weight of the huge & heavy ship's pistols that he could not raise himself erect."

Gansevoort was one of the few who got to go ashore. Another—one of the first—was Acting Midshipman Oliver H. Perry. Almost as soon as *Somers* arrived, Mackenzie sent him on his way to Washington to report in person to Secretary of the Navy Abel P. Upshur. Mackenzie had written a long report during his stop at St. Thomas, and he wanted Upshur to read it as early as possible. With Perry safely en route, Mackenzie himself reported to the youth's father at New York Navy Yard, and to Jacob Jones, the New York squadron commander. Meanwhile he busied himself writing another, longer, more formal report, a coherent narrative woven from all the insane little fragments of the previous weeks, a report in which he depicted himself in a highly favorable light. He was too much a man of letters, too much a career officer, and too much a New York public figure not to know what was going to happen. He wanted to get in the first punch.

Perry took barely forty-eight hours to get from New York to Washington, where he delivered his dispatch to Upshur. The story the report had to tell, of mutiny, piracy, and hangings at sea, was simply extraordinary. The United States Navy had never seen anything like it. But it wasn't a matter just for the Navy Department. It included the War Department, too, or at least the head of it. Right away Upshur told John Canfield Spencer, through a private secretary, that his son had died—had been hanged—while at sea.

Young Spencer may have been troubled, even delinquent, but he had still been a son, and his parents reacted in an understandable way. Elizabeth Spencer, the boy's mother, was in the middle of planning another of the social functions that were always going on in the capital when she found out. It was one of those horrible moments in life. One minute she was engaged in mundane, day-to-day business; the next she was in shock, trying somehow to deal with the totally unexpected news that one of her children was gone. She was a delicate woman; the blow was all the harder for that.

Her husband was tougher, and his was a typically male, testosterone-driven response. The navy, a group of men trained in the arts of organized violence, a group over which he utterly lacked jurisdiction, had killed his son, and he wanted revenge. Almost immediately he started trying to come up with a way that he could get at Mackenzie and hurt him.

John Canfield Spencer's stake was large, and very personal, too, but it wasn't the only one, at least not for long. The United States, born a republic, was fast growing more democratic. But the United States Navy had always been an insular world, a place of inequality, of aristocracy and caste borrowed wholesale from the service of Drake, Rodney, and Nelson. It was out of step with the rest of America, at least in America's view. And when the country heard about *this*—a multiple killing of common sailors at the hands of a captain, without any due process or judicial review, in peacetime . . .

The news had to break before long, and it did, in New York and Washington both, spreading out quickly from there. *Somers* arrived on Wednesday night; two days later wild rumors began, and by the next day the newspapers had them. The first stories favored the officers, probably because those stories sprang from Mackenzie's report, and probably because the idea of mutiny made more sense than the image of a captain running amok. "A dreadful mutiny," prominent Whig merchant Philip Hone had called it. "Two-thirds of the crew were engaged in the plot; but Captain Mackenzie appears to have acted with the utmost decision and bravery." Hone *would* write that, of course; as a Whig, he would have been bothered less than a Democrat would by notions of "aristocracy," and anyway, he was related to Mackenzie by marriage.

Hone's account shows that a lot of the detail was common knowledge by Saturday. But a lot of the detail was wrong. "The mutineers were confined under hatches," he told his diary. "A court-martial was held." The meeting of officers in the wardroom had not been a court-martial. It couldn't have been. Congress had spelled out exactly who could convene such a court, and exactly who had to serve on one. Mackenzie had lacked the authority, and even if he had had it, he had lacked the requisite number of senior officers. But a lot of folks mistakenly used the term "court-martial" in the following days. They were mistaken about other things, too.

At any rate, Hone approved of how things had turned out. "The imminent danger of the captain and lieutenant," he decided, "with so large a proportion of the crew in a state of insubordination, no doubt rendered this dreadful and summary exercise of power unavoidable, as an example and measure of safety." Hone might have used the term "court-martial," but he still recognized that, by whatever name, the wardroom proceedings had been most irregular. Despite that, he still backed Mackenzie.

He had a lot of company, at least in the first few days. Mackenzie was well thought of, and initially he had public support. "A more humane, conscientious and gallant officer does not hold a commission in the navy of the United States," one newspaper editor wrote. If Mackenzie had done what he did, then that *ipso facto* proved its necessity. The same sentiments echoed in nearly all of the papers. "By this one act, the Commander . . . has done more to sustain the supremacy of naval authority and to vindicate outraged law, than anything which has ever occurred in our Navy," the *New York Herald* proclaimed. "It is indeed fortunate that on such a man as Slidell Mackenzie devolved the high responsibility of such a critical hour."

While some people lauded Mackenzie, others attacked Philip Spencer. "A very dare-devil," one newspaper called him. "From his childhood almost there are many stories told about his freaks, that occurred while he was at college at Geneva." Others began to see proof of the youngster's treachery in a pattern of events not merely aboard *Somers* but on dry land as well. "Spencer declared before his departure that he would never return to this city," one New York paper claimed, "and on the passage out assumed to be able to tell men's fortunes, and assured his fellow midshipmen in the steerage that they had not long to live!" Clearly some facts had leaked out, but other facts were already known, and apparently had been for a while. And the paper had more to say on this point. "A rumor was circulated some week or two ago here, of the shipwreck of the *Somers*," it observed. "This may have been designed to account for her non-appearance in case the mutineers had been successful."

Given the rumors that were flying around, this story may or may not have been true. If it was, and if it wasn't coincidence, it hinted at something more serious than even a violent teenage obsession. That seems a stretch. But according to this same report, the navy took the whole episode seriously enough to dispatch a warship to the Isle of Pines to have a look around for anything that would shed light on Spencer's plans.

An aristocratic navy was something that plain democratic folks feared, or at least distrusted. But charges of aristocracy cut both ways in the days after *Somers*'s arrival. "Had young Spencer been put in irons and brought home to meet his trial, he would in all probability have escaped," the *New York Herald* announced. "We have had of late such melancholy evidence of the facility with which criminals having wealthy and influential friends can evade the hands of justice . . . that we can hardly suppose this abandoned young man would have received the just demerit of his crime." Philip Hone largely agreed. "Young Spencer was a worthless fellow," he penned, "who would have been cashiered for some misdemeanor on a former cruise but from feelings of delicacy for the respectable character and high station of his father."

Some people even thought that this was yet the case. One New York writer confided an especially wild rumor to his diary. "A man of most judicious sense [was] heard gravely to maintain that Spencer was never really hung till he was dead at sea but that he was cut down and smuggled ashore." The writer didn't believe it, but he understood how such stories could get started. "A fact like the above shows not merely a certain amount of vileness in the person who utters such a saying but a general presumption of the relaxation of law and that a guilty person with influence will most likely escape."

But the dead Spencer had his defenders, especially since his family was getting dragged into it. William H. Seward, who had known him (though "only as friends know our children") had trouble seeing him as a bloodthirsty would-be pirate. "I should as soon have

expected a deer to ravage a sheepfold," he commented. Others'
attacks were much more direct and forceful. "There was no court-
martial," one paper soon realized, and then it started to speculate.
"The officers would seem to have acted under a panic." A letter to
the editor of the *National Intelligencer* took another writer to task for
claiming that Spencer's brothers were villains, pointing out that one
currently served on a ship of the line while another was an attorney.
Given how people felt about lawyers, and Philip Spencer's own performance aboard *Somers,* these observations weren't especially helpful. Still, lawyer and naval officer were better labels than that of
inmate of Sing Sing, which the earlier writer had mistakenly
claimed of one brother.

But the strongest attack came from a widely circulated column
signed "S.," which was very likely John Canfield Spencer, still out for
Mackenzie's blood. Spencer was a first-class lawyer, and whoever S.
was, he knew his law, using it in expert and cool-blooded fashion to
nail Commander Mackenzie. The column called attention to the
officers' wardroom meeting; the proceedings there, he noted, took
place "in the absence of the prisoners and without giving them any
opportunity to cross-examine the witnesses or to make any explanation or defense, or to procure any testimony in their own behalf." It
was a blistering attack, showing as it did that the ship's officers had
broken naval regulations and federal law, had perhaps even set the
Constitution itself aside, in any number of ways. "These officers,"
continued S. coldly, had imposed the ultimate penalty on three
American citizens "without even the form of a court, without even
the obligation of an oath, and upon this ex parte secret information."
What had happened aboard *Somers,* in other words, was not martial
law; it was no law at all, except possibly, S. failed to note, the law of
the jungle.

It was a powerful challenge, and S. was just getting started. He
now moved from law into fact, slanting and bending it to his own

purpose the way any good courtroom lawyer would (and as Mackenzie was doing in his own reports). But in doing so S. was handi-
capped, for the full story wasn't available yet. He knew a lot of the
details—whoever he was, he pretty clearly had access to what
Mackenzie had written—but there were things he still couldn't
know, and he used facts selectively. "When every thing and person
were perfectly quiet," he charged, "after four days of entire security,
the three persons were, by order of Mackenzie, hung at the yard-arm
at mid-day." Those four days hadn't been "perfectly quiet," of course,
but the public didn't know that. The picture S. painted made
Mackenzie look very bad indeed; he was out to crucify the captain.
No, worse than that; by his cunning rhetoric, he made Mackenzie
into a maritime deity, killing a trinity in his lust to become his own
god. The commander had drawn sacrificial blood to punish "the
mere romance of a heedless boy."

It was a brutal, effective assault, and everyone knew it. Philip
Hone saw the threat, and he, like S., talked in law's language. "If
there exists any reasonable doubt of the absolute necessity for this
awful exercise of power, Captain Mackenzie may wish sincerely that
he never had been born to meet such a responsibility," he wrote
when S.'s column came out. "If the cabinet should take part with the
bereaved parent, who is one of its prominent members, in denying
the existence of the ringleaders of the mutiny, and if the laws should
not support the measure, Captain Mackenzie is ruined past redemp-
tion." By "the cabinet," Hone probably had in mind a single cabinet
member: Abel Upshur, the man who could order a legal investigation and make the final decision as to whether Mackenzie's acts had
been wrong. True, even Upshur was under certain constraints; as a
politician he had to heed public opinion, and a lot of that still
favored the captain. The *New York Tribune* was getting especially
strident, denouncing one competing editor's claim that "The *law of
the land*, not of the ocean, must control the whole case." To this the

Tribune gave an outraged reply. "Was not the crime committed upon the sea?" it asked, implying that the crime had not been Mackenzie's, but Spencer's.

> Was not the peril one of the ocean? Were not the interests of the ocean commerce of the world threatened by the mutiny? Was not piracy upon the deep intended, and was not the whole affair, from its black beginning to its bloody end, confined exclusively, in its origin, purposes, and issue to the sea? Why then should it not be controlled and judged by the law of the ocean—and why should doubt and suspicion be cast on the integrity of our maritime tribunal?

Yes, such things could influence Upshur, but only so much. And Upshur had only so much leeway. Despite the support for Mackenzie, he had to order a court of inquiry, a navy-run fact-finding process in which the *Tribune* showed so much faith. Even Mackenzie had probably known, from the moment he had arrested young Spencer, that that would be the result. The larger fear that the *Tribune* voiced—the possibility that others were talking about—was that whatever the secretary of the navy might do, it would not be enough for the secretary of war, that John C. Spencer would try to have Mackenzie indicted in federal court for murder. Hone saw the danger. "A more dangerous opponent than John C. Spencer," he observed, "could not be found in the United States; stern, uncompromising, obstinate in temper, determined and energetic in action, and with talents equal to any effort which his feelings may prompt, or his duty may call him to execute." If he went after Mackenzie, as he seemed to be doing, Mackenzie would land in a world of trouble.

But whatever attack Spencer managed to mount, it was going to have to come second to the navy's own process. The court of inquiry that Upshur had ordered was ready to start barely two weeks after

Somers returned to New York. Despite its name, it wasn't a court, and its proceedings weren't exactly a trial as civilians understood the term; today's navy would call it a board of inquiry instead. But it was still official, still very serious, and in ways it *did* look like a trial, right down to the calling, questioning, and cross-examination of witnesses. It was a fact-finding process whereby a panel of officers tried to discover the truth about something important. Accusations against servicemen; allegations of administrative mismanagement; strategic or tactical screwups that cost the country a victory, or made victory cost too much—a court of inquiry could investigate all of these things. Often its findings were conclusive, and the matter didn't go any further. But sometimes those findings could lead to a full-blown court-martial, especially when the inquiry's convening authority ordered it to give an opinion on the merits of the matter before it.

Upshur had ordered this particular court to give just such an opinion.

The court would consist of three senior officers: Captain Charles Stewart, who had held a navy commission since the end of the previous century; Commodore Jacob Jones, the New York squadron commander, whose time in the service was almost as lengthy as Stewart's; and Alexander James Dallas, another commodore of long service and the son of a brilliant lawyer who had once headed the Treasury Department. Dallas was commodore down in Pensacola; Matthew C. Perry, conveniently stationed in the New York Navy Yard, couldn't serve for obvious reasons.

The members of the court need not be attorneys. But a lawyer among lawyers would still be there, in the person of Ogden Hoffman, a famous and able prosecutor. Now in his forty-ninth year, he, too, had once served in the navy. He was a veteran of the War of 1812, and then he had sailed with Stephen Decatur in the war against the Algerines. But in 1816 he had turned to the bar ("I regret," said Decatur, "that young Hoffman should have exchanged an honorable profession for that of a lawyer") and soon became a gifted attorney. In 1837 he traveled to Congress, where his dazzling powers of speech brought Democratic opponents to ruin. In one brutal exchange, Churchill C. Cambreleng, an enemy New York congressmen, accused him of inconsistency, of using his navy-learned arts to "tack and veer." But then Hoffman's tongue completely destroyed the man. It was "a half-hour of the most tremendous invective that ever was uttered," declared John Quincy Adams in awe. "A shout of applause burst forth from the galleries as he closed. I told Hoffman that I had prepared for a settlement of accounts with Cambreleng myself, but that he had settled all my balances with him as well as his own. I could not call a dead man to account."

Now Hoffman, his congressional days behind him, was U.S. attorney for New York's Southern District, the district encompassing the navy yard. While the latter wasn't exactly within his jurisdiction, he still knew the navy, and he knew the law, too, and he was, after all, a prosecuting attorney. He seemed a perfect choice to serve as judge advocate, the prosecutor, the man who would be in charge of getting to the bottom of what had gone on. Mackenzie appeared to be in for a very rough time.

So, too, was Gansevoort. As the ship's first lieutenant, her de facto executive officer, he would be one of the court's natural targets. His family knew it, and it knew, too, that John Canfield Spencer could be a dangerous man. "I have at all times," Gansevoort's uncle wrote him on Christmas Eve, "believed your conduct throughout has been not only consistent with your manly course through life, but marked by the exercise of those generous & chivalrous feelings which belong to true courage." That was of limited comfort, though, when facing opponents such as Hoffman and Spencer. Ever since the latter had published his attack on Mackenzie, Gansevoort's uncle continued, "I have reflected with painful anxiety on the effect which the influence of a strong power may exert over the proceedings in the nature of an Inquiry which is about to take place," he emphatically cautioned his nephew. "You & your Commander will be placed upon the defensive under unparalleled circumstances."

He wrote none too soon. Almost before the letter could be delivered, on the 28th of December, the court of inquiry convened. And though Peter Gansevoort might not have known it for sure, he probably had his suspicions, and they were probably right: his nephew's life, along with Mackenzie's, was now in danger again.

The inquiry took place on the ship of the line *North Carolina*. On the morning of the 28th of December, the various officers were piped aboard with the usual elaborate ceremonies and all was made ready. Civilians were there as well, including reporters. This was the biggest news story in the country, and everyone's eyes were turned toward New York.

The fireworks were slow in coming. For every minute of excitement in court, a hundred minutes of tedium and routine pass by, not unlike life on a warship at sea. The first day or two centered around administering oaths, setting times to convene and adjourn, and making sure that every witness was there. Not until midday on the 29th did Captain Stewart, the court's president, begin moving toward matters of substance. He began—even though he almost certainly knew what the answer would be—by asking Mackenzie formally if he had a written narrative of what had occurred on his ship.

"I have," said Mackenzie, "but I forwarded the original document to the Department at Washington."

"No narrative has been received from the Department," commented Stewart. This meant a delay, even though Mackenzie now offered to go get another copy. Stewart returned to procedural matters. "Are there any witnesses in this case present?"

"None but one or two summoned to prove matters not connected with the transactions on board the ship," answered Mackenzie.

That was still too many. When Mackenzie came back with his narrative, Stewart wanted to hear it, and he didn't want any witnesses, *Somers* men or not, to be exposed to it yet. "All witnesses present will be required to retire from the Court," he ordered. At the same time he made sure that various witnesses were aboard, so they could be rounded up quickly when needed. This included most of *Somers*'s officers, and so Stewart ordered another captain to make sure that proper watches were set aboard the brig-of-war in the interim.

By now somebody had brought Mackenzie a copy of his narrative, which he had written ten days before, less than a week after his ship's return to New York. Hoffman, the judge advocate, began to read it out loud, but then Stewart broke in. The copy wasn't authenticated, he observed. "Its reading should be delayed until an authentic copy should be received." Stewart wasn't calling Mackenzie a liar; still, *Somers*'s commander had had occasion to doctor his narrative in light of all the recent publicity. The navy's reputation was on the line here, and it couldn't do anything else that even looked slightly suspicious.

Mackenzie said that he could locate an authentic copy of the report in a half-hour's time. But it was already late in the day, so the court adjourned instead. The next morning would be soon enough.

Despite its concern over form, the court was giving Mackenzie every advantage. Rather than starting with witnesses put on by the judge advocate, which would be the normal way in a trial, it was letting Mackenzie get in the opening pitch, telling his own story first. The judge advocate wanted him to read every word before the witnesses began speaking; that way they could trip him up, impeach his account. Stewart disagreed, expressing the view that Mackenzie could read or withhold whatever he chose. Then, too, there was the fact that Mackenzie was an accomplished writer. He had had nearly three weeks after hanging young Spencer to decide how to justify what he had done, and to use all of his skills, grammar, and rhetoric to convince readers that he had been right. The court seemed sympathetic, willing, perhaps, to close ranks. The navy, and not just Mackenzie and Gansevoort, was in for some rough weather. That was unavoidable. But a heroic commander and a disturbed young acting midshipman would play a lot better with people than an innocent, victimized youth and a latter-day Captain Bligh, especially if the former were true. Nothing suggests that the court had pre-judged the facts, but it did seem inclined to give Mackenzie a break.

It began the next morning, shortly before noon. Mackenzie read his account, every last bit of it, taking one and a half hours to do so. It was dramatic and polished, and obviously self-serving. All this was to be expected.

He called what had happened a mutiny, not hedging, not fudging. He told of how he had worried about Spencer from the very beginning, how he had asked Commodore Perry to transfer the youngster. His desire for that transfer had been all the stronger, he said, because of Spencer's identity. "On this point, I beg that I may not be misunderstood," he explained. "I revere authority, and in this republican country I regard its exercise as an evidence of genius, intelligence, and virtue. *But I have no respect for the base son of an honored father.* On the contrary, the conduct of that man who sullies by his crimes the pure fame and the high honor of his parent seems to me to be far more base than one equally guilty from an humbler station. But I wish nothing to do with baseness in any shape; least of all on a vessel belonging to the United States. On this account I wished to get rid of Spencer."

It was an interesting passage, showing deference to the father and contempt toward the son in almost the same breath. Mackenzie knew that John Canfield Spencer would be watching from Washington; he nodded in the man's direction, acknowledging his station, his power. At the same time he told him exactly what he thought of young Philip. Perhaps he was appealing to the secretary of war's sense of honor, trying to make him understand the horror that had happened at sea. But if that was what he was attempting to do, he was failing to take into account the parental anger and grief that John Canfield Spencer was bound to be feeling.

On he went with his narrative. He told, in sinister fashion, of the declining morale, the news of the mutinous doings, and the arrest of young Spencer. He described Small at the braces, the carrying away of the topgallant mast, and the boy Gagely's narrow escape. "The night was the season of danger," Mackenzie half-chanted, trying with words to re-create in the court the mood that had captured his ship. "Some mysterious agency had evidently been at work since the departure of the *Somers* from New York." After Cromwell's arrest and the rescue attempt in the dark, things had gotten more desperate. "The whole crew, I soon found, were far from tranquil," he recounted. "They collected in knots upon the deck; seditious words were heard among them, and they assumed an insolent and menacing tone."

Then came the strange doings of Wilson, McKinley, and Green, the missed musters, Wilson's African dirk—"an extraordinary knife," Mackenzie called it, "broad in the middle, and running to a point. He had made it very sharp on both sides. It was a singular weapon, of no use except to kill."

The commander described the rising tide of danger, the evaporation of options as he started to lose control of the crew in the small hours of late November. "Where, I asked, was this to end?" he appealed to his listeners. "If the men upon a bright night like this seem mutinous and disposed to undertake the rescue of those confined, on a bad night, in a storm, in the midst of utter darkness, how much greater will be the probability of a rescue? If all suspected should be ironed, would the danger be over? What sympathy might not be felt for the prisoners? These matters crowded upon my mind."

Mackenzie had had no alternative; he made what had happened on the first of December seem completely inevitable. Once his decision was made, he said, "I put on my full uniform, came on deck, and proceeded to execute the most painful duty that ever devolved upon any officer in the American navy—the announcement to the prisoners of the fate that awaited them."

Spencer, as Mackenzie described it, had shown little courage. A few days before his death, when Mackenzie had stopped his tobacco allowance, "his spirit gave way. He would sit for a long time with his face buried in his cloak, and when he raised his head his face was bathed in tears." Then, Mackenzie continued, when the midshipman heard his fate pronounced, he "was overcome with emotion. He burst into a flood of tears, sank on his knees, and said he was not fit to die." It was just the sort of unmanly performance to earn him a manly society's contempt, and to make Mackenzie look good by comparison.

There wasn't much else left to tell. Spencer's claim that Cromwell was innocent needed some explanation. "This, I confess, staggered me," admitted Mackenzie, "but the evidence of his guilt was conclusive." Rather unfairly, he shifted some of his command responsibility to his executive officer: "Lieutenant Gansevoort said that there was not a shadow of doubt of it." Mackenzie himself had feared that by keeping Cromwell alive he would have played into the acting midshipman's hands. "Spencer wished to save him, probably from the hope that he would yet get possession of the vessel and carry out his original design," he theorized, "and perhaps that Cromwell would in some way effect his rescue."

Mackenzie kept the description of what followed as stark as he could, passing over the details of death. He told of the cheers of the crew after the deed had been done. "From that moment," he emphatically stated, "I felt that I was again completely master of my vessel, and that I could do with her whatever the honor of my country required." He described the burials at sea; he lauded his officers' conduct, recommending them all for promotion. "For myself," he concluded, "I ask only that I may not be deprived of my command until I am found unworthy of it."

Mackenzie had had his say. With that he yielded the floor.

The day was only half over. Now that Mackenzie was done, the court summoned James W. Wales, who also gave a very long statement.

The crew had been talking to Gansevoort. The lieutenant had to have known that an inquiry was going to happen, and he wanted to be prepared. Soon after *Somers*'s return, he and some of the other ships' officers had held a new wardroom meeting, an eerie echo of the tribunal that had recommended the deaths of Spencer, Cromwell, and Small. This one, too, was concerned with possible hangings. Gansevoort and the other officers asked several crew members if they knew anything about the plot; whenever someone said that he did, they ordered him to report to the wardroom. The meeting was designed to discover the truth before the official inquiry started—either that, or else it was meant to make sure that everyone got his story straight before the judge advocate took a crack at the case. Trial lawyers call it "woodshedding." If trials were designed purely to get to the truth, then witnesses could just tell their stories and answer whatever questions were put to them. But neither party to a trial is normally interested in the truth. Instead, each party is more concerned with winning. And with such an agenda and a capable courtroom lawyer, the truth often suffers a mauling. To prepare for a ruthless cross-examination, then, an attorney will take witnesses out to the woodshed for a little heart-to-heart talk, a lesson in how to answer the other side's questions . . . without violating, of course, the witness's oath to tell the truth.

Woodshedding is a commonplace practice in any big case. An

attorney might even be failing in his duties if he doesn't woodshed his clients. But Gansevoort was no attorney. Still, he instinctively followed the practice. The problem was that if the other side could paint the inquiry as a nonadversarial search for the truth, then what Gansevoort was doing would look like an effort to color, or even conceal, that truth, making the process an adversarial one.

James Wales, the boy who had blown the whistle on Spencer, may or may not have been one of the ones whom the wardroom group had woodshedded. But when he was called to testify after Mackenzie ended his narrative, he gave a long and well-thought-out speech of his own. It wasn't as long as Mackenzie's had been, although it was detailed and thorough. But it wasn't the most highly organized; Wales was clearly nervous. After telling the story of how Spencer approached him, after going over the execution's awful details, he backed up and recounted Spencer's strange doings in the weeks before his arrest. Other witnesses would also give jumbled accounts; the purser's steward's was merely the first.

Wales finally concluded late in the day. But the court wasn't finished with him. Mackenzie now had a chance to examine (or as the record put it, to cross-examine) him. The captain had spent some time preparing his questions. These questions, which Mackenzie gave to the court in writing, were designed to put him in a favorable light.

The very first one caused a face-off. "Did you ever hear Cromwell speak of his wife?" asked Mackenzie.

Judge Advocate Hoffman could spot right away that the question wasn't relevant to the inquiry, but he didn't move fast enough to head off Wales's reply. "I have," the boy said. "Two or three days after we were out we had a heavy gale. Cromwell came down and began to speak about friends at home. He spoke of his wife in a light manner for a man who had just been married." The words he had used, added Wales, had been about her chastity.

Now Hoffman objected, asking Mackenzie the point of the

question, and Mackenzie responded, "It was merely to counteract any feeling of sympathy that might be sought to be drawn from his wife and family." The captain's strategy was perfectly obvious, and this was part of it. Having killed Spencer, Cromwell, and Small at sea, he was now going to have to assassinate their characters in court. If they were as he portrayed them, then he had been justified in what he had done. But if they'd been virtuous, if he'd overreacted, he might soon join them in death. He thus had to portray them in the blackest way that he could, without making it seem incredible.

This wasn't a formal trial, and certainly not a civilian proceeding, and the rules of evidence were slack. Dragging in Cromwell's wife was irrelevant. What he had thought or said of her had no bearing on the fact of whether there had been a plot. But the court overlooked it, and the questions continued. "Did you hear Mr. Spencer make any remark about dead men telling no tales?" Mackenzie asked next.

"I did," replied Wales. "He said his motto was 'dead men tell no tales.' He alluded to this in connection with what he said of scuttling vessels that he might capture."

"What effect, if any, did Mr. Spencer's remark about throwing Commander Mackenzie overboard have upon the crew?"

"It rather pleased them," said Wales. "I saw smiles upon the faces of several of them; Cromwell and Small were among them."

"What was the conduct of Commander Mackenzie generally during the difficulty on the *Somers?*"

It was a crucial question. This was an age of duty and honor among all white men of status, and most especially among those in the profession of arms. A display of fear, a show of cowardice, could ruin a man, could even cause duels. If the witnesses proved that the ship's officers had overreacted in fear, then their careers would be over and their lives would be shattered. They might even swing for what they had done.

Wales came through for his captain. "He appeared to labor under no fear, was humane, and did everything he could for the comfort of the prisoners."

It wasn't enough. Mackenzie had to push harder, had to speak of things that were nearly taboo. "Did you observe any conduct in Commander Mackenzie exhibiting unmanly fear, a despotic temper or any quality unbecoming a commanding officer and a gentleman?"

The very thought was a slap in the face. One might as well have asked about details of the captain's sex life. "NO!" shouted Wales, aghast. "Sir, I did not!" His conviction was unmistakable.

It was late in the afternoon, and the outburst showed that people were getting tired. The court adjourned for the day, but Wales wasn't finished. The following morning Mackenzie kept going, doing his best to draw out more damning details of the conduct of the three dead men. Now and then Wales strayed into hearsay, telling the court what other people had told him they said they had heard, and sometimes the court stopped him from going on. But there were ways of phrasing questions that circumvented the hearsay problem. "How soon after your interview with Mr. Spencer," the captain inquired, "did you understand the mutiny was to take effect?"

Wales's answer was emphatic, deliberate. *"I understood that it was to be very shortly—before our arrival at St. Thomas."* The answer underscored the emergency. It was sufficient. And at last Wales was through.

Now it was Gansevoort's turn. His would be some of the most important testimony. He had acquiesced in, advised, and helped with the hangings. He had as much on the line as Mackenzie.

The tale that he told was far different from Mackenzie's polished account and the self-conscious statements of Wales. It was densely factual, spelling out the details of what had happened on the disastrous cruise. It dwelled on the things that the lieutenant had heard from the crew, and on the things its more troublesome members had done. He told of Wilson's knife; as he did he produced it, and the court took in the sharp six-inch blade and its handle of bone.

Gansevoort's testimony was long, and the court had to adjourn for the day—and for the year, too—before he could get through it all. It was December 31, a Saturday, and not until the following Tuesday could he resume his tale. But before he could start talking again, Mackenzie had a point to bring up. All along he had felt as if his own actions were on trial, even though this was simply an inquiry. Why, people were asking, had Spencer acted the way that he had? The suggestion was that something—or someone—had driven him to it.

That bothered Mackenzie, and he had to respond. He had already tried to put Spencer on trial; now he invited investigation himself. He mentioned mutinies of the past hundred years, some of the most famous in history: *Hermione; Medusa;* and of course *Bounty.* All of them, he conceded, shared one common thread. They were, as he said, "provoked by gross tyranny on the part of the commanding officers." The inference was clear. In light of this pattern, people could claim that whatever young Spencer had done, Mackenzie's ill-treatment had somehow forced him to it.

Mackenzie felt he had to prove otherwise, and he wanted the court to let him. "It concerns me, therefore, and my professional honor," he told it, "to show that there has been on board the *Somers,* and of every vessel I have had the honor to command, no cruelty, no disregard of the comfort or the feelings of any of the crew, no weakness, no incapacity which could provoke or encourage any of the crew to this act of mutiny." Here, again, he called it an act; not a plot or a plan, but an actual mutiny.

Hoffman didn't like it, and he said so. On top of that, he pointed out, Gansevoort was in the middle of testifying, and the court shouldn't let procedural matters interrupt it. This time he won; the court postponed Mackenzie's request.

Mackenzie's timing was unfortunate. Just minutes after he claimed that he was a kinder, gentler captain, he heard Gansevoort describe what had happened on execution day. "The orders of Commander Mackenzie to the officers," said the lieutenant, "were that if they saw an attempt made to rescue the prisoners, to blow out the brains of both the prisoners and those making the attempt." It was a poor choice of words, one hardly designed to paint Mackenzie in the light of beneficence. But now came some help that was quite unexpected, help from Judge Advocate Hoffman.

While Hoffman had objected now and then on procedural points, he had not been too eager to ask critical questions of substance about what had happened on board. At last, though, as Gansevoort finished his narrative, Hoffman got busy, but the things he asked Gansevoort were decidedly friendly. "Was there any change," he began, "in the conduct of the crew after the execution from what it had been before?"

"There was, sir," Gansevoort responded. "I think orders were obeyed with more alacrity; and there was less sullenness than there had been before in the manner of some of the men." Hoffman had passed him the ball, so he ran with it. The morale and discipline issues were critical, and Gansevoort lectured the court about them as if it were a panel of lubbers. "A change of manner on board ship is very easily observed," he pointed out, knowing reporters were listening, "and I had observed it in this case, but could not trace it to any cause until I was told that there was a mutiny aboard, and then my mind turned back to many instances which had occurred." He went on to describe a lot of the sinister doings, and Hoffman obligingly let him keep talking. Then he posed another question that helped the lieutenant. "At the time of the execution," he asked, "how far were you from St. Thomas?"

"I am not positive but think that it was five or six hundred miles."

It would have been a logical time for Hoffman to ask if *Somers* had met other vessels, ships that might have given her aid. He didn't. Instead he stayed friendly. "Was the conduct of the rest of the crew after the arrest of Spencer, Cromwell, and Small improved or otherwise?"

"Otherwise, decidedly," said Gansevoort. "So far as I could judge it *was and is my firm belief that an attack and a rescue were intended.*"

Next Mackenzie got to work examining Gansevoort, but while he could match Hoffman's friendliness, he couldn't outdo it. For a time he stayed on the point of morale. Based on how the crew had behaved, he asked, did Gansevoort believe that the officers could have gotten the ship to St. Thomas? Did the killings have to happen?

"I think she never could have reached port in the hands of her Officers, if the execution had not taken place," Gansevoort stressed. *"I thought so then; I think so now."*

Finally came the query that had smashed Wales's composure. "Did you see in the commander or any of the officers of the *Somers,* during the difficulties, any trace of unmanly fear, of a despotic temper, of any qualities unbecoming an American officer?"

"I saw nothing of the kind," replied Gansevoort easily. "Too much praise cannot be awarded to all the officers." With that, he was off the hot seat, at least for now.

Hoffman was an enigma. He was a prosecutor both by profession and nature. His training in the arts of taking the fight to the enemy went back to his days with Decatur, for the offensive has always been the best tactic at sea. But now here he was, the principal legal officer of a court of inquiry, and he seemed to be playing favorites, helping Mackenzie and Gansevoort, closing ranks with his former service.

This wasn't a trial, of course. The traditional adversarial system wasn't fully in play here. But the country was watching, a country that distrusted the aristocratic ways of the navy. Hoffman had been in politics. He wasn't blind to the popular temper, not in Jacksonian America. But he was acting as if he were. If he didn't ask the difficult questions, nobody else at the inquiry would. And he wasn't asking. In short, the whole thing was starting to look like a whitewash.

That wasn't all. While Hoffman the judge advocate was doing little to pin down Mackenzie and Gansevoort, Hoffman the federal district attorney was doing still less. He had not gone to a civilian grand jury with the facts that he had in hand; he was outright refusing to do anything in his capacity as a civilian prosecutor, despite the undenied, undeniable fact that Mackenzie had admittedly had three people killed. That was a source of outrage to some, including Margaret E. Cromwell, only lately a bride and now a new widow.

During Margaret's brief marriage, Samuel Cromwell had probably treated her poorly, at least to judge from how he had talked of her aboard ship. Still, she must have seen something in him, and now he was gone, dead and buried more than two thousand miles away in the depths of the sea. She needed closure, and maybe revenge.

The problem was how to get it. Mackenzie had ordered her husband's death, and Gansevoort had helped. That sounded like murder. But it hadn't taken place in New York, or in any other state. So getting an indictment from a New York grand jury was pretty much out of the question. That meant federal court. But here, too, she faced roadblocks. Thirty years earlier, the United States Supreme Court had declared that there was no such thing as a federal common law of crimes. What that meant was quite simple: she had to find some positive, written law, probably a federal statute, that said what Mackenzie had done was illegal. In January she and her lawyer found it.

It was a provision of an 1835 act that involved federal maritime jurisdiction. Persons on the high seas, beyond the reach of state but not federal law, who committed the act of murder, the act proclaimed, were guilty of a felony and subject to capital punishment. On the surface it seemed to say what Margaret Cromwell wanted, and needed, for it to say. But still problems remained, and the biggest one was that the local U.S. attorney—Hoffman—didn't agree with her reading. Or, if he did, he wasn't doing anything about it. He gave no sign of sending the case to a grand jury.

So Margaret seized the initiative and made an end run right around Hoffman's office. As the court of inquiry continued to sit, she and her lawyer went to federal district court and demanded warrants for the arrest of Mackenzie and Gansevoort for murder.

It was an irregular sort of proceeding, and District Judge Samuel Rossiter Betts knew it. Attempting to bypass a grand jury, as well as the prosecutor, was strange. Betts had to know what was going on, and he had to know why; he was aware of what Hoffman was up to in Brooklyn, and he could read the newspapers as well as anyone else. Still, what Margaret Cromwell was asking was not without precedent, but Betts had to go gently. He did. He went too gently, in fact, for Margaret, refusing to issue the warrants.

He explained why in a longish opinion. A mere assertion that a crime had occurred, he announced, is not enough by itself to let a judge go forward. Margaret had pointed out that Mackenzie himself had already admitted, in the navy's inquiry, to giving the orders that ended her husband's life. That seemed pretty conclusive to her, meeting Betts's requirement of proof (or as he more technically put it, a "strong presumption") that the crime had occurred. But Betts didn't think that it was enough.

In the opinion he wrote, the judge took the opportunity to lecture the absent Mackenzie and Gansevoort, and the court of inquiry, too. Mackenzie had claimed that he had been facing a mutiny. That might have been so, Betts conceded, but it might not be enough to excuse what he had done. "The necessity of the case must be made apparent beyond any fair ground to doubt," he pronounced, "before any functionary, under whatever plenitude of power, can, on his own mandate, take the life of a citizen." Betts's tone suggested that he wasn't convinced of the need to kill the three prisoners, and he wanted the navy to know it.

But this was as far as the judge was willing to go. The words of the 1835 statute seemed broad enough to reach the decks of a United States warship, but the fact was that the Constitution, and a pattern of older congressional acts, showed that Congress had the power to set up a separate system of justice for the armed forces, and that it had actually done so. If the statute on which Margaret Cromwell was relying had meant to change that system by giving civilian courts jurisdiction over the navy, then it would have said so explicitly. It didn't. Thus, held Betts, he couldn't get involved in "this most solemn and melancholy transaction," especially since the navy, with Hoffman's help, was investigating already. With that he threw out the case.

But Margaret Cromwell wasn't done yet. Neither were others.

Meanwhile, at the eye of the storm that swirled in the press and the courts, the inquiry aboard *North Carolina* continued. Witnesses came and witnesses went, giving longer or shorter statements, being asked much the same questions by Commander Mackenzie. First up were the officers; then the crew had its chance. Even the stewards, remarkably—African-Americans all—got to have their say, once they told the court that they were Christians and that they knew what oaths meant. In this respect, at least, the navy was more democratic than many civilian courts, which would not tolerate African-American testimony. Nearly every witness, black and white, heard variations on the same queries: "Did you observe in the commander or other officers an indication of unusual fear, a despotic temper, or of any qualities unbecoming an American officer?" "What sort of usage had you on board the vessel—was it worse than on board other vessels?" and, nearly always, "At the time of the execution did you, or do you now believe, that the *Somers* could have been brought into port if the execution had not taken place?" And each time—

mostly—the answers resembled each other. To the first: "No, sir." To the second: "It was good—better than I had on other vessels." And, usually, to the third: "I did not then, and I do not now."

Some crewmen gave different answers. A few said that the ship could have made port; one or two others opined that she might have gotten as far as St. Thomas, but never all the way to New York. But Oliver Browning, bo'sun's mate, wasn't one of them. He knew ships and he knew men. He wouldn't have been a bo'sun's mate otherwise. "In dark nights and squally weather the officers might be engaged taking in sail, and it was hard to tell who were engaged in it or not," he explained to a panel of officers who might or might not have known as much about sailing as he did. "It would be easy in a dark night for a parcel of men, where the officers were running about the deck, for each man to pick out his mark, stick his knife in him, and after killing all the officers but the commander, it was easy to take command of the vessel."

But there had been a way to bring an end to the danger, and Mackenzie had taken it. Browning didn't think that any crew member except for the two dead ones could have managed the ship. As for the dead midshipman, Browning was quite dismissive. "I do not believe Spencer was seaman enough to sail the brig without the assistance of Cromwell and Small," he declared. "I do not think he knew a dozen ropes aboard of her." Of course, in the end, the boy had gotten acquainted with one rope, at least.

Still, Browning had been worried—scared, even. "I feared a rescue would be made very much, and was afraid to turn into my hammock at night," he said frankly. "I was afraid to go to sleep, I had such a dread on my mind; I never unbuckled my arms from me, and slept with them from the time they were given me until our arrival in New York off the Navy Yard."

The testimony wasn't all about witnesses' unmanly fear, though, or lack of it. Other people spoke to different concerns. Ship's surgeon Leecock described Small's demeanor on the day of Spencer's arrest; the seaman had claimed to be ill, but Leecock instead had thought him terrified. Midshipman Hays told of how the topgallant mast had gone after Small had ignored the orders to slacken the brace. Commander Joshua R. Sands, who had supervised *Somers's* construction, spoke to the brig's small size: there was no place below, no cabin, no locker, where the officers could have secured Spencer, Cromwell, and Small, much less all the others. "If the prisoners had been confined in the cabin, and guarded from the deck," he told his fellow officers, "there would have been no interruption to their release by the crew but the bulkheads, which a single round shot would have demolished." So much for battening down with all the men below. And it could have gotten much worse. "Had the deck been in possession of the crew, and the officers below," he continued, "one man at each end of the trunk, with a billet of wood in his hand, could have prevented the officers from coming on deck." And this was even if mutineers were willing to put up with the trouble of prisoners. Spencer might not have known the ropes, but according to Sands, his plan to take the ship would still have been very effective.

Through it all, Hoffman said little. Maybe his navy blood was reasserting itself, but whatever the reason, he wasn't going after Mackenzie. Now and then he did ask a question, but hardly an adversarial one. Once, Mackenzie asked Sergeant Garty what he inferred from remarks he had heard on the cruise regarding what Mackenzie wryly referred to as "the change of administration." That drew an objection from Hoffman; it was up to the court, he said, to draw inferences. But more often he and Mackenzie seemed almost a team. At one point Mackenzie asked a young sailor about possible bias. "Have any inducements of any sort, any promises, or any threats, been held out to you to induce you to tell what you knew about the mutiny?"

"No sir," the sailor answered, "none."

Hoffman chimed in. "By anyone—your commander, or others?"

"No, sir."

"Any promises or threats?" the judge advocate kept up.

"No, sir."

"By anyone—officer or civilian?"

"No, sir."

"Have you been told by anyone," Hoffman persisted, "what it was necessary for you to testify to, or to prove?" No doubt he had heard of the wardroom woodshedding, but the sailor stuck with his story. "No, sir." Finally Hoffman let it go, without any attempt at impeachment.

Every once in a while Hoffman got a response that injured Mackenzie, but it seemed almost happenstance, since he always asked the same questions—questions about the officers' fear or whether they could have kept control of the ship. In mid-January, two weeks into the inquiry, George Warner found himself on the stand. His name had been on Spencer's list; suspicion had fallen on him pretty strongly, and Mackenzie had ironed him when *Somers* arrived off New York. When Hoffman asked him the usual things, one of his answers was different from those of the others. "The brig could have been taken to St. Thomas at any rate without the execution taking place," he claimed. "The day of the execution the officers and petty officers being all armed, I was satisfied we could proceed to any port in safety." Still, he didn't deny that something was going on. He had said so at the time, to the officers in the wardroom just before the hangings, and he reiterated it now. He had thrown suspicion on Cromwell, maybe in an effort to save himself. "I might have said," he admitted, "that 'Cromwell deserved to be hung,' but I did not think at the time that they were going to hang him. I think he was the most desperate character in the ship."

It was partly on the basis of Warner's opinion, then, that Cromwell had swung, and Hoffman chased it awhile. "Is that or was that a serious opinion of yours," he asked, "that 'Cromwell deserved to be hung'?"

Warner fudged. "If he was guilty, he deserved to be hung."

"Did you think he was guilty?" Hoffman persisted.

"I did think he was guilty," declared Warner, defensive. "I don't know how many others were concerned in this mutiny; I cannot say how many others I thought were concerned." He was obviously worried. Whether or not he was involved, he was under suspicion, and he had watched three of his shipmates die for what he was now suspected of. That would make anyone nervous. As to whether he was telling the truth, that was up to the court to decide.

The court was also the one to decide the right answer to procedural issues, and a few days later Mackenzie raised one. The media circus hadn't abated, and Mackenzie was watching his name and his case dragged through every newspaper. Worse, he suspected that someone at the navy yard was leaking news to the press. One of the items that had lately shown up was an account of the punishments that he had meted out during the cruise. Floggings and such were par for the course aboard practically every warship, but they didn't play well to an increasingly democratic and libertarian society, and anyway, these accounts flew in the face of Mackenzie's attempt to pass himself off as a lenient captain. The immediate problem was that the account had to have come from *Somers*'s log, the same log that was in the court's custody. Mackenzie wanted to stop the leaks, and he asked the court to investigate.

The court wasn't obliging. Hoffman pointed out that it lacked the authority to conduct any other inquiries, and the panel of captains agreed. They had to ignore the newspaper statements. "If any incorrect ones have been made," Commodore Stewart remarked, "Captain Mackenzie had better reply to them. All the court can do now is to take precautions to prevent a similar occurrence."

That wasn't enough for Mackenzie, who was under full-scale assault in the press. The next day he kept pushing the court to investigate. Henry Eld, Jr., acting master of *North Carolina*, described for the court the precautions he had taken to keep the log secure, noting the people who had had access to it, pointing the finger in their directions. But the court had decided; this matter was out of its hands. Finally Mackenzie gave up, and turned his efforts to a different line of attack.

Since he wasn't able to get the press under control, he renewed his efforts to vilify Spencer in the inquiry's official records. As the proceeding entered its eighteenth day, the captain asked leave to bring in the dead midshipman's background. Mackenzie had been busy; he had collected witnesses and evidence that would show that a pattern of piratical thoughts had plagued Spencer's mind for years. The boy had talked of them, claimed Mackenzie, during his days at Geneva College; he had thought about ways of taking *Potomac* as he sailed home from the South Atlantic aboard her. Mackenzie was also ready to show, if only the court would let him, that McKinley and Cromwell had been talking of mutiny shortly before *Somers*'s departure, and that Cromwell had turned mutinous once before while serving in Florida. Hoffman didn't like it. The question was what had happened on *Somers,* and he dismissed most of what had gone on before as irrelevant. He did concede that anything the victims had said just before sailing could probably come into evidence, but the rest was out of bounds. The court agreed.

Hands effectively tied, Mackenzie summoned John Ford, a former *Somers* wardroom steward who, luckily for him, had not been aboard for the African cruise. The night before the brig sailed, he had gone ashore in one of her boats. McKinley, who had been in the boat with him, had taken him aside once they reached land and told him that a mutiny was going to happen. It was a brief enough statement, which Hoffman didn't bother to follow up. About the same time, Mackenzie called two other witnesses, both *Somers* crewmen, who swore that they heard Cromwell ask Gansevoort's forgiveness just minutes before the hangings. Mackenzie was worried about

Cromwell; the bo'sun's mate had maintained his innocence until the last, and Mackenzie was trying hard to punch a hole in that story. Would Cromwell have asked forgiveness, he posited, unless he'd done something that needed forgiving? Why ask forgiveness, he undoubtedly figured, unless there was guilt?

But Mackenzie was worried about the whole thing, and not just about the Cromwell angle. Hoffman had run through all his witnesses; Mackenzie, too, was nearly done. But he wasn't through addressing the court, officer to officers, gentleman to gentlemen. He now asked them to let him explain, in his own words, why he'd done what he'd done. The court had heard his report to the Navy Department; still, he wanted to set forth again the reasons for his actions. The court agreed to hear him, but Hoffman would read the statement.

That statement painted an ugly black picture of what should have been an innocent training cruise. Into this fairly short address Mackenzie crammed everything evil that he claimed to have seen and heard on the voyage. It was the only way. "First," the statement began, "I was influenced by my deep conviction of the reality of the plot disclosed by Mr. Spencer to Mr. Wales." Mackenzie stressed that he hadn't gullibly gone along with Wales's revelation at first; only after critically judging Wales's demeanor had he accepted the statement. "The nature of this plot," he continued, "involving the murder of the officers and a large portion of the crew, and the commission of almost every crime, convinced me that those who had agreed to it were capable of carrying it into execution and committing any atrocity." That most of the crew were apprentices only made things more dangerous: "Many of them, although men in strength and size, were still boys in age, and consequently would be little likely to resist temptation and more easily allured by the pleasures held out to them as accompanying the life of a pirate." The only recourse had been to arrest the ringleader.

But what was at issue here was not the arrests but the hangings. Mackenzie knew this, and he carefully spelled out the things that went into his decision to kill. The crew's insubordinate manner was one; the unknown extent of the plot, another. "Let us suppose the whole crew had been examined, and all had protested their innocence and ignorance," he suggested, doubtless aware that this had effectively happened here in the inquiry. "Could we have believed and trusted them? Would the uncertainty have been removed or diminished? On the contrary, must not the universal denial have increased and justified our suspicions of universal guilt? We must still have believed that many were guilty, and could not have known that any were innocent." He may have been stretching with this last statement or two, but not very much, given that he had been a thousand miles at sea, his officers outnumbered by as many as ten to one.

Mackenzie wasn't yet finished. The statement went on to mention the officers' exhaustion, the greatly increased danger that a squall or storm would have brought, and the small ship's inability to house more prisoners. The message's final point stressed the captain's belief that only by killing those who knew how to navigate could he put down the mutiny.

There was no doubt in Mackenzie's mind, or if there were, he could never give voice to it. To do so would have been suicide. "I was doing my duty faithfully," he concluded, "to my God and to my country." With that, the statement closed.

That was nearly the end, at least of the court of inquiry. Mackenzie called one last witness, a man named Rice, whom he wanted to testify as to things that Cromwell had said and done in the month before the cruise. Hoffman objected; it was inadmissible, irrelevant. The court agreed. Testimony was over. The day was January

19, a Thursday. The court was cleared, and the officers began to deliberate.

Mackenzie was worried. The press was still calling for blood—his blood—and Margaret Cromwell's attack in the regular courts had just recently failed. He could feel others coming. Word was spreading that John C. Spencer had put her up to the job, and Spencer wouldn't let go so easily. Even a complete vindication from the court of inquiry might not shield Mackenzie from Spencer or Cromwell, from the regular courts, or from the public at large.

The court of inquiry hadn't yet reached a decision when Mackenzie made one of his own. He wrote to Abel Upshur, requesting a full-blown court-martial. For all that he knew, the secretary might order one anyway, whatever the inquiry said. He had that authority. And Mackenzie had the right to ask for a trial. So, facing the whirlwind, he threw his fate into the hands of the navy and asked.

Meanwhile the inquiry reached its decision. It exonerated Mackenzie, giving all of his actions a ringing endorsement. In almost every way possible it supported the captain. It found that a mutiny had in fact taken place, and that Spencer, Cromwell, and Small were the ringleaders. It accepted Mackenzie's position that he had intended, wanted, and tried to bring the three home alive. It fudged a bit on the issue of the loss of the topgallant mast, saying merely that the crew's odd and sullen behavior "justly excited in the Commander and the officers the belief that an attempt would be made to rescue the prisoners and take the brig." Had such an attempt taken place, found the court, especially in a storm or at night, it might well have succeeded, given the officers' run-down condition. "Under these circumstances," it concluded, Mackenzie "was not bound to risk the safety of his vessel, and jeopardize the lives of the young officers and the loyal of his crew, in order to secure to the guilty the forms of trial . . . the immediate execution of the prisoners was demanded by duty and justified by necessity."

There was one final word the court had to utter before it adjourned. It had held Captain Mackenzie officially blameless; now it needed to clear his personal image. His conduct, said the court clearly, and that of his officers, "was prudent, calm, and firm . . . he and they honorably performed their duty to the service and their country." This opinion was signed by Charles Stewart, the court's president. Under his signature was Judge Advocate Hoffman's.

It hardly mattered. The opinion did little to shut up Mackenzie's critics, and already Upshur was having the court-martial charges prepared. By January 23 they were ready, five in all. The first, the most dangerous, was for murder; it specified that Mackenzie did "without form of law, willfully, deliberately, and with malice afore-thought" hang Philip Spencer, Samuel Cromwell, and Elisha Small. The second charge averred that these killings had constituted oppression; the third argued that in ordering them, Mackenzie had imposed illegal punishment, one far in excess of what Congress allowed him to do.

The other two charges were different, both of them slaps in Mackenzie's face, adding insult to injury. One was the charge of conduct unbecoming an officer. It claimed, in particular, that Mackenzie had unfeelingly taunted young Spencer on the day of the execution. The fifth and final charge tried to explain Mackenzie's motive: it alleged that for the whole of the cruise, Mackenzie "did oppressively and cruelly use and maltreat the crew," inflicting need-less, extreme punishment. Mackenzie had asked for a trial; he was obviously going to get one.

This time it would be a real trial, not a mere fact-finding process. The inquiry's vindication meant nothing now. Mackenzie was about to face a panel of officers who would feel pressure from both the public and the Cabinet. They could clear him again, or they could convict him of murder.

And if they convicted him, everyone knew, then Mackenzie's fate could be the same as that of his own three victims. He would hang by the neck from some yardarm, until he was dead.

The die, as Philip Spencer had said, would shortly be cast.

PART SEVEN

Court-Martial

NORTH CAROLINA was a ship of the line. Nearly two hundred feet long, with a crew of close to a thousand, the multidecked vessel could bring massive striking power to bear anywhere in the world that she could find water enough to keep her afloat. On paper, she was rated at seventy-four guns, somewhat modest armament for a battleship, but the American navy tended to stuff extra artillery into its hulls, and in *North Carolina*'s case it had taken this practice to an extreme. She likely outgunned much more highly rated opponents. In fact she was arguably the planet's most powerful warship, the most lethal weapons platform of the mid-nineteenth century.

At least she had been. Laid down just after the War of 1812, by 1843 she was a quarter of a century old. Age was no real problem, but technological changes were. Steam was making headway, quite literally. So were chemistry, metallurgy, and armor. Slowly she was growing outmoded, though she was always expensive. Some of her sister ships were still hanging on, but ever since 1839 she had been a permanent fixture in New York's navy yard. She was now a receiving ship, a mixture of barracks, administrative office, and training vessel—and site of courts-martial and inquiries. Mackenzie had been grilled on board in December and January, and his formal trial would begin there in February's first days.

She might have been old, but she was still big, dwarfing the minuscule *Somers*. Many civilians might not understand the difference between a brig and a ship of the line. Even frigates, long the stars of the United States Navy, made *Somers* seem tiny, and frigates were little compared to *North Carolina*.

Richard Henry Dana, Jr., tried to get this point across as the court of inquiry met. He was one of the nation's most famous nautical men, even though he had not been to sea for some years. Still, he had written his famous account *Two Years Before the Mast* firsthand, so most people rightly considered him an authority. But he was a lawyer, not a sailor, by trade, and something in him wanted to see Mackenzie get a fair deal. So, after visiting *Somers,* he described for a newspaper audience what he'd seen. First he spoke in his persona of mariner. "No one ought to form an opinion upon the issue of this conspiracy without first seeing the *Somers,*" he told his audience. He tried to get across to the readers the very small size of the vessel. "You feel as though half a dozen resolute conspirators could have swept the decks, and thrown overboard all that opposed them before aid could come from below." As for securing the prisoners belowdecks, Dana was positive that it would have been impossible, describing the cramped berth deck spaces and cabins, explaining how flimsy the bulkheads were. He threw the whole weight of his considerable reputation behind the beleaguered officers. "One must have been at sea, or be willing to receive something on faith from those who have," he declared, "to judge fairly of this case."

Thus wrote Dana the mariner; now Dana the lawyer took over. To require the officers to have refrained from acting until they had incontrovertible evidence of mutiny would be unreasonable. The mutineers, he pointed out, would have tried to hide their own plans. "If the officers had waited for that evidence," he said, "they would have waited just too long for their own safety, and for the prevention of dreadful crimes on the whole ocean."

Anyway, Dana continued, the officers had had evidence enough as it was. They had witnessed overtly mutinous acts. The men who missed muster on the night of the 29th of November, for instance: "If this was, as the officers believed, a deliberate combination to disobey a lawful order and carried out, it was of itself a mutiny, and would forfeit the lives of the parties by martial law," he opined. "It is open defiance of authority, and, connected with the event of the others, would alone go far to make out the required case." The pattern of small and not-so-small things; the incident with the topgallant mast; the sullen and rowdy crew, its refusal to obey orders; all this convinced Dana. As he wound up his narrative, he made another plea for the officers. "They could call on no aid from abroad," he reminded his audience, "there was no place for retreat, and no concession would avail them. Must they await the onset and its chances?" Dana, lawyer and sometime sailor, was sure of the answer: "Not so at sea, in a case like this."

If Dana had hoped to convince the public to side with Mackenzie, he failed. James Fenimore Cooper, Mackenzie's longtime nemesis, had things to say, too, and, like Dana, he could draw on a maritime background. He'd been a midshipman once; maybe that helped him identify with young Philip Spencer. So, too, might the fact that his own son had once been a classmate of Spencer's. But whatever the reason, Cooper thought that Mackenzie had done something wrong.

Cooper was putting the finishing touches on a pamphlet called *The Battle of Lake Erie* when *Somers* arrived in New York. It was the latest salvo in his running feud with Mackenzie. But when news broke of what had happened aboard the small brig, he stopped and took time to castigate her commander for his decisions and actions during the cruise. Even before Dana's comments became public knowledge, Cooper had made up his mind. "Mackenzie's affair looks bad enough," he told his wife. "The report he sent to Washington is considered to be the work of a man scarcely compos mentis. I never read a more miserable thing in my life."

Later, as Mackenzie's legal battles proceeded, Cooper got even more strident. "I think the affair one of the most discreditable events that ever occurred in the service, since it exhibits a *demoralized quarterdeck*," he declared. "I can find no necessity for the executions, and certainly nothing like substantial *proof* against Cromwell. I have serious doubts whether this man had any connection with Spencer's mad schemes at all. Mackenzie, however, reverses the maxim of the common law, which says that if there be a doubt of guilt, the prisoner is to have its benefit; he reasons, if there be a doubt of his innocence, hang him."

Among the public, in the press, all over New York and the nation, the controversy continued to blaze as the court-martial proper began. Attendance at the proceedings was so heavy, in fact, that even the huge *North Carolina* couldn't hold all the people. After a few days the court started meeting ashore in the roomy navy yard chapel. But at first it took place aboard ship, with all of the nautical pomp and circumstance that declared to the world that a naval officer was on trial for his life. As the court convened on the morning of February 2, the special flag was run up; a naval gun boomed from the battleship's side, signaling that naval justice was about to be done. The court of thirteen officers appeared; among them were Captains John Downes, George Read, Daniel Turner, and John D. Sloat, all veterans of the 1812 war. Turner, in fact, had commanded a vessel at the Battle of Lake Erie, and Sloat would go on to play a key role in the U.S. conquest of California. Mackenzie, of course, was on hand with his counsel, as was a new judge advocate. Mackenzie had two attorneys, in fact, George Griffin and John Duer. Duer, his lead lawyer, was part of the close-knit New York community, a former federal district judge and collaborator with John Canfield Spencer in various legal endeavors. Not so the judge advocate. William H. Norris of Baltimore was an outsider here, and not in the same professional league with the likes of Ogden Hoffman. "The appointment of the Judge Advocate was a bad one," an insider pronounced. "He is a young man and little known in his profession even in Baltimore." But unlike Hoffman, Norris had a desire, as he would soon show, to go after Commander Mackenzie.

As the court-martial got under way, though, Norris seemed somewhat restrained, even more so than Hoffman had been. As the court finished organizing itself, reading aloud the orders that had caused it to be, giving and taking all of the requisite oaths, Mackenzie gave the judge advocate a large, easy target. The charges against him had just been read when he arose and made a statement. "I admit that Acting Midshipman Philip Spencer, Boatswain's mate Samuel Cromwell, and Seaman Elisha Small were put to death by my order," he freely stated, "but, as under the existing circumstances this act was demanded by duty and justified by necessity, I plead not guilty to all the charges."

Although not under oath, Mackenzie had just confessed, in the hearing of the court and judge advocate, something he had never denied, something everyone knew to be true. He had had three people killed. So Norris need not go to the trouble of showing it. All that he had to prove was that Mackenzie had had no legal justification, that he had had no legal excuse. Actually he didn't really need to prove even as much as that. Since the fact of the killings was clear, the law now gave Mackenzie the burden of showing excuse or justification. Theoretically Norris could simply sit back and cross-examine defense witnesses while Mackenzie tried to prove one of these things. But as soon as Mackenzie ended his statement, Norris made one of his own.

The American common law process is mostly adversarial, with each side in a case arguing its position before a neutral judge and jury. If no one sees any need for bringing up a particular point, then that point doesn't get raised. And it doesn't stop there. In the old days, if party A saw party B fail to make a legal argument or discover some useful evidence that could help B win its case, party A had no obligation to mention the oversight. Party A wasn't out for justice, or fairness, or truth; party A was out to win, just as was party B. Justice was up to the judge and jury. Much of this is still true today. Even the system of military and naval law followed this same general outline, although it was not, strictly speaking, a part of the common law system. In the military proceeding, Norris's job was to convince the court to convict Commander Mackenzie, and it was up to Macken-zie and his attorneys to object if Norris violated the rules of exami-nation and evidence while he was trying to do it.

But Norris now warned his listeners that he had other ideas, ideas that grew from centuries of Anglo-American military law. "I shall not expect to be restricted by the technical rules in these partic-ulars, and be treated and restrained as an ordinary prosecutor," he lectured the court. "I wish to elicit the whole truth, whether favor-able or adverse to the defendant, and if I do not extract what legally ought to serve him, equally with his own counsel, it will be only from inferior capacity, knowledge, and that sagacity which a partisan feeling does only give."

This was a radical twist, an upheaval in the adversarial system. On the surface it seemed like a good deal for Mackenzie. Here was a prosecutor who claimed to be after the truth, whether or not it meant a conviction. It also seemed as if the apparent whitewash that Hoffman had seemingly helped carry out would continue, since Norris acted more concerned with truth than with victory. But Nor-ris's offer came with conditions. "I must be apprised in advance by defendant and his counsel of their intended course," he warned. He wanted the right to ask any question at all, without running the risk of Mackenzie's objection on grounds of relevance, hearsay, or any other rule of evidence. That was the only way that Norris could search for the truth. Would Mackenzie and his counsel give him the leeway he wanted? Or would they claim the rights that were theirs under the adversarial system?

It took them a day to answer. They didn't trust the judge advo-cate, or at any rate they lacked enough trust to surrender their legal teeth and claws. The traditional, adversarial weapons, they told both court and Norris, were "essential to the discovery of truth, the administration of justice, the preservation of the rights of the navy." In short: no deal. They wouldn't give free rein to the officer whose job it was to see Mackenzie swing.

So be it. The defense wanted an adversarial trial; that was what Norris would give it, then. He started calling his witnesses.

First up was Midshipman Hays. At once the judge advocate went on the attack, asking him if Spencer had been executed on Commander Mackenzie's orders. There could be only one answer to that, and Hays gave it, to no one's surprise. Then Norris began asking questions that made Mackenzie's actions seem darker. "From the time of his arrest to the time of his execution, was Philip Spencer furnished with any charges and specifications of crime?"

"Not to my knowledge," replied Hays.

Had Mackenzie, pressed Norris, extended to Spencer any procedural safeguards? Right to confrontation of witnesses? Cross-examination? Right to offer his own evidence? Right to object to others' evidence?

"None that I know of," the midshipman admitted.

Norris moved on to the matter of Cromwell's death, asking much the same questions, and then he proceeded to Small's. Next he returned to Spencer, beginning the litany all over again. The first time around had been in relation to the first of the five charges against Commander Mackenzie, the accusation of murder; Norris now repeated it for the second, and then again for the third. Over and over Hays had to restate the same answer, the repetition further damning his captain: "He was executed by order of Commander Mackenzie, at the time and place specified." Mackenzie didn't even try to cross-examine the witness.

But Mackenzie did persuade the court to let him go ahead and call James Wales. Just as he had at the court of inquiry, the purser's steward told his story of how Spencer had tried to enlist him. But this time, unlike the last, Norris was waiting for Wales at the end of it, with a cross-examiner's questions.

First he interrogated Wales about the mysterious lists—the lists, he got Wales to admit, that had gone unseen the night before Spencer's arrest. The ones that Gansevoort and Rogers had found later among Spencer's belongings were nothing that Wales had ever encountered. For all that Wales knew, Norris was hinting, Spencer had simply been joking. To reinforce this suggestion, he then asked a long and complex question, a question that dragged on interminably, recounting many of the supposed plan's details, to ask Wales's opinion of Spencer.

Right away Mackenzie objected. He objected so much, in fact, that that evening he and his lawyers wrote out a long argument to show why the question was pointless. The next day they read their objection aloud. The question, John Duer declared, wasn't designed either to get information from Wales or to impeach his credibility. It was designed to make what Spencer had said look like a joke, a game of some kind. That wasn't a good enough reason to ask it.

The court agreed, but Norris hadn't finished with Wales. "Did you have any difficulty with Commander Mackenzie at Puerto Rico," he asked, referring to the shakedown cruise of the previous summer, "and what was it?"

"I had a difficulty," Wales admitted, "but decline explaining it." Norris, strangely, let it go.

Already, with these first witnesses, Norris was firing harder and faster than Hoffman had done at any point during the inquiry. But his firing was erratic, even blind. With his first questions to Wales he seemed to imply that there hadn't been a conspiracy, only a boy's overactive imagination and perhaps a planted document. But his next attack on the steward, whose name appeared on the list, suggested that there *had* been a plot, and that Wales, disaffected because of his earlier run-in with Captain Mackenzie, had been in on it, that he had perhaps decided to squeal when he saw that Spencer was getting in over his head. This latter tack didn't much help the judge advocate's case, but at least he was cross-examining, which was more than Hoffman had done. His assaults would get more effective in time.

Norris showed little concern for Wales, but the court was more forbearing with the young man. By now he had been on the stand for the better part of three days, and Norris wasn't through yet. So the officers on the bench began to jump in with friendly, yet important, questions. "Did Commander Mackenzie in any way taunt Mr. Spencer?" one asked, a clear reference to the "conduct unbecoming" charge that Mackenzie was facing.

"No, sir, he did not," replied Wales, doubtless relieved that the focus had shifted away from himself for a time. Next came a still gentler question, although it, too, was critical. "Were you ever on board a man-of-war before?"

"Never to sea in one," said Wales. "I have been on board of the *Ontario* for a month." This helped paint a picture of Wales as a scared youngster, though one who lacked any frame of reference for what he had seen aboard *Somers*.

The court's softball questions continued the next day. "Had you never any idea," an officer queried, "that a mutiny was intended before your conversation with Midshipman Spencer on the booms?"

"No, sir," came Wales's firm response. "Never."

Later came another leading question. "Was not the conduct of Mr. Spencer generally wayward or eccentric, otherwise?"

"I don't know, sir," Wales cautiously said; then he threw caution to the winds. "I noticed sometimes he was rather singular, dull, stupid!" This helped take some of the pressure off the boy. In light of all of these questions from the bench, Spencer was back on trial.

But not for long. A day or two later, as Wales was winding down, Mackenzie tried to keep going, offering—as he had offered in the earlier inquiry—to show that Spencer had had a mutinous plot while serving aboard *Potomac*. But this time, too, the court prevented him. And by then it was Gansevoort's turn, and the focus returned to him and Mackenzie.

Gansevoort began with a long narrative, much as he had in the inquiry, with few interruptions from the lawyers. Toward the end of the day he referred to the letter Mackenzie had written on the eve of the execution, the letter in which he had asked the advice of his officers on what action to take with the prisoners. The next step would be to go over the testimony and the notes that the officers had taken down in the wardroom just before the hangings, but Norris decided to fight Gansevoort. The record of the officers' meetings, he argued, wasn't admissible. "It is not the proceedings of a lawful court," he insisted. Mackenzie was seeking to keep the dead men on trial, and Norris was going to stop him. "As evidence to show the guilt of any of their parties and their connection, it is wholly unallowable."

Norris wasn't being unreasonable, merely adversarial. He didn't even deny that Mackenzie and his officers had had the right to protect themselves against mutiny. But that didn't mean that they'd had the power to carry out trials when the law didn't say that they could, much less that they'd had the authority to string sailors up. The judge advocate didn't even mind the use of the wardroom evidence and the letters between captain and officers. But he did think them admissible for only one reason, which related to the issue of malice.

The law does strange things to words. It can take a dead Latin phrase and turn it into a crucial, mysterious concept, a phrase such as habeas corpus, for instance, or res ipsa loquitur. It can infuse a meaning into a term that only history can fully reveal, as is the case with "corruption of blood" and "fee simple." Or it can take a commonplace word, a word that seems very straightforward, and contort it so utterly that its new legal meaning has little or nothing to do with its everyday definition. *Malice* is one such word.

To most of us malice signifies evil, ill will, or hatred. But it means something else in the law, something very specific: it means a wrongful act done with intent, even if ill will is absent. For Norris, what Mackenzie had done was clearly malicious, in the legal sense of the word. Ill will, or lack of it, was irrelevant. Norris was happy for

Mackenzie to offer the letters and the officers' wardroom record to show that there hadn't been any garden-variety malice. It didn't matter at all. None of the charges against him required a showing of *that* kind of malice. So if Mackenzie wanted to show that he had no hatred of Spencer, no ill will toward him or the other two victims, then let him, and much good might it do him. He still had the kind of malice that counted in court. He had done an illegal act, and he had intended to do it, and that was all that legally mattered. Still, to the degree that those minutes showed the desperation, the fear, that the wardroom had felt, they might help acquit Mackenzie. So Norris tried to block their use.

The court split the difference. It refused to let in the records at all, but it let in the two letters between captain and officers, although just for the purpose of showing absence of ill will on the part of Mackenzie. That was a blow to *Somers*'s commander, but there was nothing to do but play out the game.

But Norris could play the game, too, and before long he got to take his own shot at Gansevoort. After the lieutenant had told his story and answered Mackenzie's friendly questions, it was the judge advocate's turn. Gansevoort had said that the crew had been acting strangely, and that he had finally grown convinced that the executions were the only way out. So Norris concentrated his fire on these statements, trying to trip up the witness, forcing a self-contradiction to destroy his credibility.

One of the first things Norris brought up was the question of what Spencer had been doing just before his arrest. His usual duties, Gansevoort replied, except when he was up in the foretop, or climbing down the Jacob's ladder with that "menacing look" of his. Gansevoort made it sound sinister; Norris tried to correct that image. "Was he on duty when he was in the foretop?" he asked.

"No, sir," Gansevoort answered.

"Was it an unusual thing for Mr. Spencer to be in the foretop?"

"I think I may have seen him there before," Gansevoort admitted.

"Have you not seen other young officers in the foretop, when not on duty?"

"Yes, sir, I have."

The next question went unasked. It was so obvious that Norris didn't need to reduce it to words. *Then what was so odd, Mr. Gansevoort—what was so strange and suspicious—about Spencer hanging out in the foretop?* Norris moved on, leaving the query to echo inaudibly in the minds of his audience.

Another vulnerable point concerned the rescue attempt in the night after Spencer's arrest. According to Gansevoort, the crew had been rushing aft, probably with some of that ill will with which Norris was unconcerned. Norris tried to shake that story. "Did you not afterward express to the commander and some of the officers," he challenged, "that you had been under a wrong impression as to the meaning of the men at the time?"

Gansevoort fought back. "I think I did afterward express my satisfaction that I had not shot among them, as I was near doing," he corrected the judge advocate. "My impression was, when they were coming down, that it was for the purpose of destroying us. . . . I don't recollect having said I was under a wrong impression, to the commander or any other officer."

"Why were you gratified that you had not shot?" queried Norris, still trying to find an opening.

Gansevoort gave some ground. "Because I might have killed an innocent man." It wasn't necessarily an admission that he had been wrong—not every sailor on deck had been involved in the rush—but it could have been taken that way. Norris moved on.

The judge advocate might not have needed to show ill will, but a little such malice on the part of Mackenzie might make the conviction easier, and he wanted Gansevoort to help him reveal it, whether or not Gansevoort was willing. Cromwell had kept proclaiming his innocence, so he was the one on whom Norris focused, bringing up an exchange that had taken place just after his arrest. "Did Commander Mackenzie," he asked the lieutenant, "tell Cromwell he regarded him as a dangerous man?"

"I don't recollect," said Gansevoort.

That wasn't good enough. "Did you not swear before the court of inquiry that Commander Mackenzie then told Cromwell he regarded him as a dangerous man?" Norris reminded him.

"I don't recollect," Gansevoort repeated. "The records of the court will show." Norris had him pinned down.

Then there was the issue of when Mackenzie had decided on death, and why. The officers' letter recommending the hangings was written on the 1st of December, when things had grown very rough. Norris wanted to show that the actual decision had come about earlier. He asked Gansevoort if he had brought up the matter three days before, on the 28th of November.

"I don't recollect as to the day," Gansevoort fudged. "I think I spoke to the doctor, Mr. Perry, and Mr. Rogers, and I think their conclusion was that they should be disposed of."

The court was now interested, and it wasn't going to let the lieutenant gloss over the issue of timing. "Was that before the council of officers was held?" asked one of its members.

"Yes, sir," Gansevoort said simply.

Talk of execution *before* the wardroom meeting? That certainly sounded malicious, and Norris began circling, starting to close in like a wolf. "Was it a day or more before the holding of the council of officers?"

Gansevoort tried damage control. "I don't think it was more than a day," he replied. "I am not positive as to the time." He probably knew that Norris lacked friendly witnesses who could blow a hole in his story, if a story was what it was.

Norris kept taking Gansevoort back to a day or two after Spencer's arrest. "Turn the log-book under the date of the 28th of November," he told the witness. "Was there a vessel reported on that date three points to the larboard bow? Was there any endeavor to hail or overhaul her? Was there any consultation about placing any of your prisoners aboard of her between you and Commander Mackenzie?" Here was an indication, if not of malice, surely of recklessness or negligence. If there had been a chance for some help, Norris was saying, then Mackenzie definitely should have taken it. If he hadn't, then he should bear the blame for the hangings.

He scored. Gansevoort, consulting the log, read of the sighting of sails. It probably made him squirm; all he could do was cut himself out of the loop on this one. "I don't recollect to have heard of that sail, excepting after we arrived here, when I heard some of the officers talking about it," he said defensively. "I have no recollection about it."

Gansevoort's reserves were running low. By now he had been on the stand for four days, and Norris wasn't through with him yet. On the fifth day the judge advocate kept up the pressure, turning the heat still higher, confronting him more directly. He decided to try to discover a motive that suggested some malice, at least as far as regarded Gansevoort. "Did you, in any of your consultations with any of the officers before the execution," he asked, "mention the likelihood that the prisoners would escape punishment if taken to the United States, by the influence of money or of their friends?" The euphemism didn't fool anyone. Norris was referring to John Canfield Spencer, and anyone should have been able to see it. "Did the commander make any such intimation to you?"

If Gansevoort had answered yes to those questions, it would have meant that the officers hadn't hanged the three prisoners out of necessity, in order to safeguard the ship, but instead because they had wanted to, because they had been feeling vindictive, had been scared for their own careers. Gansevoort couldn't answer yes even if that were the true answer. "I did not," he said. "I don't recollect that the commander made such intimation to me." But the suggestion still hung in the air.

A few minutes later, from Norris: "What injuries had Mr. Spencer done you?" A suggestion of a personal grudge between victim and executioner.

Gansevoort bristled. "None that I know of," he retorted, "except having meditated taking my life, and taking the vessel out of the hands of her officers."

Another day came and went, with tempers getting shorter, like fuses. Norris now dwelled on the sailors' strange meetings and mutterings and Cromwell's unusual actions, suggesting that they were mere molehills, out of which the officers had made mountains. "Have you not seen similar behavior in other seamen aboard of other vessels, without their being in a mutiny?" he asked.

"No, sir." Gansevoort was obstinate. "Not in a regular system continuously."

"If this conduct was so continuous and unusual," asked Norris sarcastically, "how comes it you did not report it?"

"I stated that before." Gansevoort, too, was warming up. Norris let it pass and moved on. "Is it not your opinion," he asked in an argumentative fashion, "that during the troubled state of the brig, if an action had impended, that such facts would waken the crew to a sense of their duty?"

The statement was hypothetical. The chance of action had been very small. *Somers*, far out at sea in peacetime on a boys' training cruise, hadn't met any slavers or pirates. Even so, Gansevoort wouldn't give in. "No, sir," he shot back. "My impression is that they would have taken charge of her and run away from an enemy." Not merely mutiny: cowardice. An ugly charge indeed.

By this point, Norris had lost Gansevoort. The mutual hostility was obvious. Many of the judge advocate's questions were argumentative, designed not so much to entrap the lieutenant as to get across to the court the judge advocate's own interpretation of what had happened on *Somers*, as well as why it had happened. Mackenzie jumped in with another long, friendly interrogation, but the taint of Norris's queries didn't dissipate very quickly. Finally the questions came to an end. Gansevoort was done. He had been on the stand for six days.

John Canfield Spencer had kept up the attack. He had maintained a low profile, largely acting through proxies; still, people knew and acknowledged that he wanted Mackenzie's head. And he was watching the legal battles, sometimes even going so far as to stick his nose into the navy proceedings. When he learned during the inquiry that Mackenzie planned to put his dead son on trial by impugning his character, the Cabinet member understandably bristled. The idea of bringing up young Spencer's indiscretions at college was especially upsetting. "Nothing of the kind can afford any excuse to Mr. M for his own conduct," he complained to Ogden Hoffman. But if Hoffman took a different view, Spencer rumbled, then the secretary demanded "to be allowed an opportunity to cross-examine the witnesses and to bring other evidence on the same point." He didn't get his way.

Since he couldn't control the navy, Spencer had to try to use the civilian courts. Cromwell's wife, Margaret, had been endeavoring to do the same, of course; so far she'd failed, but she was still trying, and others were succeeding. The efforts were bothering Commodore Perry. Once the court-martial got underway, various New York state judges started issuing habeas corpus writs to the navy authorities, demanding release of some of *Somers*'s sailors. Habeas corpus is a simple and powerful writ; it is a court order requiring someone to show that he has a legal right to hold someone else in custody. In this instance, the detainees in question were George Warner, Charles Van Velzor, Eugene Sullivan, and George Kneavels, all of whom were *Somers* crewmen and candidates for mutiny charges. Their enlistments were up, and since they hadn't been charged so far, their families and friends were using habeas writs to get them out of the navy's hands before it was too late.

Perry didn't like it. It was subversive of naval authority. The very morning he learned of the attempt to release Warner, he dashed off a letter to Hoffman in his capacity as U.S. attorney. He was so anxious to hang on to the sailor that he told Hoffman the story of how he himself had once served on a court-martial in Boston that had tried a seaman for hitting a master-at-arms on the very day his enlistment expired. The commonwealth courts had let the navy keep hold of the man, and, Perry happily noted, he had drawn a sixty-lash sentence.

But Hoffman wasn't able to help. Over the next few days the civilian courts came for others of *Somers*'s complement, and soon Perry was complaining to Upshur. "Should these prisoners be released from naval jurisdiction upon such grounds," he griped, "the act will be subversive of all future military authority in this yard."

After getting several such letters, Upshur started to tire of the problem. His hands were tied, and he wanted his commodore to calm down. "I regret the ill-timed and most improper interference in this business," the civilian head of the Navy Department informed his inferior, "but have no power to prevent it." That, after all, was the essence of civilian control and a libertarian legal tradition.

And these were just flank attacks on the navy's authority. The main assault was still going on in federal court. Despite Hoffman's efforts, a grand jury had finally gotten hold of the matter. Grand juries can sometimes be willful things, and as the court-martial continued, Margaret Cromwell, together with John Canfield Spencer's son-in-law Henry Morris and another man, someone named Cleaveland, had managed to get their case in front of one. By early March the jurors had questions, and they brought them to District Judge Betts.

Betts had already ruled that, given the circumstances, he lacked the authority to commit Mackenzie for trial. But a grand jury probe

was different from a bench warrant or a judge's commitment decision, or at least it looked different. Betts seemed willing, at least, to
entertain the idea. The jurors now wanted to get his thoughts on
two points. The first was whether any grand jury could ever look
into possible crimes committed on American warships. If the
answer was yes, then the second point needed addressing: could this
particular jury examine what had happened aboard *Somers?*

What Betts had said in his earlier ruling, however, suggested that
the answer to both questions was no. But technically these were new
questions, given that that earlier ruling went to the judge's authority
and not to a grand jury's. He couldn't just dismiss them. Instead he
went in the other direction. He called for legal arguments.

Hoffman, as U.S. attorney, refused to take part. His opinions, he
said, "were known on the subject"; as a prosecutor he couldn't argue
against the court's jurisdiction, and because of those personal opinions of his, he would make no argument *for* it. He suggested, rather,
that Mackenzie's and Gansevoort's attorneys, Duer and Robinson,
take on the job. Then Charles O'Conor and Benjamin Butler, well-
known New York attorneys whom John Canfield Spencer had sent
to observe the court-martial, piped up. Morris, who had pressed
young Spencer's cause, had asked the two to speak for him.

Betts was willing, but Robinson and Duer weren't there. They
were busy in Brooklyn, defending Mackenzie at the navy yard
chapel, holding on the court-martial front. So Betts put off the
debate until the following morning. But when the arguments
started, they lasted for hours; then hours turned into days. For nearly
a week the battle raged. Butler went first, on the 10th of March,
talking for more than four hours, taking a very broad view of the district court's power. He took too broad a view, in fact. He claimed
that the court had the authority to try defendants for common law
crimes, a very old-fashioned and largely discredited argument. If
that was the best he could do, then he was in trouble.

His troubles increased when the new week began. He had spoken on Friday; John Duer had then asked to have the weekend to prepare his response, and Betts had agreed. When Monday arrived, Duer took the offensive.

It was masterful. "Never was there a more powerful or eloquent appeal presented before a court of justice," one observer proclaimed. Given the level of legal talent that practiced in front of this bench, he declared, "it requires ability of richest order to rivet in an unusual manner the attention of the audience," and Duer had managed to do it. He went for two and a half hours, meeting Butler head-on, decrying young Spencer's malice, championing Mackenzie's heroism, citing the same statutes, relying on the same arguments, on which Betts had built his first opinion. He also threw in a brilliant twist.

Criminal procedural rights; indictment and trial by jury; all very democratic-sounding things, for an increasingly democratic society. Who in America *wouldn't* want such protections, protections that weren't found in courts-martial? The answer to this unspoken question was clear: Alexander Slidell Mackenzie. His best hopes lay with the navy, not with that mob called "the people," its common-man passions, and its representatives in the grand jury. The navy understood the ways of command, the customs of the sea. Public second-guessing, carried out in the regular courts, would only be meddling in the affairs of the profession of arms. Mackenzie was safest right where he was, in front of that court-martial he had demanded. But of course Duer could say none of these things. He could only look at the hard rules of a court-martial and say, with apparent regret, that the Constitution and Congress had spoken. It may seem wrong, he lamented, but the law firmly declared that the federal courts had no jurisdiction here.

Duer spoke so long and hard that he finally grew faint and had to stop for the day. He was back the next morning, though, but his vitality had left him for the time being, disappointing the people who had hoped to see a reprise of the past day's performance. Still, he was winning, and after he had sat down, George Griffin took up where he had left off.

Spencer's attorneys had to be angry. They had their hands full. They were arguing to a judge who had already decided against the position that they were pressing upon him, at least in a different context. Duer and Griffin were giving them fits. And as if that weren't enough, James Kent, the aristocratic, conservative dean of the American common law world, had come down strongly and in public against district court jurisdiction. If America had a Blackstone, Chancellor Kent was he, and he was no friend of King Mob. If the navy was an aristocracy, then it had a friend in James Kent. "Crimes and offenses committed on the high seas by a person in the actual service of the United States, on board one of their vessels of war, and duly commissioned and claiming to act under that authority," Kent had said in one long, legalistic breath, "are not cognizable under the jurisdiction of the courts of the United States." O'Conor and Butler had suffered another blow.

On Wednesday O'Conor finally lost his composure. He quit arguing law and started making personal attacks on Duer and Griffin both. He claimed that Duer had drawn first, "indulging in observations unjust to my colleague and those with whom we are engaged." And like a typical lawyer, he went on to give as good as he got, or at least he tried. Duer had talked of young Spencer's malice, but where, asked O'Conor, was the fairness in that? "I would ask your honor," he entreated, "how you could have been entertained by an eulogium on the persons for whom he acts, and criticisms as to private malice and private revenge. Where was the proof of malice on one side and of amiability of character on the other?" This was a legal debate, he insisted, not a popularity contest.

He wasn't even close to being done with his diatribe. "The counsel, in excuse, speaks of his friend and the wife of his friend," he taunted Duer, and through him Commander and Mrs. Mackenzie. "The relatives of those who have gone, and who have feelings as well as himself, have a right when *their* friends, condemned without color of law, have been deprived of life suddenly and at a distance from home, put to death, to speak also." He built up to a blistering pitch. "If the counsel has a right to be excused for what he pleads," he asked rhetorically, "has not the father of one of the departed a privilege to appear at the threshold of the temple of justice and inquire why and wherefore his son has been slain?"

O'Conor kept up the emotional drive, asking, demanding, justice. Finally he calmed down and summed up. "The whole argument," he restated, "has been conducted on their part by a want of consideration for one side and of feeling for the other."

It was as good as any other possible argument. The deck was stacked against him, and against the others, too. They had to know it, and a few days later, on Monday, March 20, Betts showed it. That was when he delivered the grand jury charge in which he answered the jurors' original questions.

He might just as well have handed the jurors a copy of his earlier ruling, for he now said much the same thing as he had before. "The circuit court is a special court of statutory jurisdiction," he held, "in precisely the same sense as a court-martial. The circuit courts have no residuary or general jurisdiction, and none whatever over the subaltern courts except it be bestowed by positive law." So much for Butler's common law arguments. Congress, Betts found, had given the jurisdiction to try offenses on warships to courts-martial. Congress hadn't, either expressly or by implication, given that same power to the Article III courts, the type of court over which Betts presided. In plain, nonlegal language, Mackenzie and Gansevoort couldn't be tried here. They could only be tried by court-martial.

And that was that. Spencer's only hope for justice now lay with the navy.

Norris was starting to try harder, and soon Mackenzie would feel it. Like a falling glass in clear weather at sea, his questions to Gansevoort, though not particularly effective, foretold what was building. But weather at sea, and the ocean itself, while often vicious and brutal, were never quite personal, not in the way that Norris was beginning to be.

After the judge advocate had finished with Gansevoort, he moved on to young Matthew C. Perry, Jr. Perry, like Gansevoort, would stay pinned on the stand for days while Norris and the court wore at him. Mackenzie threw him questions as well, but Norris was the one to watch out for. His queries were sharpening as he got in more practice.

One of the things he focused on was the loss of the topgallant mast, or rather, what had been going through the acting master's mind the afternoon that it went. "Did you think at the time," he asked Perry, "that the mast was carried away by design to afford an outbreak to the mutiny, or to rescue Mr. Spencer?"

No harm in answering that one, or so it would seem. "I did, sir."

"Were you on deck at the time of the occurrence to the mast?"

"I was not." A slight question mark. Perry hadn't seen it himself, so how could he know for sure? Norris continued the subtle attack. "How soon did you come up, and how long did you stay up on deck?"

"I was on deck immediately," explained Perry, "and went below after half an hour and stayed a few minutes, and remained on deck, with the exception of a few minutes, until sail was set on a new mast."

"Why did you go below?" Innocent enough question. "The first time I don't remember why," said Perry. "The second time for my meal."

The trapdoor sprang open without warning. "Did you not swear before the court of inquiry," charged Norris, "that you went below because you found nothing to do?"

A small inconsistency, but one that needed explaining. "I might have done so," Perry agreed, "and by refreshing my memory, by referring to the records of the court of inquiry, I do recollect having sworn so." Fair enough; but now Norris stoked the fires of suspicion. "If you supposed the occurrence to the mast was meant to afford an outbreak to the mutiny, would it not have been your duty to remain on deck?"

"I did remain on deck," Perry protested, "as long as there was any confusion or any likelihood of there being any." But the confusion seemed to be Perry's. He *said* he'd feared a mutiny, but he kept going below for reasons so trivial that he could barely recall, under oath, what they'd been.

Norris, scenting blood, held on. "If you feared a rescue while first on deck, why did you not arm yourself? Were there not battle-axes on the ship's bulwarks?"

"Yes, there were," said Perry. No use denying the obvious. "I did not think of it at the time; it was immediately on my arrival on deck, after hearing how the mast was carried away, that the idea of a rescue struck me." But Norris's questions raised the idea that the possibility of a rescue attempt had only struck Mr. Perry very much later, when he saw that he needed to protect himself and the officers from a legal inquiry.

Norris kept picking at him, trying to trip him up further, trying to find inconsistencies. He asked Perry when Gansevoort had first discussed the idea of executing the three prisoners. During a conversation on the 29th of November, Perry replied, the day before the officers had first met in the wardroom.

"Did you swear before the court of inquiry," Norris reminded him, "that this conversation with Mr. Gansevoort was on the 28th of November?"

"I may have done so; I don't remember." Perry was evasive. "If I did so, it was correct."

"How was it that, on the 28th of November," Norris persisted, "you told Mr. Gansevoort that Mr. Spencer, Cromwell, and Small should be put to death, when you now state that you did not think the execution necessary until the day before the council of officers was held?"

"I said I think it was the day before," replied Perry, trying to find a way out of the maze. "I am not quite positive; I do not mean to be positive as to dates, except when I refer to the log book." He had a point, of course. Stress, sleep deprivation, and danger could play games with the memory, and Mackenzie's own counsel should have brought that up with more force. Nevertheless, Norris was starting to hold Perry up as a mass of small contradictions, and worse, as someone who advocated a multiple killing well before a crisis had come. It looked like premeditation, and a lot of it.

But whether or not Perry's explanations made sense to the court, he stuck to his story, especially when answering Mackenzie, that he'd feared a mutiny and a rescue attempt. He emphasized that he'd been against asking Caribbean authorities for help—"I said I would rather go overboard than go into St. Thomas for protection," he swore—and that was a pretty strong statement. It appealed to the virtue of honor, something not easy to question. When asked why he had said such a thing, his answer was simple, straightforward, and stock. "Because I thought it would be a disgrace to the United States, the navy, and particularly the officers of the brig," he explained. "My reasons were that if an American man-of-war could not protect herself, no use in having any." It was a good stratagem; Norris couldn't attack that without himself seeming to attack America.

Still, Norris showed signs of wanting to prove that *Somers* could have made port without the officers killing anyone, that the ship had been close to land and making good headway. But Mackenzie cut him off, basing his position, as had Perry, on the unassailable bastion of honor. He had never considered asking for foreign help, he declared in a written, signed statement. "A naval commander can never be justified in invoking aid in reducing an insubordinate crew to obedience," he wrote. And his officers, he continued, had known these views of his. He was throwing down a gauntlet. If he was to be hanged for doing his duty, for refusing to tarnish America's image abroad, for putting national security before his own career, so be it.

Norris knew better than to go there. Rather than assail the fortress in which the officers had taken refuge, he kept picking away at more concrete details, trying to prove that there was a truth that hadn't yet surfaced. On February 21 he went after William Neville, the nineteen-year-old sailor. Mackenzie and his lawyers asked Neville if he had seen Spencer talking with Cromwell, if he had seen the acting midshipman show any papers to the chief bo'sun's mate.

"Yes, sir," said Neville. "I saw him show him a paper at the store-room door; it was about the size of half a sheet of paper; it was yellower than writing paper—had marks on it like crosses; it was not English writing, and geometrical figures on the back."

This was quite a description, based on a glance in the dim confines of the berth deck. "Did the paper you then saw resemble either of those now shown to you?" asked the defense, holding up a couple of sheets.

"Yes, sir," Neville replied. "It resembled the one marked No. 2 by the court of inquiry."

Now it was Norris's turn at the sailor. "Was Cromwell's face or back to you when you first saw them?"

"His back was to me."

"Was Spencer's face toward you?"

"No, sir."

So Neville had been looking over their backs in the twilit belowdecks, seeing the same side of the paper they had. "Take a piece of paper," Norris told him, "and show the court how the parties were standing, and how Mr. Spencer was holding it."

Neville did so. "He was standing this way."

The trap sprang. "How then did you see the back of the paper?"

Neville quickly corrected himself. "Part of it was turned over this way," he said, folding the sheet.

"Did you show that it was doubled at first? And why not?" Norris asked, accusing.

"Because I understood you to ask me to show you their position," Neville protested. "I did not understand you to ask if the paper was doubled up."

Now Norris was firing questions at Neville, keeping him off his balance. "Look at that paper," he told the witness, "and see if the part having geometrical figures on it were doubled over, whether it would not have been in Mr. Spencer's hand upside down where the writing was?"

A slow stubbornness started to smolder in Neville's responses as the logic of his story began to unravel. "I could not say it would have been upside down; I saw geometrical figures." He saw where Norris was taking him, and he didn't want to go. The judge advocate was suggesting that Neville had seen nothing, nothing at all—that his recollection, to put it in delicate terms, was in error. In plainer terms, he was suggesting that Neville was lying.

Norris fired another broadside. "Is not the lower half of the paper without geometrical figures on it?"

"No, sir; not half—about a quarter." Neville was struggling, sensing himself being driven onto a lee shore.

Norris was relentless. "If as much as half had been doubled over, could any of the writing be seen?"

"No, sir."

"How much of the paper was doubled over?"

"I can't say how much—there did not appear to be much."

"If there was not much doubled over, and there are no geometrical figures on a quarter of the lower part," Norris said, crowding Neville onto the shoals at last, "how did you see the geometrical figures?"

Neville was wrecked. "I saw it, sir," he insisted. "I cannot tell how I saw it; I saw it!"

It was one of the few moments of classic cross-examination during the whole of the trial, involving a string of questions, many of them leading, that revealed inconsistencies in the witness's story, showing that his claim to having seen both sides of the paper was simply implausible. Neville stuck to his claim, in the end, but as far as Norris was concerned, that was just fine. He had shown, through his questions, that there was no rational basis behind it. In short, Neville was mistaken or lying; and that might be true of others as well.

But Norris was at a tactical disadvantage. In fact most of the disadvantages were on his side, not Mackenzie's. If there was a cover-up, which the judge advocate seemed to believe, he was going to have a very hard time proving it in the traditional way. He was dealing with an insular little community—*Somers*—wrapped inside of a larger insular community—the navy. Every witness to what had gone on, every sailor and officer aboard *Somers,* was likely biased somehow, and most of them toward Mackenzie. Even the sailors who might not like their captain had seen for themselves where dislike could get someone: high up on the yardarm, at the end of a rope. That kind of lesson stayed with a man. The officers, for their part, had to maintain that what had gone on was a mutiny; the sailors, in light of that fact, were safer in saying that they had seen others talking and acting in mutinous ways than in claiming the officers were liars.

It was a plausible theory, but it meant that Norris had no witnesses who would give an account that he wanted the court to hear. For the court was part of the larger machine of which *Somers* was just a small cog, the naval community that would try to protect itself. The protection could take two forms: the navy could purge and police itself and keep itself clean, or it could deny that its officers had done any wrong, that the trouble had lain with the scum in the ranks and a young troublemaker, a traitor to his class. Norris seemed to believe that it was taking the second approach, as the court of inquiry's outcome seemed to suggest.

So all Norris could do, since he would have trouble rounding up folks who would challenge the mainstream account, was to poke holes in witnesses' stories, uncovering prior inconsistent statements, internal contradictions, statements that flew in the face of common experience and knowledge. He might try to show facts that hinted of deceit and dissembling. Woodshedding, or at least talking to witnesses before putting them on the stand, was a perfectly normal thing; but Norris brought it up a couple of times, getting sailors to tell that they had met with Gansevoort and the other officers at the end of the cruise to get their stories straight, that they had been examined in private by John Duer and Commodore Perry. The other side might argue that this was a standard way to find out what had happened, to prepare testimony; Norris's response was to call not for prepared testimony, but instead for the truth. But he wasn't playing to a common law jury, and this court would look down on theatrics. He had to be careful and subtle.

One of the things he tried to do was to suggest that the officers, and maybe even the crew, had tried to build a coherent story after *Somers*'s return to New York. By doing so he probably hoped to make them all look as if they were covering themselves, getting ready to dodge and dance with the questions they knew were certain to come, fabricating a story, cooking up a sinister plot. On its face Norris's tactic made sense; but there was too much against it, the log entries for instance, and the near-certainty of an inquiry from the moment of Spencer's arrest, which would serve to keep the people on board honest with themselves about what they were doing. If the officers had wanted to fabricate anything, they could have done so in a lot greater privacy while out on the deep; why wait until reaching New York, where they could be watched? Of course, Norris probably feared that they *had* all gotten together at sea, that the meetings after *Somers*'s arrival were just for fine-tuning. But nothing suggests that that happened; Norris never seemed to have made such a claim. All in all, trying to prove a conspiracy by concrete evidence was beyond him. He could only suggest.

He tried it with William Neville. "Did you not hear, before the execution," he asked, "that a paper with strange characters had been found in Mr. Spencer's locker?"

"I had heard some of the boys mentioning it about the decks," Neville acknowledged.

"Why did you not tell anyone before the execution, or before your arrival, what you say you saw between Cromwell and Mr. Spencer?"

"I was not asked anything about it," Neville said shortly.

Very convenient. "Did I understand you then to say that you never mentioned having seen this paper to any of your messmates, or people at the gun with you, or to any of the crew, before your arrival in New York Harbor?"

"No, sir," disagreed Neville. "I have mentioned it to Clark, one of the apprentices."

"When did you mention it to Clark?"

"After the execution."

Now Norris was getting somewhere. William Clark had deserted, had disappeared, after testifying at the court of inquiry. There was talk that somebody had bribed him. And, better still, Neville had contradicted himself. "Did you not first say you never mentioned it to anyone?" asked Norris. "How is it you recollect having told it to Clark?"

"I don't know that I said I never mentioned it to anyone," Neville disputed. "I said I did not recollect mentioning it to anyone." That wasn't the way that Norris had heard it, or the court reporter either. Norris had scored again.

The prosecutor didn't stop there. "As you say that you are not particularly intimate with anyone, how is it that you told only Clark?"

"I don't know how it come." Neville became mulish again—what else could he do? "I recollect that I told him on the spar deck; I don't recollect how it come."

Norris's questions were taking a toll on Neville's credibility. But Neville was only one witness. He might genuinely be confused or mistaken. The strain of taking the stand is enough to make anyone jumpy, especially in a life-or-death trial. Norris needed to go a step further, to show that Neville's inconsistencies weren't happenstance but design—to show, in effect, a conspiracy. He had no direct evidence of that. His proof was circumstantial at best, resting on inference. But that was what he had to try to do.

Beginning with Neville, he made a point of getting some of the witnesses to admit that they had been woodshedded. He had Neville say that Mackenzie's attorney John Duer had examined him in private prior to the court of inquiry, and that he had done it at Commodore Perry's house. This last bit was an insinuation that the navy command structure was pushing a whitewash, a dangerous assertion that Norris could never have made in so many words. When Neville was finally finished, Edward English came next, and Norris brought up the same point with the eighteen-year-old apprentice. Under Norris's questioning, English admitted that he had never told any of the officers about seeing Cromwell and Spencer in the fo'c'sle looking over an old, yellow paper. Never, that is, until raising New York, when Gansevoort summoned him to the wardroom. When Norris asked him why he'd kept his mouth shut, English had a simple reply. He'd kept it shut, he said, "until I was asked."

Fifteen-year-old Billinger Scott stated much the same thing when he was called to the stand. He, too, had seen Cromwell and Spencer conversing. Spencer had given Scott tobacco sometimes and had tried to recruit him; his name was on Spencer's list. The youngster didn't seem to realize that he was implicating himself. It was powerful testimony, and Norris wasn't ready for it. He even gave Scott a way out, but the boy didn't take it. "Did not the men spin yarns about such things?" he asked. "Think—have you not heard from the seamen many stories about such things?"

Scott was oblivious. "No, sir."

Norris moved on to the woodshedding. Scott, like English, had said nothing until after *Somers*'s return to New York. "How came you to have your first conversation with Mr. Gansevoort after you came in?" Norris asked.

"He called me in the wardroom," recalled Scott, "and asked me if I knew, or ever heard, Mr. Spencer, Cromwell, and Small talking."

So far, Scott seemed to be truthful—too truthful for his own good, in fact. So Norris took a small gamble, asking a crucial question to which he didn't yet have an answer, usually a dangerous thing for a lawyer to do with a witness. "What did Mr. Gansevoort say to you when he called you in? Tell everything."

"He asked me," said Scott, "whether I heard Spencer and Cromwell, or Small, talking; I told him just as I have stated here."

"Did he tell you it would be better for you to tell everything?"

"Yes, sir."

Norris shouldn't have asked that. Scott's veracity was pretty clear, and now he had sworn that Gansevoort had told him to tell the truth, rather than asking him to help cover things up. The conspiracy theory had taken a blow.

Norris wasn't a bad sort, and he hated to see what Scott had done to himself. So with his last questions he let the boy off the hook, whether or not Scott knew it. "Did you know that your name was down on the paper?"

"No, sir."

"Have you ever told Mr. Spencer you would join him in a mutiny?"

"No, sir."

"Did you know what Mr. Spencer was arrested for at the time?"

"No, sir."

Scott was free; but Norris's struggle continued. He was fighting not only Mackenzie, not only the system, but two defense lawyers who were playing by tag-team rules. On February 24 John Duer bowed out, called away by the demands of his caseload, to be replaced by Theodore Sedgwick. A methodical, Columbia-trained lawyer from a prominent family, Sedgwick was a good fit for Mackenzie, since he, too, was a historian and author on the side. As Sedgwick geared up to fight Norris, attention started to shift to the crew and its sinister doings, especially Charles Wilson and his African dirk.

A lot of people recalled that dirk, recalled Wilson threatening sailors about it. One was sixteen-year-old Jonas Humbert, who had borrowed it for a while. Wilson had taken it from him, saying that he wished Spencer could have it.

Mackenzie and his attorneys used the occasion to show the court the weapon. "Is this the knife of Wilson, which he told you not to touch?"

"Yes, sir," Humbert replied. It was exotic, impressive; there wasn't much room for mistake.

Norris tried to show that Humbert had been the one in the wrong. "Was he not using the knife in mending sails, or cutting ropes?"

"No, sir."

The judge advocate tried again, firing blindly; he never knew for certain what the witnesses were going to say, a massive handicap for an attorney. "Have you not often seen him using this knife in his work?"

"No, sir."

The lawyer's frustration had to be growing. "At the time of the talk," he tried yet again, "was the knife or dirk lying alongside Wilson?"

"He took it out of my hand and laid it alongside of him," Humbert corrected. He should have stopped there, but he didn't. "I took it out of the sailbag first."

Bingo. Humbert had rummaged around in Wilson's belongings, a major offense on so small a vessel. Norris closed in. "Did he look at you very fierce when he told you it would cut your throat?"

"Yes, sir." Wilson had had some excuse for his violent reaction, then; still, his words had been strong ones.

Then Mackenzie counterattacked. "Do you call that a knife or a dagger?" he asked.

"A dagger," said Humbert.

"Is that a good instrument to split canvas or cut rope?"

"No, sir."

"Did Wilson use the dagger for such purposes, or did he always have with him a sailmaker's knife, similar to a shoemaker's knife, to use in his work?"

"No, sir," Humbert answered the first part of the question. His reply to the next part hurt Norris, too. "He always had a sailmaker's knife which he used in his work."

It wasn't merely about the knife; it was also about the man who owned it. Fourteen-year-old James B. Travis made that point. He, too, had borrowed it, and Wilson had torn it away, telling the boy that the blade had some slaughtering to do. One of the panel of officers interrupted the witness's story. "Did you ever know Wilson to threaten to take the life of the commander, or anyone else, on board the *Somers* during her late cruise, previously to the execution of the prisoners?"

"I heard him say," declared Travis, "he would take the lives of two boys, Weaver and Tyson, the first chance he got."

Norris objected. This attack on Wilson's character was irrelevant, having no bearing on whether he was involved with any alleged mutiny. The court ignored the objection.

Hours stretched into days. "Was Wilson the brig's butcher?" Norris asked Peter Tyson.

Tyson's choice of words was provocative. "Him and Warner used to kill."

"How long was it before Mr. Spencer's arrest when you and Wilson quarreled?"

"About a week," recalled Tyson. "Not over a week."

"Before this conversation," asked Norris, "had Wilson been flogged about striking Weaver?"

"Yes, sir." That made it all seem like Weaver's fault because he had made Wilson angry. "Have you not frequently heard seamen and boys, after being flogged, threaten a great deal of revenge?" Norris continued.

He'd pushed too far. "No, sir," said Tyson. "I never recollect anyone threaten to have revenge but Wilson."

Norris had to be frustrated. He had tried to show many things: that witnesses had lied about getting a good look at whatever Spencer had written; that the loss of the topgallant mast had been an act of God and not the design of Elisha Small; that when the crew had rushed Mackenzie and Gansevoort, it had merely been trying to get away from Bo'sun's Mate Browning and his busily swinging colt. But without knowing what the witnesses were going to say, he had trouble showing anything. With some of the witnesses, a single unexpected answer could destroy an otherwise good line of cross-examination. With others it was simply a matter of attitude, as was the case with Henry King. The gunner's mate's answer to Mackenzie was friendly: "I had to stand nearly night and day in our watch," he had said, "and when below we could not get much sleep, from the noise of the boys, and we did not know what minute we might have a knife put into us." But the moment that Norris started asking him questions, everything changed. "Did you, before the council of officers, give it as your opinion," the judge advocate queried, "that Mr. Spencer, Cromwell, and Small should be put to death?"

"I gave it as my opinion that the vessel was not safe with them aboard." Evasive, perhaps nonresponsive.

"What did you intend should be understood by that?" A stupid question, followed by a sarcastic reply. "It was to be understood that I did not think the vessel safe." The answer's subtext was perfectly clear: *What do you* think *I intended to be understood?* But Norris, in the dark as he was, never could tell what the witnesses meant. He had to have more latitude, and he finally asked for some.

His chance came on the 8th of March, more than a month into the trial, as he prepared to call his rebuttal witnesses. Since, just as before, he never knew at the outset what they were going to say, he in effect asked the court for permission to treat them as hostile, to pose leading questions. The request was surprising, but reasonable. A leading question is a very adversarial thing. It is a question phrased in a way so as not to be neutral, to lead the witness toward giving a particular answer, even suggesting a particular answer. Because it is so obviously partisan, it is usually allowable only when witness and lawyer really are adversaries, that is, during a cross-examination. There are exceptions, of course. The law sometimes lets attorneys lead their own witnesses, when for some reason leading is needed. Norris now argued that this was just such an occasion.

He had seen signs of hostility, he claimed. Midshipman Hays, when told to report to the judge advocate prior to taking the stand, had told Norris frankly that he would answer none of the lawyer's questions. Norris had then gotten much the same treatment from Acting Midshipman Tillotson. The officers, though polite, had been firm. And so Norris had stayed in the dark.

There was only one thing he could do, one stance he could take. "All the officers and crew of that brig were furnished by the department for witnesses at my selection," he reminded the court. "With neither have I had any opportunities of conversation. I have never sought any with the crew. My duties to the case compel me to offer these gentlemen, wholly in the dark as to their disposition and acquaintance with facts, except as shown in the record of the court of inquiry." What this meant, he probably figured, was clear. "Under these circumstances," he concluded, "it is conceived that the privilege asked for is but fair and reasonable."

Mackenzie and his people had other ideas, and they said so. Witness hostility is the principal reason that justified leading. But there was no question of these witnesses being hostile to Norris, Theodore Sedgwick claimed. Quite the contrary, in fact. "They are notoriously willing witnesses for the charges," he stated, "and to give the counsel for the people liberty to put leading questions to willing witnesses would be, in a capital case, to give it a ruthless and appalling character." If Sedgwick believed they were willing, that was more than Norris knew. The two sides had developed competing conspiracy theories: the prosecutor suspected the officers of trying to hush up the truth of their own panic and fear, while the defense charged that the real conspiracy had been to take over *Somers*, a conspiracy that nobody in his right mind would admit under oath to having been part of.

But Sedgwick had more to say. "It is idle to speculate," he argued, "upon the relative position of these witnesses and the defendant. The true question is not whether the witness *may* be biased, but whether he is in fact biased, and that can only be established by the test of examination." But he had it backwards; Norris was claiming that he couldn't truly examine the witnesses unless he could treat them as biased.

The parties were at an impasse, and so Norris now accused the defense of obstruction. Had the officers been forthcoming with him before trial, he complained, things would have gone more quickly and smoothly. But that hadn't happened. "A bunch of keys has been thrown the judge advocate," he fumed. "One word would have told the one fitted to each door, but he has been compelled at every lock to try the whole bunch."

It was to no avail. The court denied his request to lead his witnesses. The fishing expedition would have to go on.

Signs of conspiracy lay everywhere, although which of those signs were true, no one could say. Both sides fixed on the disappearance of Clark. Norris took pains to try to show that he couldn't use the absent apprentice's earlier account to corroborate Neville's testimony, while Mackenzie claimed that someone, presumably pro-prosecution (John Canfield Spencer, perhaps?), had paid Clark to get out of town, to sail home to England.

Norris called Benjamin Green and Alexander McKee to the stand. Each of them denied involvement with whatever Philip Spencer had been up to, struggling to find other believable reasons for their odd behavior. Daniel McKinley took the stand, too, claiming that he had been hunted, that it had been persecution. "I saw Mr. Gansevoort watching, chasing, and following me all around the vessel," he swore. That, coupled with the first three arrests, had made him think that he was in trouble.

Then there was Richard Leecock. The ship's surgeon was in a strange situation; while not really a line officer, his status put him among the little group in the wardroom with which his loyalty would probably lie. He was tight-lipped and he seemed nervous while he was on the stand. Over and over again he gave the same answer to Norris. "Do you know," asked the lawyer, "how Mr. Spencer was employed the day of the arrest?"

"No sir, I don't recollect."

"Have you had any conversation with Mr. Spencer, or any other of the executed persons, from their arrest till executed?"

"No, sir, not that I recollect."

"Prior to the council of officers, were you consulted as to putting them who were executed out of the way?"

"I don't recollect."

"Did Mr. Heiskill leave the wardroom till he signed the letter of the officers on the first of December?"

"I don't recollect."

And so it went. Only when asked about the physical state of the officers did he unbend somewhat, opining that by the time of the hangings they had been nearly exhausted.

But the most crucial witness of all was Commander Mackenzie himself, even though he never actually took the stand. Still, Norris got him before the court and managed to keep him there, asking witnesses about what he had done and second-guessing his judgment. And more and more, as the trial ran on, he focused the spotlight on Mackenzie's actions in the final hour of Spencer's life.

That was a crucial hour, an hour, Norris was certain, that Mackenzie was lying about. The lies were part of a cover-up; and the very fact of a cover-up suggested Mackenzie's guilt, if only Norris could show that it was really a fact. By the middle of March he was devoting more and more time to proving it.

Things started to get serious on March 9, when seventeen-year-old Oliver H. Perry began his testimony. He was Mackenzie's clerk; he knew about keeping records. That was something in which Norris was interested, keeping records. He was particularly interested in records of the last conversation that Spencer had had with Mackenzie, records that Mackenzie might have destroyed. He began to ask Perry about it. "Do you know whether Mr. Spencer wrote home to his friends?"

"No, sir."

"Do you know whether, at his request, anyone else wrote for him?" By this he meant none but Mackenzie, who had talked with Spencer for most of the time immediately before the hangings.

Perry stuck with his story. "No, sir."

"Did you not say," Norris led him, "in the presence of the secretary of the Navy and other gentlemen, that you were of the impression that Spencer did send a written message home?"

Perry gave in. "At the time of the execution," he acknowledged, "it was my impression he did send a message home; the captain was copying something."

A message? Nobody had heard of a message. Norris began to explore. "How near were you to the commander when he was writing when you were of this opinion?"

"I was standing between the binnacles, about four or five feet off." A ringside seat.

"Did you hear Mr. Spencer say he could not write with his irons on?"

"No, sir."

"Did Mr. Spencer take the pen and try to write?"

"I did not see him."

"Did you hear the commander tell him he would write for him?"

"No, sir."

But Mackenzie had written *something*, and Norris was going to find out what it had been. He thought he already knew: a letter from Spencer to his parents, or maybe some other message, that somehow proved Mackenzie's guilt, that showed legal malice . . . a writing that no longer existed, a writing that Mackenzie had long since destroyed.

Norris wasn't the only one who was following this thread very closely. Mackenzie was following it, too. As the prosecutor interrogated young Perry, the commander got up and walked over to Norris.

"Why do you ask this question about Mr. Spencer's not being able to write in irons?" he wanted to know. "He declined to write."

If the confrontation surprised the judge advocate, he concealed it. "Yes, sir," Norris replied, "but I am told he afterwards dictated to you what to write."

"He said he did not wish to write," claimed Mackenzie.

"Yes, sir," Norris repeated, "but I am told he afterwards dictated to you what to write."

"Yes," Mackenzie conceded, "he did."

Norris suddenly saw a door open. "Then he did dictate to you what to write." It wasn't a question.

"Yes, he did," said Mackenzie again. "The substance of it is in my report—my official report," he added. But Norris seemed not to notice. He turned to the court.

"There is no use of further examination on this point," he announced, "as Captain Mackenzie admits that Mr. Spencer did dictate to him what to write."

The panel seemed inattentive. "What is that?" an officer said, not having caught the exchange. Theodore Sedgwick also asked what was up. Norris repeated himself again. "Captain Mackenzie says," he uttered distinctly, "Mr. Spencer did dictate to him what to write."

Sedgwick was puzzled. "What has that to do with the examination?"

Everything, Norris believed. Mackenzie had effectively denied that he had written a message for Spencer, and then he'd contradicted himself. He seemed to be hiding something. Norris even offered to take the stand himself to swear to what Mackenzie had said just moments ago.

Mackenzie could see the danger, and he promptly submitted a statement of his own, in which he admitted to passing on a message to Spencer's family. That he could have forgotten such a detail seems odd; still, he had had to hang three people that morning, after days of exhaustion and lack of sleep. Recollections were bound to be hazy. McKinley testified, for what it was worth, that he had seen Mackenzie writing. Gansevoort, summoned back to the stand, said the same thing, but he didn't recall hearing that Spencer had dictated a personal message to anyone. After finishing up with Gansevoort, Norris started on Midshipman Thompson.

The young officer was in agreement with McKinley and Gansevoort. "The commander was writing some of the time," he stated, "and conversing with Mr. Spencer some of the time."

The writing was now a given; what Norris wanted to show at this point was that the commander had been taking dictation. "Would

Captain Mackenzie raise his head, seem to listen, and write?" he asked.

Mackenzie and his lawyers objected, claiming irrelevance, an interesting point to bring up. Actually the question seemed quite relevant, and the court, after talking things over, agreed. But the answer was a disappointment to Norris. "No, sir," said Thompson. "I did not notice it particularly."

But Norris wasn't going to let him off that easily. "Did the commander address to you any observation when he commenced to write?"

"Not that I recollect," answered Thompson. Then a new thought struck him. "Ah, yes: after he had spoken to the others, he told Mr. O. H. Perry, I think, to note the time; Mr. Perry and myself both noted it." Mackenzie had told them to let him know when ten minutes had passed. He had evidently decided that that was how many minutes of life remained for Spencer.

"Did you report the end of the time?" Norris asked.

"I think I did." Thompson was somewhat offhand. "It is so long since those things occurred that it is impossible to remember these trivial things, such as the way Mr. Spencer held his head or his hands."

That was a terrible answer, and Norris let Thompson know it. "Do you regard it as a trivial thing to report the expiration of ten minutes," he asked acidly, "which were the limits of Mr. Spencer's life?"

"I did not say that was a trivial thing," bristled Thompson. "My remark referred to some trivial questions which you have put to me."

Norris kept on, unflappable, trying to find out what Mackenzie had said as well as what he had done. "Did he not tell you," he asked Thompson, "Mr. Spencer 'is writing home, or sending a message to his friends,' or words to that effect?"

"Not that I recollect," said Thompson, reflecting. "I think not."

Norris was getting impatient. "On such a matter can't you be positive?"

"My impression is," said Thompson again, "that he did not."

It was all very frustrating for Norris. He felt that he had the key, if not in his grasp then at least within reach, if only he could discover what Mackenzie had written. It couldn't have been merely a message to Spencer's parents; they would have turned over anything that would help prove Mackenzie guilty of their son's murder. No, Norris seemed sure that there was something else, something incriminating, and he was obsessed with finding it.

The next day, the 14th of March, he grew even more certain that he was onto something. Mackenzie didn't show up. Leecock sent a message instead, certifying that his captain was ill. Norris suspected that Mackenzie was simply fearful, especially after the exchange of a few days before. "I wish the world could have seen," he wrote much later, "the shaking agony, and the craft at the same time with which he made his admission." The possibility that Mackenzie had simply been getting sick seemed out of the question to him. There was a sinister writing, or at least there had been. He was sure of it. He meant to prove it, and thus win his case.

Mackenzie missed another day, and then still another, making Norris more and more certain. But finally the captain came back to court and launched a counterattack. The trial had been polite enough—as polite as a murder trial can be—but Mackenzie's temper now showed. Norris's arguments, he said, were based on "a gratuitous and offensive assumption," and the accusation that Mackenzie had destroyed a letter of Spencer's was not only "utterly unfounded" but "flatly contradicted by every fact that has yet appeared." Mackenzie was tired of it all. So he produced a writing, a writing that he had sworn before a local magistrate was the thing he had penned while talking with Spencer. It was no letter; it was merely a record of what the two had discussed. Mackenzie had later written the gist of it into his official report, which was why he hadn't submitted it earlier. "The memorandum was hastily and roughly written," he pointed out, "and did not in fact detail the conversation with as much fullness as it is given in [my] report."

It *was* a rough memorandum, in some places nearly illegible. Mackenzie's execution day stress clearly shows through. Still, except for his oath, there was no proof that this was the document that Norris was trying to find. Between gentlemen, such an oath should have done the trick. But Norris kept trying to find out more, kept hoping that something more remained to be found.

He never did find it. The trial was winding down. He had exhausted his few avenues of attack, never coming up with a witness or a writing that could conclusively prove his conspiracy theory. As the flood of witnesses slowed to a trickle, he seemed to see that his cause was lost. That band of brothers, the navy, was simply too strong for him. The last witness was Quartermaster Charles Rogers; he was as little help to the judge advocate as the others had been, insisting that the talk and behavior of the crew had suggested mutiny was looming.

After that, Norris gave up. At least he partly gave up. Once Rogers had left the stand, the lawyer moved to drop two of the five charges that Mackenzie was facing—the charge of unofficerlike conduct and the oppression article. The first, he decided, was a charge that the naval code didn't allow for, even though people had been tried for it often before now. The charge of oppressing the crew, he decided, was simply void for vagueness. That left only three charges: murder, imposing illegal punishment, and conduct unbecoming.

Maybe they would be enough. Norris had one last chance to convince the court that they should be, in his closing argument. But before he could sum up, Mackenzie's lawyers had their own chance.

The task fell to George Griffin. His summation was long, but it was straightforward. A mutiny had happened, he declared. Spencer, Cromwell, and Small had been at its head. The officers hadn't over-

reacted; they weren't conspiring to hide the fact of "unmanly fear."
There hadn't been any of that, not in the United States Navy, not
with its hero-filled past, not among *all* of the officers. It was
unthinkable. The real threat had been exhaustion, an exhaustion
that made the hangings the only way out. "From the arrest of Mr.
Spencer to the execution, the officers of the *Somers* had upon them a
heavy weight of labor and responsibility," Griffin submitted.

> They took sentinels on the deck, and ultimately had no
> alternative but to remain there under arms day and
> night, watch and watch about. To the refreshing influ-
> ence of quiet sleep they had become strangers. Fatigue
> and consuming care were wasting away their youthful
> frames. Nature would have endured the struggle but
> little longer. And while their physical strength was
> hourly becoming less and less, the danger was hourly
> becoming greater and greater.

And what was the danger? Griffin had already argued that this was
unlike a mutiny on land, in the army or the militia, with its chance of
escape and evasion. Here the ship was an insular unit. There could
be no retreat, and *Somers* herself had been the objective. He
described what had been at stake.

> An American vessel of war was about to become a pi-
> ratical cruiser. A vessel which had been born into our
> naval family, and consecrated as a defender of her
> country's glory, and one of the protectors of the great
> commonwealth of civilized man, was about to be torn
> from her sphere, and let loose a lawless wanderer upon
> the deep, carrying along in her devious course, like a
> comet loosened from its orbit, devastation, and terror,
> and death. Perhaps no vessel could be found better fit-

ted to become the pest of the ocean. Seldom surpassed in speed by anything propelled by sails; of sufficient strength to overcome merchantmen; so small and light that, if pressed by superior force, she might retire beyond their reach, and hide herself in shoal water; capable of supplying herself, from her prizes, with men, naval stores, provisions, and water—she might have made her home on the seas, without ever entering port. There, swift and destructive as the pestilence, by turns showing herself on the Atlantic, and then in the Pacific and Indian Oceans, she might have been the world's terror for years, without its being known whence the scourge came, or whither it went.

Given the circumstances, Griffin continued, Mackenzie had had no alternative. The positive law of the navy and Congress might not have given him power to convene a court-martial; still, said the lawyer, "he had with him a volume of nature's laws, written by the finger of God on the human heart." This natural law, argued Griffin, had been all the authority that Mackenzie had needed. The hangings had been a necessity.

It was a powerful pitch. The dramatic and colorful passages couldn't conceal the close legal reasoning that Griffin was using. Now Norris had to counter his arguments.

It was a very tough job. It always had been, given what little he knew, and given the presumption of innocence that the law, and the navy's heroic image, forced him to confront. His only hope now was to shift that presumption somehow, to make Mackenzie have to justify what he had done at sea.

"In the case of a wreck," he admitted, "and two persons have hold of a plank which is sufficient to buoy only one, the right to force off the other into the sea has been allowed by the law, by virtue of the privilege of self-preservation. It can, from necessity, consign even innocence to death." So much was clear. "But," he warned, "the necessity must be extreme, absolute, and impending."

This, Norris contended, had not been the case aboard *Somers*. Mackenzie had been in a bad spot, he agreed, but that in itself wasn't enough. "The position of an officer so circumstanced is, in extreme cases, one of great trial, full of peril, and which can be adequately and justifiably sustained only by the exercise of the greatest caution, prudence, and firmness." This was crucial. "No matter how innocently he is removed from the resource of a court, he cannot become a judge to try or execute an unallowed sentence without taking on himself the risk of establishing the guilt of the criminal by legal evidence, and of vindicating his usurpation of authority by the fact of a reasonable necessity."

Necessity wasn't unlimited, pointed out Norris. "Mutiny," he conceded, "is treason at sea." That statement spoke for itself; there is no worse crime in the world. But had a mutiny happened? No, Norris argued. There had been no trial, no determination of guilt; and "necessity could give no jurisdiction over any but a guilty man." If the court found necessity, he concluded, it had to acquit Mackenzie. But otherwise it had to convict. The law, and good order and discipline, demanded it. Mackenzie had had no discretion. Nor did the court. If it found no necessity, Mackenzie had to suffer the punishment.

That was really all that Norris could say. And so the court began to deliberate, the officers meeting day after day to discuss what they'd heard and seen. And when they reached their decision, rather than making it public at once, they informed the Navy Department.

A court-martial cannot go so far as to pronounce a binding judgment. Its finding as well as its sentence are only recommendations. The military, the navy, are instruments of authority and order. The final word, by tradition and law, lay with the convening authority— in this instance the secretary of the navy and ultimately the president, the commander-in-chief. So the court informed these men of what it was about to do.

On March 28 the officers entered the chapel-turned-courtroom. The finding it issued read like a mantra. First specification, first charge; second specification, first charge; third specification, first charge. And then on to the second and third charges, each with its specifications. In every last instance, the final two words in each recitation were the same: "Not proved," the old standby of Scottish law that waffled between guilt and innocence. The officers refused to declare Commander Mackenzie guilty, but they hesitated to vindicate him as well. They punted instead. What Upshur and President Tyler decided to do with this finding was entirely up to them.

The decision came during a Cabinet meeting on March 29. President Tyler was there; so were Abel P. Upshur and John Canfield Spencer. Exactly what happened isn't quite clear, but the general outline seems plain enough. Spencer, refusing to recuse himself from the discussion, urged Tyler to order another trial. Upshur opposed him, and the rest of the Cabinet backed Upshur. So, too, did the president. The issue for both Upshur and Tyler was that of double jeopardy. "When a man had once been fairly tried," Tyler explained needlessly, "he should not be tried again upon the same charges & evidence." But the president went even further, emphasizing the court's independence. "I could do nothing but approve the sentence," he protested. "If it had ordered Mackenzie to be shot, I would not have interposed to save him."

No doubt Spencer, a most able lawyer, didn't appreciate a lecture on constitutional doctrine, especially when that doctrine might not reach into the world of military discipline. He had always had a hot temper, and most accounts say that after this exchange it exploded.

Upshur, too, then flew into "a glorious rage," and a fistfight erupted between the two men, a fight that Tyler himself stepped in to stop. He had made his decision; the sentence would stand, although he refused to dignify it with his signature. Mackenzie was effectively acquitted. But he didn't escape the cloud on his name.

Spencer had tried and failed. Mackenzie, though not his reputation, survived. Others were not so lucky. Three days after the court-martial made public its findings, ship's surgeon Leecock, belowdecks aboard *Somers*, picked up a pistol and blew off his own head.

Mackenzie had demons, too. They chased him out of New York, pursuing him into the countryside. Norris stood prepared to hear the commander's complaints against the sailors whom he'd clapped in irons; there was a chance now that they would face mutiny trials. But Mackenzie didn't stop to make any charges. He simply rode up the Hudson, heading for his Tarrytown home as fast as he could go. Behind him, in New York City, Norris gave up, recommending that the court-martial adjourn. The legal battle had ended. The storm that had swept all of them up—the captain, the officers, the sailors, the lawyers, the court—swirled, and faded, and died.

EPILOGUE

Rough Waters

SOMERS's EARLY CRUISE was a rough one; but there was another, still rougher.

Mignonette's keel was laid down in Brightlingsea, Essex, in the spring of 1867, the year before Gansevoort's death. She was no warship, and she was small even compared to the little brig *Somers*. She was a yacht; her two masts and her rigging made her a yawl, half *Somers*'s length with just half her beam. For her size she carried a huge spread of canvas, just as *Somers* had done, but she was heavily ballasted and very stiff-handling. Like *Somers*, too, she was fast. Although she could serve as a fishing boat, she was designed mainly for pleasure cruising. Yachting was an upper-class sport in Victorian England. The Royal Navy reigned supreme, unchallengeable on all the earth's oceans during this century of the Pax Britannica, and the land's aristocracy flaunted its rule of the waves. But the sea can never be peaceful.

As a small pleasure craft, *Mignonette* was no deep-ocean creature. She lacked true intercontinental range and duration, though with careful provisioning, crewing, navigation, and handling, there was no reason why she couldn't—if luck favored her—sail halfway around the globe. That was her goal when she set out from Tollesbury in May of 1884. Her captain and sailing master, Tom Dudley, was fleeing his native land, hoping to start a new life in Australia. His small crew shared his hopes: Edwin Stephens, Ned Brooks, and even his new cabin boy, Richard Parker, all wanted to build new worlds for themselves.

Parker was young, only fourteen or so, and he was new to the life of the sea, even newer than Spencer had been on the mutinous cruise. He had a lot of growing up to do and he recognized the fact.

He said that he'd signed on for this voyage, someone later reported, "to make a man of himself." Manhood through putting oneself to the test: forty-two years and an ocean away from the land that had once launched *Somers,* the idea was still predominant.

Mignonette and *Somers,* as well as their fateful cruises, resembled each other in ways. They were both dry ships, with no spirits aboard except for the medicinal kind. The Puerto Rican shakedown aside, the tragic trip to Africa had been *Somers*'s first ocean sojourn; likewise, when *Mignonette* set out for Australia, it was her first foray beyond the friendly home waters of England. And the two voyages overlapped, in space if not in time, with *Mignonette* calling at Funchal, just as *Somers* had, and skirting the Cape Verde Islands. But while *Somers* had turned west after reaching Cape Mesurado, *Mignonette* headed southwest, catching the trades and dropping below the Line, looking to round Good Hope. The seas belonged, more and more, to steamers, but *Mignonette* was still the slave of the winds. She went as they went, following paths that sailors had traced since before the days of Columbus. That kept her out of the sea-lanes, safe from the steam-powered vessels that might run her down in the night. But it also meant that she was alone, more alone even than *Somers* had been.

A month out of Madeira she was in the grip of the southeast trades, at the height of the Southern Hemisphere's winter, and nearly as isolated as it was possible to be on the face of the planet. Good Hope was sixteen hundred miles away, and South America more than two thousand. Gales shrieked through her rigging while she battled heavy cross-seas, straining to reach the Cape. By July 3, a winter storm was tearing at her; by the 5th, she was running before a howling wind, riding under only a backed jib and trysail. That was when disaster struck.

A mountainous sea, appearing impossibly huge to the crew of the minuscule vessel, came hurtling at her broadside out of the gathering dusk. It was, Brooks recounted, "a tremendous sea—reaching, I should think, quite halfway up to our masthead." He barely had time to take in hand a couple of turns of the dinghy's lashings to keep from being washed overboard. Then the wave slammed into the yacht.

Stephens put the helm hard up, trying to meet the sea, but too late. *Mignonette* was buried in foaming, phosphorescent white, then green, then perhaps even black in the failing ocean twilight as she burrowed deeper and deeper. Then the waters receded, and she reemerged, gasping, but the damage was done. "My God!" yelled Stephens over the wind. "Her topsides are stove in; she is sinking!"

The worst injury was the one that the crew couldn't see. Below the waterline at the stern, *Mignonette*'s planking had torn apart from her frames, or perhaps from her sternpost. Whatever the cause, she was taking on water and settling fast. Miraculously, all four souls had managed to stay aboard during the onslaught. Now they scrambled to get off. Quickly the dinghy was put in the water, with the crew desperately trying to round up provisions from the fast-foundering yacht. They were just barely successful, and soon they were forced into the tiny dinghy. Five minutes after being swept by the thundering sea, *Mignonette* went down by the stern.

That was on July 5. For the next nineteen days, beyond any hope of coming to land, the four survivors got by on a turtle and a couple of tins of turnips. After a while they began to drink their own urine, and then young Parker, the cabin boy who had wanted to be a man, began to gulp down seawater. It dehydrated him further, causing severe diarrhea. Before long he was in a very bad way.

Dudley, Stephens, and Brooks were not much better, but they were alert enough to know that unless something happened quite soon, they would all be dead. That was when they got the idea of sacrificing one of themselves so that the others would have food.

Exactly how it took place was unknown. Sometimes, when history draws a veil across the facts of the past, it can be merciful. Apparently the group drew lots, but their stories, the stories of sick and hungry men, were conflicting and inconsistent. Parker was in the worst shape; he appeared to the others to be dying. So on July 24, nearly three weeks after *Mignonette*'s sinking, Dudley helped him along. That morning, after checking as usual for sails on the horizon, he took his pocketknife and slit young Parker's throat.

What followed is best not described. It lasted for five days, and then, at last, the sail for which the group had been watching for nearly a month appeared, and the long-hoped-for rescue took place. Six weeks later, the German barque *Moctezumah* put into Falmouth and its three passengers, still weak, went ashore. Within hours they were under arrest for murder.

What happened next was one of the most notorious cases in the annals of criminal law, a case that produced one of the most famous judicial opinions of the nineteenth, or any other, century. Nearly every law student in every common law country knows the case of *Regina v. Dudley and Stephens*. The grisly facts are one reason. Even more important is this: the case raises, at the most basic level possible, the question of the nature and origins of the thing called law. A small group of people are cut off in nearly every conceivable way from a larger community and an established legal system. What law governs them? From where does it come? How is it known? What is its purpose?

Dudley, Stephens, and Brooks didn't simply turn off their sense of morals and decency when they were cast adrift. They knew that the taking of life was wrong, that it didn't stop being wrong just because they were alone and in danger of death. But their instincts for self-preservation had been honed to a razorlike edge now that they stared death in the face. Sanctity of life on the one hand; self-preservation on the other; both in perfect balance. What was the proper solution?

The answer, the courts decided, lay in the rule of necessity, precisely the same legal rule that Mackenzie had relied upon when he had decided to hang three people. His case wasn't so very different from what happened among the *Mignonette*'s crew. It was a case of kill or be killed. If anything, Mackenzie had had a better excuse than Dudley, Stephens, and Brooks. It wasn't just *his* life in the balance. It was the lives of the other innocents he had aboard with him, the lives of civilians and merchantmen who might have come under *Somers*'s guns. That had been his judgment, at least, and his officers had agreed.

Mackenzie had been prepared for an inquiry. Still, the reality of landsmen questioning and second-guessing his decision, even labeling him a murderer, must have come as a bit of a shock. The only way, after all, he could have conclusively proved that his judgment had been right would have been to wait and let a full-fledged mutiny happen. But people ashore didn't care. They were happy to call him a villain.

One, of course, was James Fenimore Cooper. His pamphlet on the Battle of Lake Erie was finally out, but Mackenzie's actions aboard *Somers* had given him fresh ammunition. He was already at work on a critical account of the court-martial, an account that would treat Mackenzie to the condemnation that the navy itself had withheld. "I regard the affair of the *Somers* as one of the darkest spots on the national escutcheon," he wrote to a friend. "Apart from the feebleness of the case that is made out in justification of her officers, it is a stain on the American character that a transaction of this nature should have been treated as this has been."

To his wife, Cooper spoke even more plainly, revealing something he'd heard from Robert F. Stockton, an officer nearly as senior as the elder Matthew C. Perry. "Captain Stockton tells me," he confided to her, "he was ordered on Mackenzie's court, but frankly told the secretary his mind is made up, and *that he should vote for hanging the accused,* if he sat. On this hint, he was excused. I am told several others got off, on the same ground." Earlier Cooper had lashed out at Mackenzie for failing to give Spencer and his cohorts due process; but the idea of a prejudiced court out to hang the defendant before hearing the evidence seemed to give him no qualms at all, given that the defendant was Alexander Slidell Mackenzie.

Cooper wasn't the only one to argue that something had been wrong with the court. Not long after Mackenzie's acquittal, the *Journal of Commerce* claimed that only a procedural fluke had allowed him to escape a finding of guilt. According to the newspaper, a majority of the officers who had served on the court had thought Mackenzie guilty of *something*. Seven of the twelve, it claimed, had voted guilty on at least one of the charges. The only thing that had saved him was that no single charge had gained a majority vote.

But the claim itself was an insult, or so Mackenzie believed. He was ready, for once, to emulate James Fenimore Cooper and sue the *Journal*'s editor. "If by bringing a suit against him the entire secret of the voting of the Court could be ascertained I should be glad," he told his attorney Theodore Sedgwick. "I do not believe that more than two at the most voted against me on any charge and I am inclined to think that there was only one, and he not of sound mind."

Sedgwick began to gear up. "The papers have charged that the acquittal is merely technical being 7 to 5 against him," he wrote his friend Charles Sumner. "We are ready to disprove this by examining the officers of the court." It wasn't a bluff. Soon the suit was in progress.

That was enough. Within a few weeks, the *Journal of Commerce* caved in. After the examination of some of the officers, everyone involved was able to see that the newspaper's information was wrong, and it said so in a retraction. The vote, it conceded, was closer to what Mackenzie had believed all along: nine to three for acquittal.

Sumner, too, got in on the act, siding with Mackenzie. "We will not undertake to decide the question," he wrote in the *North American Review* the summer after Mackenzie's acquittal, "whether a national ship, on the high seas, in time of peace, and in the absence of mutiny or disturbance, is under the rule of municipal law or the martial law. But," he continued firmly, "however this may be in ordinary circumstances, we cannot doubt that, by the mutiny on board the *Somers,* this ship was placed, for the time being, in a state of war." He might as well have written "state of nature," because in both nature and war, force is the final word. And given that state, necessity had dictated Mackenzie's actions, for the safety of both *Somers* and the innocent lives that she otherwise might have threatened.

Sumner's defense of Mackenzie revealed that he knew that civilians, safe on dry land, couldn't quite grasp the autocracy of the seas and the elements, the need for something of despotism in an insular maritime world. A lot of the back-and-forth sniping between Mackenzie's defenders and critics reflected this cultural clash between the norms of life in an increasingly democratic United States, and the custom and law of the sea. It certainly caught at the literary imagination, or so many people thought. Herman Melville, Guert Gansevoort's cousin, makes mention of *Somers* in his introspective novella *Billy Budd,* and many critics from that day to this believe his tale to be based on the *Somers* affair. But whether or not the episode inspired Melville to pen *Billy Budd,* the resemblance between his story of the Handsome Sailor and that of Philip Spencer, or even that of Elisha Small or Samuel Cromwell, is not all that strong. Most people, too, have failed to see that a hanging on an American frigate during the Mexican War resembled Billy Budd's story much more closely than did the *Somers* events.

Still, memories of the *Somers* affair lingered, though they remained beyond the comprehension of many land-bound citizens. And if they couldn't fully understand the ways of the sea, seafarers had similar difficulty realizing that they would be judged by the laws of the land. Dudley and Stephens, the evidence shows, were forthright about what they had done, and they were astonished to find themselves under arrest for it. Unlike Mackenzie, they were convicted and sentenced to death, but the Crown intervened and commuted the sentence. It was the exact opposite of Mackenzie's case: in the end he had demanded a trial, the court grudgingly let him go, and President Tyler, while acquiescing in the court's finding, never trusted him with a command again. But in both cases the ambivalent stance of the people who lived on the land showed just how hard the problem was.

Mackenzie was a fairly young man. If fate had not intervened he could have gone on to be a post-captain, the royalty of the naval officer corps, and then perhaps moved on up to command a squadron, thus earning the coveted title of commodore. He might even have become an admiral someday, for Congress finally created that highly aristocratic position during the Civil War years. But it wasn't to be. There were too many officers as it was—too many for peacetime, anyway—and even a slight stain on a record could throw someone out of the race. And he was out of it; his remaining assignments were mostly on land, except for a brief post-Tyler command during the Mexican War—command of *Mississippi,* sister ship to the ill-fated *Missouri* he'd once grounded in the Potomac, and, perhaps not coincidentally, Commodore Matthew C. Perry's usual flagship. The war was the end of him; he returned from the Gulf of Mexico ill, and, half a year later, he died while still a commander in 1848.

His experiences aboard *Somers,* however, helped change the navy. For decades some of the service's more farsighted officers had been calling for a naval academy. Several navy secretaries had done the same, begging Congress for approval and money. The downside of making political midshipmen's appointments was obvious, not only to the secretaries who felt the political pressure from friends and friends of friends to give their sons commissions and warrants, but also to the senior and middle-grade officers who had to live with the results. As steam began to go in, the stridency increased; specialized knowledge required specialized training, or so went the argument.

But that made little sense. Sailing a warship—sailing any large vessel—was one of the most complex and specialized things in the world. Congress just didn't understand. The navy was expensive, and aristocratic, and perhaps not even useful; that, at least, was how the American people tended to view it in the interwar years. No point in spending more money to encourage the building up of an aristocratic officer class. Congress seemed unaware that it was encouraging just such a buildup—a buildup not of aristocracy but of incompetence, and even of danger.

The *Somers* affair sounded a wakeup call. The son of the secretary of war, a son with a spotty civilian record, had been foisted upon the navy, presumably by the pulling of strings. Three deaths had resulted, including his own. It might have ended in the loss of a ship, in civilian casualties and damage to property. This was unacceptable. The navy should be a draw for the best, not a cesspool for the worst. Some other system was needed. In the months following the Mackenzie court-martial, Congress began to reconsider the idea of a naval academy, one with competitive examinations to sort out the wheat from the chaff before the latter ever got near the decks of a warship. In doing so, it found itself being egged on by the men of the Navy Department, civilian and officer both.

It still took some time, but things finally got moving. In 1845, two years after Mackenzie's acquittal, the new secretary of the navy—the nationalist scholar-historian George Bancroft—had managed a deal between the army and navy to establish an academy at minimal cost to the people. The army agreed to give him an obsolete base in Annapolis, Fort Severn on the banks of the river that bore the same name. Classes began by the end of the year. The United States Naval Academy was at last a reality, helped on its way by Philip Spencer's appointment, his schemes, and his hanging.

The Academy came about scant months before the end of three decades of comparative peace. It had little time to contribute to the development of the officer corps, at least in the short run, although in time it would become the world's premier naval training ground. But for now, during its years of youth and adolescence, the Old Navy whose ways had produced it was still very much alive. It was this navy, bred in the decades of peacetime, that would have to fight the war for the conquest of Mexican lands. And *Somers* would be part of that war.

She was a young ship commanded by a young officer when she met her end in the thick of combat. Near obsolescence when her keel was laid down, she seemed to know she was cursed by the circumstance of her birth and by the reputation that she'd promptly acquired. Sailors serving aboard her swore they could hear the hanged men's cries when the wind sighed through the rigging in hours of darkness. She wouldn't grow old, not gracefully, not any other way. She would die as Philip Spencer had died: in youth and in violence.

She was on station off Vera Cruz when it happened. America's first true foreign war, a war of expansion and conquest, was in full bloody flower, and she was at its center. By now the small American army was well on its way to being a truly professional force. Winfield Scott, Robert E. Lee, Ulysses S. Grant, George B. McClellan, Thomas J. Jackson, not yet a "Stonewall"—they were all in the crucible there as the United States assailed the gates of Mexico. The navy, too, had its role, a major one; the storming of Vera Cruz, the New World Gibraltar, by sea was the biggest amphibious landing in all of American history until the Second World War. For the very first time, the United States was using the navy to fire the army like a projectile at a foreign enemy shore. The navy, though still adolescent, was now coming of age.

Somers had not yet felt the professional touch when she raised the Mexican coast; the academy on the Severn, far to the north, was just in its infancy. She was still of the old school, and here, in the Gulf, she wasn't too far from the old pirate lairs—for instance, the Isle of Pines—that had been her original targets. The bad, romantic old days of the pirates were a fast-fading memory, but her lines and her rigging still dreamed of them. And the subsequent career of her last captain would be an echo of the life of a freebooter. His name was Raphael Semmes. Fifteen years later he would become one of history's most famous commerce raiders when he took command of the vessel that was destined for him: CSS *Alabama,* the most celebrated ship of the Confederate States of America.

But there, off the Mexican coast, Semmes was just a lieutenant in the United States Navy. He was somewhat young for *Somers,* being a mere lieutenant, but he doubtless knew her history. Mackenzie was gone, though; this quarterdeck and all its memories now belonged to Semmes. Gansevoort, too, was gone; Spencer was gone. But like a stain, the memories lingered.

Seventy-odd others were here with Semmes, and it was to be their misfortune. *Somers* was still as fast and as handy as she had ever been, and she wasn't tied to the shore by a hunger for coal; a good thing, too, since she stood off an enemy shore, where coal was scarce indeed. She had been on blockade duty for months when Semmes's predecessor collapsed of exhaustion. That was how Semmes came to have her in her final few weeks.

One morning he had her set out from her anchorage, patrolling the waves, daring the blockade runners to come out and try her. He kept an eye on the weather; it was late in the fall, and even here in the cloistered Gulf, the wind could come around fast as northerlies sprang up without warning. Day by day he had walked the deck where seven boys and men had been chained, under yards where three had swung, waiting to see ships hull-down on the far horizon. Four years and a week after the hangings, a lookout spotted one. The wind was from nearly out of the west as *Somers* started the chase, but then it began to come out of the north. She continued to be one of the fastest ships in the world, and by this point in her cruise she was dangerously light; her crew, nearer to the end of their long patrol than they thought, had eaten and drunk their way down to the bilges, and she had almost nothing for ballast. So when the breeze grabbed her sails, everybody would know it, for she would start racing the winds themselves. Her prey had no chance at all.

That was when it happened.

She was giving chase under mainsails and topsails, close-hauled on the larboard tack, the wind more or less off her larboard bow. She was cleared for action, gunports open, guns run out, heeling hard over to starboard. Still, she was handling well. And then Semmes's first lieutenant warned his captain of a darkening, a squall to windward where none had been a few moments before. Semmes quickly ordered the mainsail taken in and the helm put up, to take the brig off the wind, but it made no difference. The squall hit just a few moments later, rolling *Somers* neatly onto her beam-ends.

Semmes, knowing that the ship was in terrible trouble, ordered the rigging and masts cut away to make her less top-heavy, but it was no use. The masts were already touching the waves, and water was pouring in through the open gunports. She was capsizing. Most of the boats were already underwater; only the port quarter-boat was available, and Semmes and his men got it free of its davits. The squall had grown, becoming a gale, and heavy seas were running. Semmes got about twenty men into the boat and had it shove off, hoping to get them to land and then use the boat to shuttle some more to safety. But *Somers* was sinking too fast; the first load just barely had time to get off. "Every man save himself who can!" bellowed Semmes—and then she was gone, taking dozens of souls with her.

Semmes's account of the sinking is sketchy. Not until 1986 did divers find the wreck and piece together the brig's last few minutes. But while we now have the final answers about *Somers* herself, we will never know the full story of what happened aboard her on her ill-fated training cruise of four years before, no matter how many more centuries pass. *Somers*'s waterlogged corpse may have spoken;

but as for her crew and her officers—as Philip Spencer had once noted—dead men tell no tales.

Legend tells of the Flying Dutchman, the captain cursed by God to be the evil spirit of the ocean. All who sight his ship are doomed; *Somers* must have spotted him early. In the end she went to join Spencer, Cromwell, and Small in a common watery grave. As God first moved upon the face of the waters, so waters spelled the end of the journey, not only for *Somers,* but for the three troubled souls who sailed her to the horizons of fate. Only the sea knows the truth; and she will not give up her answers, not until Judgment Day.

Author's Note

SHIP'S CAPTAINS OF LONG and distinguished service don't usually arrest officers and sailors without good reason. Even more rarely do they arbitrarily hang them. But disaffected young men do sometimes plot and commit acts of irrational violence, as the recent wave of tragic school shootings and other current events all too clearly show. These are the premises on which I have based my interpretation of what happened aboard *Somers*.

Of course, I could be wrong. For one thing, the above statements are nothing but generalizations, and *Somers* might be the exception. Then there is the problem of incomplete knowledge. Historians and courts have differing rules of evidence, but in this particular case, neither set of rules helps us explain everything. Given the size of the ship, the fact that she was at sea, and the inherent nature of conspiracy and mutiny, there could be no disinterested witnesses to what took place on *Somers*'s African cruise. Stories and testimonies conflicted; motives were complex; and the stakes were literally life and death. Each man and boy who took the stand in New York may have been telling the truth or many variations of lies. Even if they all tried to tell the truth, the stress and sleep deprivation, combined with the horror of ordering, witnessing, or taking part in a more or less cold-blooded execution, all while going about the extraordinarily complex business of sailing a ship, had to affect people's memories. The real story of what happened on *Somers,* in short, can never be known.

Yet I think that my premises come as close as anything to explaining what really took place. Philip Spencer gave signs of mental disturbance, or at the very least an unhealthy obsession with weapons and violence, and without doubt he showed very poor judgment. Mackenzie, for his part, had no obvious motive to persecute Spencer, although no one can know what unconscious pressures he might have been feeling. Nobody, except for Spencer himself, admitted to seeing any hostility in Mackenzie's treatment of the acting midshipman, or anyone else on the ship, before the arrests. Still, the step from arrest to hanging is an extreme one. Maybe Mackenzie wasn't justified in doing what he ultimately did. But, even if the execution was unreasonable, he might still have carried it out in good faith. As for Spencer's arrest, it was almost certainly reasonable. Thus, while both Mackenzie and Spencer might have gotten carried away, it was likely Spencer's morbid obsession that started the chain reaction that finally spun out of control. Such, at least, is my understanding. Different premises may lead to different conclusions, and the reader is free to accept or reject them.

In writing this brief account of a complicated subject, I have had the help of many people. I here have the pleasure of thanking my editors, Chad Conway, Rachel Klayman, and Bruce Nichols; the other members of the fine team at The Free Press, including Dominick Anfuso, Suzanne Donahue, Leslie Ellen, Carisa Hays, Amy Heller, Maris Kreizman, and Martha Levin; Professor John V. Orth of the University of North Carolina at Chapel Hill; Professor Stephen Beall of Marquette University; Dr. Robert J. Schneller of the Department of the Navy's Naval Historical Center; Vicki Arnold; John Bonds; Fred Chase; Kimberly K. Elbert; Tara C. Hogan; Jaime Humphries; Anna Jett; Elizabeth G. Joyce; John C. Kuzenski; Jennifer J. Miller; Daniel J. Palmieri; Oscar Spivey, M.D.; Captain Jack Walp, U.S.N. (Ret.); and Major Mark Whitson, U.S.M.C.

A special note of appreciation is, as always, due to my parents, particularly Lieutenant Commander Buckner F. Melton, U.S.N.R. (Ret.). My greatest thanks, as always, go to my wife, Dr. Carol K. W. Melton, who worked long and hard on this book with me and who is truly, as another historian once said, the power behind the drone. My final word of appreciation this time out goes to my agent, Ed Knappman, to whom I dedicate this book.

Notes

I have occasionally altered spelling, punctuation, and capitalization in primary source quotations to conform to modern standards. Readers should consult those sources directly for the most accurate renderings.

PART ONE: SOMERS

3 *Even tied up at dock: Dictionary of American Naval Fighting Ships* 6 (Washington: Naval History Division, Department of the Navy, 1976), pp. 549–50; Howard I. Chapelle, *The Baltimore Clipper: Its Origin and Development* (Salem, Mass.: Marine Research Society, 1930), *passim;* Howard I. Chapelle, *The History of the American Sailing Navy: The Ships and Their Development* (New York: W. W. Norton, 1949), pp. 430–33; Howard I. Chapelle, *The History of American Sailing Ships* (New York: W. W. Norton, 1935), pp. 121, 123, 166; James P. Delgado, "Rediscovering the *Somers,*" *Naval History,* Mar./Apr. 1994, pp. 28–31; Spencer Tucker, *Arming the Fleet: U.S. Navy Ordnance in the Muzzle-Loading Era* (Annapolis: Naval Institute Press, 1989), ch. 5.

6 *A ship is a device:* The classic statement is that of Alfred Thayer Mahan:

> The first and most obvious light in which the sea presents itself from the political and social point of view is that of a great highway; or better, perhaps a wide common, over which men may pass in all directions, but on which some well-worn paths show that controlling reasons have led them to choose certain lines of travel rather than others. These lines of travel are called trade routes; and the reasons which have determined them are to be sought in the history of the world.

Alfred Thayer Mahan, *The Influence of Sea Power Upon History, 1660–1783* (Boston: Little, Brown, 1890), p. 1.

6   *The Mediterranean was the earliest ocean frontier:* Cecil Torr, *Ancient Ships* (Chicago: Argonaut, 1964), p. 1.

6   *Egyptians were perhaps the first:* Veres László and Richard Woodman, *The Story of Sail* (Annapolis: Naval Institute Press, 1999), p. 9.

7   *Human beings, whether free men or slaves:* John Keegan, *The Price of Admiralty: The Evolution of Naval Warfare* (New York: Viking, 1988), p. 3.

7   *This was a lesson:* Ibid., pp. 3–4.

7   *A lumbering merchant ship can be slow:* Torr, *Ancient Ships*, p. 20; Clark G. Reynolds, *Command of the Sea: The History and Strategy of Maritime Empires* (Malabar, Fla.: Robert E. Krieger Publishing Company, 1974), pp. 22–24.

10   *There rose up from the water:* Richard Henry Dana, Jr., *Two Years Before the Mast* (New York: Harper & Brothers, 1840), ch. 33.

12   *Navies are different from armies:* Karl Lautenschläger, "Technology and the Evolution of Naval Warfare," in *Naval Strategy and National Security* (Princeton: Princeton University Press, 1988), pp. 173, 175.

12   *The more firepower, the better:* Reynolds, *Command of the Sea*, 1:107–9.

12   *Now that warships relied on the wind:* Bernard Brodie, *Sea Power in the Machine Age* (Princeton: Princeton University Press, 1943), pp. 99–100, 120–21.

13   *Steam engines had been around for years:* Ibid., ch. 2.

13   *Steam power at sea:* Ibid., pp. 36, 99–121; Kenneth J. Hagan, *This People's Navy: The Making of American Sea Power* (New York: The Free Press, 1991), p. 123; Donald L. Canney, *The Old Steam Navy* 1 (Annapolis: Naval Institute Press, 1990), pp. 15–28; Samuel Eliot Morison, *The European Discovery of America: The Southern Voyages, A.D. 1492–1616* (New York: Oxford University Press, 1974), ch. 10; Lautenschläger, "Technology and the Evolution of Naval Warfare," pp. 173, 177–79 ("The perennial concern of military planners is that technological surprise will give an opponent a decisive advantage in event of war.").

14   *"Seeing how energetically the Anglo-Americans trade":* Alexis de Tocqueville, *Democracy in America;* George Lawrence, trans., J. P. Mayer and Max Lerner, eds. (New York: Harper & Row, 1966), p. 373.

15   *Right after the War of 1812:* Hagan, *This People's Navy*, p. 102.

16   *One of the first to notice the problem:* Samuel Eliot Morison, *"Old Bruin": Commodore Matthew C. Perry, 1794–1858* (Boston: Little, Brown, 1967), pp. ix, 3, 27–29, 58, 77–84.

17   *Life in the Old Navy:* Lieutenant Matthew C. Perry to Samuel Southard, 5 Jan. 1824, RG 45, Officers' Letters, 1824, I, No. 13 and enclosure, RG 45, National Archives, Washington, D.C.

17   *Perry even tried to go:* National Gazette (Philadelphia), 8 Feb. 1828, p. 2; 14
      Feb. 1828, p. 1.

18   *So Southard submitted another report:* Samuel L. Southard, *Report from the
      Secretary of the Navy, in Compliance with a Resolution of the Senate of 20th
      May, 1826, in Relation to the Difficulties in Obtaining Seamen for the Navy, the
      Cause of Such Difficulties, and the Measures Necessary to Remove Them* (Wash-
      ington: Duff Green, Serial Set 167, 1828), p. 11.

19   *Eventually a viable bill emerged:* Act of 2 Mar. 1837, 2 Stat. ch. 21, § 1, at
      153. For a brief history of the boys' program, including the role of the *Somers*
      affair, see Harold D. Langley, *Social Reform in the United States Navy,
      1798–1862* (Urbana: University of Illinois Press, 1967), ch. 5.

20   *But the program wasn't a total debacle:* Morison, "*Old Bruin*," pp. 124, 144–47.

PART TWO: SPENCER

26   *In a way it all started in the Caribbean:* William Preston Vaughn, *The Anti-
      masonic Party in the United States, 1826–1843* (Louisville: University Press of
      Kentucky, 1983), ch. 1; Alice Felt Tyler, *Freedom's Ferment: Phases of Ameri-
      can Social History from the Colonial Period to the Outbreak of the Civil War*
      (New York: Harper Torchbooks, 1944), pp. 351–63.

28   *Seward wasn't the only Anti-Mason:* "John Canfield Spencer," Dumas Ma-
      lone, ed., *Dictionary of American Biography* 9 (New York: Charles Scribner's
      Sons, 1964), pp. 449–50.

28   *Spencer had a young son:* George W. Ray, ed., *The Chi Psi Story* (Ann Arbor:
      Chi Psi Educational Trust, 1995), pp. 57, 59; William Harwar Parker, *Recol-
      lections of a Naval Officer, 1841–1865* (Annapolis: Naval Institute Press,
      1985), p. 7.

30   *He was a cutup:* Ray, *Chi Psi Story*, pp. 56–60.

32   *Spencer himself seemed to have chosen the sea:* Ibid., pp. 60–61; Diary of R. H.
      Dana, Jr., in Charles Francis Adams, ed., *Richard Henry Dana, A Biography* 1
      (Boston: Houghton Mifflin, 1890), p. 60.

33   *America, at the time, had no naval academy:* Charles Todorich, *The Spirited
      Years: A History of the Antebellum Naval Academy* (Annapolis: Naval Institute
      Press, 1984), pp. 5–8; Jack Sweetman, *The U.S. Naval Academy: An Illustrated
      History,* 2nd ed. (Annapolis: Naval Institute Press, 1995), pp. 4–5.

34   *He was still a rebel:* Adams, *Richard Henry Dana,* 1:60–63; Edward W. Calla-
      han, ed., *List of Officers of the Navy of the United States and of the Marine Corps
      from 1775 to 1900 . . .* (New York: L. R. Hamersly & Co., 1901), p. 137.

36   *His estimate was probably right:* Acting Midshipman Philip Spencer to Com-

modore M. C. Perry, Commanding U.S. Naval Station, New York, 11 Feb. 1842, Naval Branch, National Archives, Washington, D.C.

36   *The navy was small:* Hagan, *This People's Navy,* p. 142; James E. Valle, *Rocks and Shoals: Order and Discipline in the Old Navy, 1800–1861* (Annapolis: Naval Institute Press, 1980), pp. 36–38.

37   *Alcohol was a staple:* William Manchester, *The Last Lion: Winston Spencer Churchill: Visions of Glory* (Boston: Little, Brown, 1983), p. 443.

37   *Spencer, however, was young:* Robert C. Rogers, "Some Reminiscences of Philip Spencer and the Brig 'Somers,'" *United Service,* N.S., 4:23 (July 1890), pp. 24–25; Acting Midshipman Philip Spencer to Commodore Charles Morris, Commanding U.S. Naval Station, Coast of Brazil, 25 May 1842, aboard U.S. Ship *John Adams,* Naval Branch, National Archives, Washington, D.C.

38   *Morris wasn't interested in the defense:* Commodore Charles Morris to Acting Midshipman Philip Spencer, 27 May 1842, Naval Branch, National Archives, Washington, D.C.

38   *Morris had called Spencer's bluff:* Commodore Charles Morris to Acting Midshipman Philip Spencer, 30 May 1842, Naval Branch, National Archives, Washington, D.C.

39   *It was a reprieve:* Philip Spencer to John C. Spencer, Jr., 31 July 1842, Naval Branch, National Archives, Washington, D.C.; Secretary A. P. Upshur to Philip Spencer, 6 Aug. 1842, Naval Branch, National Archives, Washington, D.C.

PART THREE: MACKENZIE

44   *Herman Melville, who would go on to write* Moby-Dick: Herman Melville, *White-Jacket, or the World in a Man-of-War* (Evanston and Chicago: Northwestern University Press and The Newberry Library, 1970), p. 23.

44   *Mackenzie, however, didn't seem to fit:* Morison, *"Old Bruin,"* p. 145; Charles Lamb, "The Old Benchers of the Inner Temple," in *The Complete Works and Letters of Charles Lamb* (New York: Modern Library, 1935), pp. 78, 80; Alexander Slidell Mackenzie, *Proceedings of the Court of Inquiry Appointed to Inquire into the Intended Mutiny on Board the United States Brig of War Somers, on the High Seas: Held on Board the United States Ship North Carolina Lying at the Navy Yard, New-York: With a Full Account of the Execution of Spencer, Cromwell and Small, on Board said Vessel* (New York: Greeley & McElrath, 1843), p. 5. Hereafter referred to as *Court of Inquiry.*

46   *The war was technically over:* Canney, *Old Steam Navy,* 1:3.

48   *Post-captains were bad enough:* Lawrence Fasano, *Naval Rank: Its Inception and Development* (New York: Horizon House, 1936), *passim.*

49   *His rise in the service was fast enough:* Morison, *"Old Bruin,"* ch. 6.

49   *He was a studious sort:* Charles Oscar Paullin, *Paullin's History of Naval Administration, 1775–1911* (Annapolis: U.S. Naval Institute, 1968), pp. 200–201.

50   *In 1833 he published:* Alexander Slidell Mackenzie, *Popular Essays on Naval Subjects* (New York: George Dearborn, 1833), p. 165.

50 .   *One thing Slidell did discuss:* Hagan, *This People's Navy,* pp. 82–87; Mackenzie, *Popular Essays,* pp. 159–63.

51   *That battle eventually led to a different kind of conflict:* Philip McFarland, *Sea Dangers: The Affair of the* Somers (New York: Schocken, 1985), p. 34.

51   *But there were big differences:* Morison, *"Old Bruin,"* p. 145.

51   *But Cooper could write, when he chose to:* Hugh Egan, "Introduction," in *Proceedings of the Naval Court Martial in the Case of Alexander Slidell Mackenzie (1844)* (Delmar, N.Y.: Scholars' Facsimiles and Reprints, 1992), pp. 23–24. Hereafter referred to as *Court Martial.*

52   *In those days the greatest strength of the American navy:* Hugh Egan, "Enabling and Disabling the Lake Erie Discussion: James Fenimore Cooper and Alexander Slidell Mackenzie Respond to the Perry/Elliott Controversy," *The American Neptune* 57 (No. 4, Fall 1997), pp. 343, 343–45; Hagan, *This People's Navy,* pp. 85–87.

53   *Whatever the merits of each man's case:* James Fenimore Cooper, *The History of the Navy of the United States of America* (Philadelphia: Thomas, Cowperthwait & Co., 1846), pp. 388–91.

53   *It was a good enough work:* Egan, "Lake Erie Discussion," pp. 345–49; James Franklin Read, ed., *The Letters and Journals of James Fenimore Cooper* 4 (Cambridge: Belknap Press of Harvard University Press, 1964), p. 389. Hereafter referred to as *Cooper Letters.*

54   *the steam frigate* Missouri: Evert A. Duyckinck, Biographical Sketch of Commander A. S. Mackenzie, Duyckinck Collection, New York Public Library.

55   *It wasn't just the technology:* Paullin, *Naval Administration,* ch. 5, pp. 167–68, 202–3.

55   *Abel P. Upshur, President Tyler's superbly competent naval secretary:* Ibid., p. 209.

55   *So he set about modernizing the system:* Ibid., pp. 209–11.

57   *It was no intercontinental, transoceanic voyage:* Court Martial, pp. 162, 166.

57   *Still, she was new, with a young and raw crew:* Ibid., pp. 59, 62, 124, 218.

58   *Perhaps this day-in, day-out normality:* Ibid., pp. 23, 30–31.

58   *Despite the unpleasantness, the ship and her crew survived:* Morison, *"Old Bruin,"* p. 145.

59   *The record of their first meeting is scant: Court Martial,* p. 139.

PART FOUR: CRUISE

66   *This was* Somers's *next weapon:* Valle, *Rocks and Shoals,* p. 3.

67   *The rest of the time these men provided:* Dana, *Two Years Before the Mast,* ch. 3.

67   *Sanding, scraping, painting and varnishing:* Ibid.

68   *On other ships rum was the answer: Court Martial,* p. 195n.

68   *Discipline on a warship was crucial:* Valle, *Rocks and Shoals,* pp. 80–81; Act of 23 Apr. 1800, 1 Stat. ch. 33, § 1, art. 30, 45, 49.

71   *Mackenzie had other punishments:* Valle, *Rocks and Shoals,* pp. 41–42.

71   *One of the favorites aboard* Somers: Ibid., pp. 15, 81.

71   *The flogging of American citizens:* Langley, *Social Reform in the United States Navy,* p. 127.

76   *Some modern theories hold:* Larry J. Siegel and Joseph J. Senna, *Juvenile Delinquency: Theory, Practice, and Law,* 5th ed. (St. Paul: West Publishing, 1994), p. 301.

76   *Spencer's adolescent years were behind him: Court Martial,* p. 88; *Court of Inquiry,* pp. 19, 47.

76   Somers *may have been a happy ship: Court of Inquiry,* pp. 21, 37; *Court Martial,* p. 148.

76   *This wasn't his only run-in: Court Martial,* pp. 118–19, 148.

77   *He was rough on the apprentices: Court of Inquiry,* p. 19; *Court Martial,* pp. 24, 88.

77   *Then . . . Cromwell calmed down: Court of Inquiry,* p. 18; *Court Martial,* pp. 22, 153, 171.

77   *The night before* Somers *sailed: Court of Inquiry,* pp. 19, 36, 40; *Court Martial,* p. 90.

78   *He seemed to spend most of his efforts: Court of Inquiry,* p. 40; *Court Martial,* pp. 100–101, 195n.

78   *Spencer had another commodity: Court Martial,* pp. 1, 25; *Court of Inquiry,* p. 28.

78   *With the officers and the other midshipmen: Court of Inquiry,* pp. 26, 30–31.

78   *But sometimes he showed some impatience:* Ibid., p. 41.

78   *People noticed them all the time: Court Martial,* pp. 84, 90, 94–95, 96, 107, 160, 224.

79   *Spencer's station, after all, was forward:* Ibid., p. 96.

79   *There was all of the tobacco and alcohol: Court of Inquiry,* p. 46.

79   *Far more serious was what began aboard* Somers: *Court Martial,* p. 63.

80   *Along with the Azores and the Canaries:* Bernard Brodie, *Sea Power in the Machine Age* (Princeton: Princeton University Press, 1943), pp. 105–6.

80   *A few months before* Somers's *arrival:* Charles Roberts Anderson, ed., *Journal of a Cruise to the Pacific Ocean, 1842–44, in the Frigate* United States (Durham: Duke University Press, 1937), p. 25.

81   *Sixty years earlier, His Majesty's Armed Transport* Bounty: William Bligh, *An Account of the Mutiny on H.M.S. Bounty* (New York: Signet, 1961), ch. 1; Leonard F. Guttridge, *Mutiny: A History of Naval Insurrection* (Annapolis: Naval Institute Press, 1992), pp. 14–33.

81   *History's great maritime powers:* "[S]ea power has never led to despotism," the great sailor-historian Morison once wrote. "The nations that have enjoyed sea power even for a brief period—Athens, Scandinavia, the Netherlands, England, the United States—are those that have preserved freedom for themselves and have given it to others. Of the despotism to which unrestrained military power leads we have plenty of examples from Alexander to Mao." Samuel Eliot Morison, *The Oxford History of the American People* 1 (New York: Oxford University Press, 1965), p. 82.

82   *from the time* Somers *arrived at Funchal: Court Martial,* pp. 18, 25, 37, 170.

82   *Spencer began acting more strangely: Court of Inquiry,* pp. 30–31, 33; *Court Martial,* pp. 168–69.

82   *after Madeira his complaints came more often: Court of Inquiry,* p. 34; *Court Martial,* p. 86.

83   *At Funchal he was involved:* Ibid., p. 54.

83   *After the brief early October days: Court of Inquiry,* p. 18.

83   *The rigging really bothered Cromwell:* Ibid., pp. 24, 54.

84   *The Articles had an ancient lineage:* Charles Francis Adams, ed., *The Works of John Adams* 3 (Boston: Charles C. Little and James Brown, 1851), pp. 68–69.

84   *The thirteenth article was the one:* Act of 23 Apr. 1800, 1 Stat. ch. 33, § 1, art. 13, 45, 47.

85   *A bo'sun's mate, too, was supposed to be loyal:* Valle, *Rocks and Shoals,* pp. 21–22.

85   Somers *had no marines: Court Martial,* pp. 119, 124; *Court of Inquiry,* p. 35.

87   Somers *dropped down the latitudes: Court Martial,* p. 23; *Court of Inquiry,* pp. 18, 28.

88   *At other times he turned outward: Court Martial,* p. 88.

88   *Young Matthew C. Perry: Court of Inquiry,* pp. 28, 29.

88   *Spencer sometimes talked of commanding a ship: Court Martial,* pp. 91, 101.

89   *He made similar overtures:* Ibid., pp. 27, 79.

89   *Sleeping on duty was a grave enough matter:* Act of 23 Apr. 1800, 1 Stat. ch. 33, § 1, art. 20, 45, 47–48.

89   *Spencer did nothing to hide his anger: Court of Inquiry,* p. 40.

90   *One day in early November:* Ibid., pp. 17–18; *Court Martial,* pp. 14, 156.

90   *Sometimes Spencer moved beyond words: Court Martial,* p. 156.

91   *The Liberian coast brought out the worst: Court of Inquiry,* p. 25; *Court Martial,* pp. 78, 135.

91   *It infuriated McKinley: Court Martial,* p. 115.

91   *McKinley again went ashore:* Ibid., p. 101.

91   *Now he had found a knife:* Ibid., pp. 115, 118, 176–77.

91   *Wilson told him to put it down:* Ibid., pp. 105, 106.

91   *Cape Mesurado was Somers's last contact:* Ibid., p. 194.

91   *Her size and her speed, and the rake of her masts:* Richard A. Lobban, Jr., *Cape Verde: Crioulo Colony to Independent Nation* (Boulder: Westview Press, 1995), pp. 35–40.

92   *the English ship probably had the weather gage: Court of Inquiry,* p. 34; *Court Martial,* p. 121.

92   *the small arms' appearance set Spencer thinking: Court of Inquiry,* p. 34; *Court Martial,* p. 120.

93   *the fo'c'sle was one of the more private places: Court of Inquiry,* p. 42; *Court Martial,* pp. 84–85, 107–8.

94   *Others saw Spencer and Cromwell together: Court Martial,* pp. 79, 167; *Court of Inquiry,* p. 37.

94   *As* Somers *sailed farther into the waste of ocean: Court of Inquiry,* p. 41.

94   *something Tom Sawyer–like:* Scully Bradley, ed., Samuel Langhorne Clemens, *Adventures of Huckleberry Finn* (New York: W. W. Norton, 1961), chs. 2, 3, 39. Cf. Hugh Egan, "Introduction," in *Court Martial,* p. 13.

94   *Spencer was too old for the role of Tom Sawyer: Court Martial,* pp. 101, 167.

94   *The easy part about navigation:* For the story of maritime chronometers, see Dava Sobel, *Longitude: The True Story of a Lone Genius Who Solved the Greatest Scientific Problem of His Time* (New York: Walker, 1995).

95   *Spencer decided to learn just how accurate: Court of Inquiry,* p. 30; *Court Martial,* pp. 128–29, 174.

95   *James Wales, the purser's steward, had been in trouble: Court Martial,* pp. 28–29, 41.

96   *"Are you afraid of death?": Court Martial,* pp. 11–12, 154-56; *Court of Inquiry,* pp. 14–18.

98   *He had to tell the captain: Court Martial,* pp. 41, 75.

99   *he sensed that speed was crucial:* Ibid., pp. 11–12, 41, 154–56; *Court of Inquiry,* pp. 14–18.

99 *Wales was probably right to worry: Court Martial,* pp. 41, 111, 155; *Court of Inquiry,* p. 38.

100 *The warning of spies came from Small: Court Martial,* p. 31.

100 *Wales went above and found Gansevoort:* Ibid., p. 12.

101 *When Gansevoort got to the wardroom:* Ibid., pp. 30–33, 126; *Court of Inquiry,* pp. 7–9, 18–21.

PART FIVE: CRISIS

109 *"I learn, Mr. Spencer, that you aspire to the command of the* Somers*": Court of Inquiry,* pp. 20, 34; *Court Martial,* pp. 32, 133–34.

111 *Spencer's arrest wasn't the end: Court Martial,* p. 141.

112 *Small, in particular, was acting strange:* Ibid., p. 134.

112 *Mackenzie had to have more information:* Ibid.

112 *Gansevoort went below into steerage:* Ibid., pp. 36, 134.

113 *More people knew Greek in those days:* Buckner F. Melton, Jr., "The Supreme Court and *The Federalist:* A Citation List and Analysis, 1789–1996," *Kentucky Law Journal* 58:243, 247 (1996–97).

113 *Henry Rogers, the senior midshipman, took care of it: Court of Inquiry,* pp. 4, 31; *Court Martial,* pp. 129–30.

115 *They each questioned several sailors: Court Martial,* p. 216.

115 *Green stuck to his story of ignorance:* Act of 23 Apr. 1800, 1 Stat. ch. 33, § 1, art. 30.

115 *some of the sailors were lying: Court Martial,* pp. 61, 79, 213.

116 *all of them on Spencer's Greek list:* Ibid., p. 107.

116 *he wished Spencer's plan had succeeded:* Ibid., p. 125.

116 *Perry guessed that as many as two thirds of the crew were involved:* Ibid., p. 76.

116 *some people had little idea what was happening:* Ibid., p. 111.

116 *McKee might have started this rumor:* Ibid., p. 216.

116 *Cromwell and Small took a different approach:* Ibid., pp. 111, 113, 115, 116.

117 *The two men were probably very afraid:* Ibid., p. 198.

117 *After quarters came church: Court of Inquiry,* p. 20.

118 *he was not under any special suspicion:* Ibid., p. 21.

118 *Cromwell, meanwhile, was being obstructionist: Court Martial,* pp. 101, 195.

119 *Spencer had spent the night on deck:* Ibid., p. 107.

119 *Somers had made about one hundred fifty miles:* Ibid., pp. 75, 78.

119 *in the afternoon, that breeze started to wane: Court of Inquiry,* p. 44; *Court Martial,* pp. 78, 198.

120 *With the wind on her quarter:* John Harland, *Seamanship in the Age of Sail: An*

Account of the Shiphandling of the Sailing Man-of-War, 1600–1860, Based on Contemporary Sources (Annapolis: Naval Institute Press, 1984), pp. 11–14.

120   *Mackenzie was on the weather side of the quarterdeck: Court of Inquiry,* p. 44; *Court Martial,* p. 29.

120   *Well forward on the spar deck sat Small: Court Martial,* pp. 110, 146.

120   *suddenly, everything began to go wrong: Court of Inquiry,* p. 33; *Court Martial,* p. 145.

120   *Small and one or two others went to the brace: Court of Inquiry,* p. 21; *Court Martial,* pp. 98, 99, 109, 173–74.

121   *The royal yard was now under terrific strain: Court Martial,* pp. 62, 100, 198.

121   *The loss of the main topgallant mast: Court of Inquiry,* p. 21; *Court Martial,* pp. 26, 110, 224–26.

122   *Nothing like this had happened before: Court Martial,* pp. 26, 78.

122   *During* Somers's *shakedown voyage:* Ibid., p. 62.

122   *Mackenzie and Gansevoort were both present on deck:* Ibid., pp. 215–16.

123   *Perry went below for a while:* Ibid., p. 64.

123   *Mackenzie had noticed things, too:* Ibid., pp. 21, 38.

123   *Gansevoort drew a pistol on him:* Ibid., pp. 38, 198.

124   *With two more people under arrest:* Ibid., p. 199.

124   *Spencer had been signaling Wilson again:* Ibid., p. 142; *Court of Inquiry,* p. 36.

124   *Immediately Collins went forward: Court Martial,* pp. 50, 104, 110, 135, 142.

125   *Instantly everything changed:* Ibid., pp. 37, 38, 57–58, 64, 178.

126   *By now Mackenzie was back on deck:* Ibid., pp. 37, 38, 57–58, 64, 178.

126   Somers *was almost a thousand miles from the nearest land:* Ibid., p. 75. Actually, the South American coast was slightly closer than the Lesser Antilles, whence *Somers* was bound, but given the prevailing winds, the islands were effectively nearer. See Brodie, *Sea Power,* pp. 36, 99–121.

126   *The next hundred hours passed: Court Martial,* pp. 38, 61, 74.

127   *Those boys, and their older instructors:* Ibid., pp. 25, 38, 61, 74.

127   *Both Spencer and the crew were problems:* Ibid., pp. 25–26, 43, 50, 58, 104.

127   *The crew bore watching, too:* Ibid., pp. 61, 214.

127   *Acting Master Matthew C. Perry, Jr.:* Ibid., pp. 61, 77–78.

127   *Breaches of discipline started happening: Court of Inquiry,* p. 40; *Court Martial,* pp. 39, 53–54, 78, 137, 199.

128   *The officers had tried to maintain an air of normality: Court of Inquiry,* p. 27.

128   *Gansevoort, meanwhile, kept talking with Spencer: Court Martial,* pp. 32–33, 45–48, 67.

129   *The boom was a long and heavy column of wood: Case of the Somers Mutiny: Defence of Alexander Slidell Mackenzie, Commander of the U.S. Brig Somers, Before the Court Martial Held at the Navy Yard, Brooklyn* (New York: Tribune Office, 1843), p. 16.

129 Somers *was rolling heavily:* Ibid.; *Court of Inquiry,* p. 27; *Court Martial,* pp. 62, 74.

130 *"The night was the season of danger":* Court of Inquiry, p. 10; cf. *Court Martial,* p. 199.

131 *Mackenzie had Waltham flogged again:* Court Martial, pp. 178, 200.

131 *Wales saw Charles Wilson reach for a handspike:* Ibid., p. 200.

131 *Meanwhile the officers grew more exhausted:* Ibid., p. 74.

131 *Gansevoort kept up his efforts:* Ibid., pp. 36, 46, 174–75.

132 *The crew was still surly and muttering:* Court of Inquiry, p. 34.

132 *Gunner's Mate Henry King had tried to warn Gansevoort:* Ibid., p. 21.

132 *Wilson was acting strangely:* Court Martial, pp. 138–40, 177, 200, 219.

133 *Mackenzie, irritated by tension:* Ibid., p. 200.

133 Somers *had survived another long night:* Ibid., pp. 52, 65.

133 *given Wilson's attraction to blades:* Ibid., p. 200.

133 *Mackenzie wasn't being vindictive:* Valle, *Rocks and Shoals,* pp. 61–64.

134 *Figuring out what all the rules meant:* Act of 23 Apr. 1800, 1 Stat. ch. 33, § 1, art. 35.

135 *Mackenzie faced another problem:* Ibid., art. 30.

136 *Mackenzie was thinking about taking things further:* Court Martial, pp. 49, 52, 66, 136.

136 *According to criminal law theorists:* Joshua Dressler, *Understanding Criminal Law,* 3rd ed. (New York: Lexis Publishing, 2001), pp. 13–26; Paul H. Robinson, *Criminal Law* (New York: Aspen Law and Business, 1997), pp. 10–15.

136 *Other than Mackenzie's loyal officers:* Court Martial, pp. 37, 38, 57–58, 64, 73–74, 178.

137 *The nearest land was several more days away:* Court of Inquiry, pp. 25, 27, 30; *Court Martial,* pp. 151–57.

137 *he chose to seek the advice of his officers:* Karel Montor et al., eds., *Naval Leadership: Voices of Experience,* 2nd ed. (Annapolis: Naval Institute Press, 1998), 164.

138 *he wrote a remarkable letter:* The letter appears in several different versions. See *Court of Inquiry,* p. 11; *Court Martial,* pp. 22, 33, 49, 201.

139 *The group met before noon:* Court of Inquiry, p. 22; *Court Martial,* p. 157.

139 *The council worked hard:* Court Martial, pp. 151–57.

141 *when the second dogwatch was called:* Ibid., pp. 26–27.

141 *The council reconvened in the morning watch:* Court of Inquiry, p. 22; *Court Martial,* p. 202.

142 *Mackenzie was in agreement:* Court of Inquiry, p. 22; *Court Martial,* p. 203.

143 *the captain had ropes, or whips, run:* Court of Inquiry, p. 22; *Court Martial,* pp. 180, 203.

143   *Mackenzie went to the condemned prisoners: Court Martial,* pp. 72, 179–80, 190, 203.

144   *Mackenzie came back to Spencer:* Ibid., pp. 179, 189–90, 193, 203–4.

144   *"This will kill my poor mother":* Ibid., pp. 179, 193, 205.

145   *There was no point in pressing him further:* Ibid., p. 193.

146   *The prisoners were now starting to move forward:* Ibid., p. 180.

146   *Cromwell was unrepentant:* Ibid., p. 56.

146   *coupled with Spencer's last statement:* Ibid., pp. 48, 203–4.

146   *Cromwell wasn't going to go without a show of defiance: Court of Inquiry,* p. 23; *Court Martial,* pp. 39, 48.

147   *Spencer was still penitent: Court of Inquiry,* p. 17; *Court Martial,* p. 14.

147   *Small, too, seemed remorseful: Court of Inquiry,* pp. 17, 23; *Court Martial,* pp. 15, 39.

147   *the last meeting of Spencer and Small: Court of Inquiry,* pp. 17, 23; *Court Martial,* pp. 26, 40.

148   *the three prisoners were all in position: Court Martial,* p. 207.

148   *"You may have heard that I am a coward": Court of Inquiry,* p. 23; *Court Martial,* p. 39.

148   *Small, too, had something to say: Court Martial,* pp. 39–40, 193.

148   *Something terrible was about to happen:* Ibid.

149   *The gun was primed and ready:* Ibid., p. 137.

149   *The three men stood silent: Court of Inquiry,* pp. 23, 40; *Court Martial,* pp. 206–7.

150   *Mackenzie finally ordered the crew dismissed: Court Martial,* pp. 180–81.

150   *The bodies stayed aloft for an hour:* Ibid., pp. 188, 208; *Book of Common Prayer* (New York: Henry I. Megarey, 1819), pp. 234, 238, 241, 248–49.

152   *a squall struck the brig: Court Martial,* p. 208.

152   *the final assault of the forces of darkness:* Morison, *"Old Bruin,"* p. 157.

PART SIX: INQUIRY

157   *She lay quietly in New York Navy Yard:* Bayard Tuckerman, ed., *The Diary of Philip Hone* 2 (New York: Dodd, Mead, 1889), p. 639. One or two sources report that upon their arrival, the ship's complement made for the nearest church to give thanks for a safe return, but this seems unlikely in light of the existence of prisoners and the quarantine that Mackenzie imposed. See *Morning Courier and New York Enquirer,* 19 Dec. 1842.

158   *A few men and boys came and went: Court Martial,* pp. 74, 92–94, 182, 215.

159   *They weren't taking chances:* Ibid., pp. 74, 141.

159   *nine days after departing St. Thomas:* Jay Leyda, *The Melville Log: A Documen-*

tary Life of Herman Melville, 1819–1891 1 (New York: Harcourt, Brace, 1969), p. 159; *Niles' National Register,* 24 Dec. 1842, p. 261; *Court of Inquiry,* p. 15.

159 *Gansevoort was one of the few:* New York Herald, 21 Dec. 1842; *Morning Courier and New York Enquirer,* 22 Dec. 1842.

160 *Perry took barely forty-eight hours: New York Herald,* 20 Dec. 1842; *William H. Seward: An Autobiography* (New York: D. Appleton, 1877), pp. 640–41.

160 *Her husband was tougher: New York Weekly Tribune,* 22 Dec. 1842; *Niles' National Register,* 24 Dec. 1842, p. 262; *Diary of Philip Hone,* 2:640.

161 *The news had to break before long: Diary of Philip Hone,* 2:163–64.

161 *a lot of the detail was wrong:* Ibid.; Morison, *"Old Bruin,"* pp. 50, 126; *New York American,* 22 Dec. 1842, in Harrison Hayford, ed., *The Somers Mutiny Affair* (Englewood Cliffs, N.J.: Prentice Hall, 1959); Act of 23 Apr. 1800, 1 Stat. ch. 33, § 1, art. 35. Mackenzie also lacked the authority to order a court of inquiry. See Act of 23 Apr. 1800, 1 Stat. ch. 33, § 2, art. 1.

161 *Hone approved of how things had turned out: Diary of Philip Hone,* 2:164; *Morning Courier and New York Enquirer,* 19 Dec. 1842.

162 *nearly all of the papers: New York Herald,* 18 Dec. 1842.

162 *others attacked Philip Spencer: New York Express,* 17 Dec. 1842.

162 *proof of the youngster's treachery: Niles' National Register,* 24 Dec. 1842, pp. 261–62.

163 *charges of aristocracy cut both ways: New York Herald,* 18 Dec. 1842.

163 *Philip Hone largely agreed: Diary of Philip Hone,* 2:163–64.

163 *an especially wild rumor: The Somers Mutiny Affair,* p. 6; Diary of Evert A. Duyckinck, 19 Dec. 1842, Duyckinck Collection, New York Public Library.

163 *the dead Spencer had his defenders:* Seward, *Autobiography,* p. 640.

164 *Others' attacks were much more direct: National Intelligencer,* 24 Dec. 1842.

164 *a widely circulated column signed "S.": Niles' National Register,* 24 Dec. 1842, p. 260.

165 *It was a brutal, effective assault: Diary of Philip Hone,* 2:165–66.

165 *The* New York Tribune *was getting especially strident: New York Tribune,* 22 Dec. 1842.

166 *he had to order a court of inquiry: Diary of Philip Hone,* 2:165.

166 *The court of inquiry that Upshur had ordered:* Act of 23 Apr. 1800, 1 Stat. ch. 33, § 2.

167 *Upshur had ordered this particular court:* Raymond Walters, Jr., *Alexander James Dallas: Lawyer—Politician—Financier* (Philadelphia: University of Pennsylvania Press, 1943), p. 235.

167 *a lawyer among lawyers:* Charles Francis Adams, ed., John Quincy Adams, *Memoirs of John Quincy Adams* 9 (New York: AMS, 1970), p. 406; "Ogden

Hoffman," Dumas Malone, ed., *Dictionary of American Biography* 5 (New York: Charles Scribner's Sons, 1961), pp. 115–17.

168   *a perfect choice to serve as judge advocate:* The judge advocate is part prosecutor, part court reporter. For a description of his functions, see Jay M. Siegel, *Origins of the Navy Judge Advocate General's Corps: A History of Legal Administration in the United States Navy, 1775 to 1967* (Washington: Government Printing Office, 1997), p. 34, n. 3–17.

168   *John Canfield Spencer could be a dangerous man:* Leyda, *Melville Log,* p. 159.

169   *the court of inquiry convened: Court of Inquiry,* pp. 6–7.

170   *the court was giving Mackenzie every advantage:* Ibid., p. 8.

172   *On he went with his narrative:* Ibid., p. 10; cf. *Court Martial,* p. 199.

172   *After Cromwell's arrest and the rescue attempt: Court of Inquiry,* p. 10.

173   *Mackenzie had had no alternative:* Ibid., pp. 12–15.

174   *The crew had been talking to Gansevoort:* Richard H. Underwood, "The Professional and the Liar," *Kentucky Law Journal* 87:919, 957 (1998–99); *Court Martial,* pp. 81, 91–92.

175   *a long and well-thought-out speech of his own: Court of Inquiry,* pp. 15–19.

177   *The tale that he told was far different:* Ibid., pp. 19–21.

178   *Gansevoort's testimony was long:* Ibid., p. 22.

178   *Hoffman didn't like it, and he said so:* Ibid., pp. 24–25.

180   *the offensive has always been the best tactic at sea:* Colin S. Gray and Roger W. Barnett, eds., *Seapower and Strategy* (Annapolis: Naval Institute Press, 1989), p. xi.

181   *a federal common law of crimes: United States v. Hudson and Goodwin,* 11 U.S. (7 Cranch) 32 (1812).

181   *federal maritime jurisdiction:* Act of 3 Mar. 1825, 4 Stat. ch. 65, § 4, 115, at 115.

182   *an irregular sort of proceeding: United States v. Mackenzie,* 26 F. Cas. 1118, 1118–21 (S.D.N.Y. 1843) (No. 15,690) (citing U.S. Const. amend. V; Act of 23 Apr. 1800, art. 21, 2 Stat. 45, 48; Act of 30 Apr. 1790, § 8, 1 Stat. 112, 113–14; *United States v. Bevens,* 16 U.S. [3 Wheat.] 336, 391 [1818]).

183   *Witnesses came and witnesses went: Court of Inquiry,* pp. 28, 36, 27, 32.

184   *Some crewmen gave different answers:* Ibid., pp. 36–37.

184   *Other people spoke to different concerns:* Ibid., pp. 29, 33, 43.

185   *Through it all, Hoffman said little:* Ibid., pp. 35, 38, 39.

186   *George Warner found himself on the stand:* Ibid., p. 39.

186   *It was partly on the basis of Warner's opinion:* Ibid.

187   *the right answer to procedural issues:* Ibid., pp. 41–42.

188   *he renewed his efforts to vilify Spencer:* Ibid., p. 47.

190   *Mackenzie called one last witness:* Adams, *Richard Henry Dana,* 2:49; *New*

York Weekly Tribune, 12 Jan. 1843; James Fenimore Cooper, ed., *Correspondence of James Fenimore Cooper* 2 (New Haven: Yale University Press, 1922), 497–98, hereafter cited as *Cooper Correspondence.*

191   *The court of inquiry hadn't yet reached a decision:* McFarland, *Sea Dangers,* p. 183.

191   *It exonerated Mackenzie: New York Herald,* 6 Feb. 1843; *National Intelligencer,* 10 Feb. 1843.

192   *The opinion did little to shut up Mackenzie's critics: Court Martial,* pp. 1–4.

PART SEVEN: COURT-MARTIAL

197   North Carolina *was a ship of the line:* Chapelle, *History of the American Sailing Navy,* pp. 314–16, 330–31; *Dictionary of American Naval Fighting Ships,* 5:107.

198   *he spoke in his persona of mariner: National Intelligencer,* 18 Jan. 1843.

198   *the officers had had evidence enough:* Ibid.

199   *Cooper had made up his mind: Cooper Correspondence,* 4:337.

199   *Cooper got even more strident:* Ibid., pp. 357–58.

200   *the controversy continued to blaze:* Hugh Egan, "The Mackenzie Court-Martial Trial: Cooper's Secret Correspondence with William H. Norris," Joel Myerson, ed., *Studies in the American Renaissance* (Charlottesville: University Press of Virginia, 1990), pp. 149, 149–50, 156 n.4; *Cooper Correspondence,* 2:498; Conway W. Sams and Elihu S. Riley, *The Bench and Bar of Maryland* (Chicago: Lewis Publishing Co., 1910), p. 498.

200   *Norris seemed somewhat restrained: Court Martial,* p. 6.

202   *Norris's offer came with conditions:* Ibid., pp. 9–10.

203   *the purser's steward told his story:* Ibid., p. 23.

205   *as Wales was winding down:* Ibid., pp. 30–31.

206   *Gansevoort began with a long narrative:* Ibid., p. 34.

206   *Norris wasn't being unreasonable:* Ibid., pp. 34–35. Karl N. Llewellyn, *The Bramble Bush: Some Lectures on Law and Its Study* (New York: Oceana Publications, 1930), p. 34.

207   *The court split the difference: Court Martial,* p. 41.

208   *the rescue attempt in the night:* Ibid., pp. 44–45.

208   *Cromwell had kept proclaiming his innocence:* Ibid., p. 47.

209   *the issue of when Mackenzie had decided on death:* Ibid., p. 49.

210   *Gansevoort's reserves were running low:* Ibid., p. 52.

211   *Norris now dwelled on the sailors' strange meetings:* Ibid., pp. 56–60.

212   *John Canfield Spencer had kept up the attack: New York Tribune,* 16 Mar. 1843, p. 2.

212   *he was watching the legal battles:* J. C. Spencer to Ogden Hoffman, 15 Jan.

1843, Documents relating to USS *Somers* (Private collection of Mr. Spencer Murray), Navy Department Archives, Washington Navy Yard.

212   *The efforts were bothering Commodore Perry:* M. C. Perry to Ogden Hoffman, 6 Feb. 1843, Documents relating to USS *Somers* (Private collection of Mr. Spencer Murray), Navy Department Archives, Washington Navy Yard.

213   *Hoffman wasn't able to help:* M. C. Perry to Abel Upshur, 13 Feb. 1843, Documents relating to USS *Somers* (Private collection of Mr. Spencer Murray), Navy Department Archives, Washington Navy Yard.

213   *Upshur started to tire of the problem:* Abel Upshur to M. C. Perry, 15 Feb. 1843, Documents relating to USS *Somers* (Private collection of Mr. Spencer Murray), Navy Department Archives, Washington Navy Yard.

213   *The main assault was still going on in federal court: New York Tribune,* 10 Mar. 1843, pp. 2–3; 11 Mar. 1843, p. 2; 13 Mar. 1843, p. 2; 14 Mar. 1843, p. 2; 16 Mar. 1843, p. 2.

217   *he delivered the grand jury charge: United States v. Mackenzie,* 30 F. Cas. 1160, 1166 (S.D.N.Y. 1843) (No. 18,313).

218   *the loss of the topgallant mast: Court Martial,* pp. 63–64.

219   *Norris kept picking at him:* Ibid., p. 65.

220   *he stuck to his story, especially when answering Mackenzie:* Ibid., p. 66.

220   *Mackenzie cut him off:* Ibid., pp. 72, 79–81.

224   *He could only suggest:* Ibid., p. 81.

226   *John Duer had examined him in private:* Ibid., p. 85.

228   *A methodical, Columbia-trained lawyer:* Ibid., pp. 99–100; "Theodore Sedgwick," Dumas Malone, ed., *Dictionary of American Biography* 8 (New York: Charles Scribner's Sons, 1963), pp. 551–52.

228   *A lot of people recalled that dirk: Court Martial,* pp. 101, 104.

228   *Humbert had been the one in the wrong:* Ibid., pp. 104–5.

229   *Then Mackenzie counterattacked:* Ibid., p. 105.

229   *the blade had some slaughtering to do:* Ibid., pp. 105–6.

229   *"Was Wilson the brig's butcher?":* Ibid., p. 112.

230   *Norris had to be frustrated:* Ibid., p. 139.

231   *His chance came on the 8th of March:* Ibid., pp. 162–64; Charles T. McCormick, *Handbook of the Law of Evidence* (St. Paul: West Publishing, 1954), pp. 9–11.

232   *Mackenzie and his people had other ideas: Court Martial,* pp. 164–66.

233   *Signs of conspiracy lay everywhere:* Ibid., pp. 144–45.

233   *Norris called Benjamin Green:* Ibid., pp. 214–19.

233   *Daniel McKinley took the stand, too:* Ibid., p. 183.

233   *The ship's surgeon was in a strange situation:* Ibid., pp. 220–21.

234 *the most crucial witness of all was Commander Mackenzie:* Egan, "Mackenzie Court-Martial Trial," pp. 152–53.

235 *As the prosecutor interrogated young Perry: Court Martial,* pp. 172–73, 180, 185.

236 *The young officer was in agreement:* Ibid., p. 186.

237 *"Did you report the end of the time?":* Egan, "Mackenzie Court-Martial Trial," p. 152.

238 *Mackenzie missed another day: Court Martial,* pp. 188–91.

239 *a rough memorandum, in some places nearly illegible:* Ibid., pp. 193, 211–12.

239 *The last witness was Quartermaster Charles Rogers:* Ibid., pp. 226–27.

239 *After that, Norris gave up:* Ibid., pp. 227–28.

239 *The task fell to George Griffin:* Ibid., pp. 228, 236.

240 *He described what had been at stake:* Ibid., p. 236.

241 *Mackenzie had had no alternative:* Ibid., p. 249.

242 *Mackenzie had been in a bad spot:* Ibid., pp. 249–50.

242 *"Mutiny," he conceded, "is treason at sea":* Ibid., pp. 251, 253, 257–59.

242 *The final word, by tradition and law:* William Winthrop, *Military Law and Precedents* (New York: Arno Press, 1979), p. 447.

243 *the officers entered the chapel-turned-courtroom: Court Martial,* p. 380.

243 *a Cabinet meeting on March 29:* "Edmund Ruffin's Visit to John Tyler," *William & Mary College Quarterly* (1st Series, vol. 14, January 1906), pp. 193, 210–11; Claude Hall, *Abel Parker Upshur: Conservative Virginian, 1790–1844* (Madison: State Historical Society of Wisconsin, 1963), pp. 170–71, 250 n.27; John C. Rives to Martin Van Buren, 14 Apr. 1843, Van Buren Papers, Library of Congress; *Niles' National Register,* 1 Apr. 1843, p. 80. Some papers dismissed stories of a fight as a fabrication. See, e.g., *Boston Courier,* 17 Apr. 1843; *New York Weekly Tribune,* 8 Apr. 1843.

244 *ship's surgeon Leecock: New York Weekly Tribune,* 1 Apr. 1843, p. 2.

EPILOGUE: ROUGH WATERS

247 *Mignonette's keel was laid down in Brightlingsea:* A. W. Brian Simpson, *Cannibalism and the Common Law: The Story of the Tragic Last Voyage of the Mignonette and the Strange Legal Proceedings to Which It Gave Rise* (Chicago: University of Chicago Press, 1984), chs. 1–3.

250 *one of the most notorious cases:* Ibid., p. x; *Regina v. Dudley and Stephens,* 14 Q.B.D. 273 (1884), supplemented by 14 Q.B.D. 560 (1885), 1 T.L.R. 29 (Assizes 1884). For an intriguing study of various jurisprudential approaches to the problem, see Lon L. Fuller, "The Case of the Speluncean Explorers," *Harvard Law Review* 62:616 (1949).

251   *a critical account of the court-martial: Cooper Correspondance,* 4:405.

251   *Cooper spoke even more plainly:* Ibid., pp. 357–58, 413.

252   *a procedural fluke had allowed him to escape:* A. S. Mackenzie to Theodore Sedgwick, Jr., 18 Apr. 1843, Collection of Houghton Library, Harvard University.

252   *Sedgwick began to gear up:* Theodore Sedgwick, Jr., to Charles Sumner, 21 Apr. 1843, Sumner Papers, Houghton Library, Harvard University.

252   *Soon the suit was in progress: Journal of Commerce,* n.d., reprinted in Hayford, *Somers Mutiny Affair,* p. 171.

252   *"We will not undertake to decide the question":* "The Mutiny of the Somers," *North American Review* 57 (July 1843), pp. 195, 228.

253   *his introspective novella:* Charles Roberts Anderson, "The Genesis of Billy Budd," *American Literature* 12:329 (1940); Laurie Robertson-Lorant, *Melville: A Biography* (New York: Clarkson, 1996), pp. 120–22; Hershel Parker, *Herman Melville: A Biography* 1 (Baltimore: Johns Hopkins University Press, 1996), pp. 241–43, 266–67, 295–98. All of these accounts suggest or state that the *Somers* episode was a major source of inspiration for the story of Billy Budd, though each source gets some of the *Somers* details wrong. They do note, however, that Melville himself might have had a garbled version of events, which might have made the episode more amenable to a loose adaptation. See, e.g., Parker, *Herman Melville,* 1:267. One should also note that Melville apparently drew from other sources as well. Some have argued, for example, that his father-in-law, Chief Justice Lemuel Shaw of the Supreme Judicial Court of Massachusetts, was his model for *Billy Budd*'s Captain Vere, and that the dilemma of antebellum judges (such as Shaw) who had the task of enforcing legal, though immoral, slavery laws suggested Vere's quandary to Melville. See, e.g., Robert M. Cover, *Justice Accused: Antislavery and the Judicial Process* (New Haven: Yale University Press, 1975), pp. 4–5. For a brief account of the Mexican War hanging, see Morison, *"Old Bruin,"* p. 190.

253   *judged by the laws of the land:* Simpson, *Cannibalism and the Common Law,* ch. 1; *Regina v. Dudley and Stephens,* 14 Q.B.D. 273 (1884), supplemented by 14 Q.B.D. 560 (1885), 1 T.L.R. 29 (Assizes 1884).

254   *his remaining assignments were mostly on land:* Raphael Semmes, *Service Afloat and Ashore During the Mexican War* (Cincinnati: Wm. H. Moore & Co., 1851), ch. 7; Evert A. Duyckinck, Biographical Sketch of Commander A. S. Mackenzie, Duyckinck Collection, New York Public Library; "Alexander Slidell Mackenzie," Dumas Malone, ed., *Dictionary of American Biography* 6 (New York: Charles Scribner's Sons, 1964), pp. 90–91.

254 *His experiences aboard* Somers, *however, helped change the navy:* Sweetman, *U.S. Naval Academy,* pp. 3–17; Todorich, *The Spirited Years,* pp. 16–18.

256 *a young ship commanded by a young officer:* Semmes, *Service Afloat and Ashore,* pp. 90–99; A. B. Feuer, "A Question of Mutiny," *Naval History,* Mar./April 1994, pp. 22, 27; James P. Delgado, "Rediscovering the *Somers,*" *Naval History,* Mar./April 1994, pp. 28–31.

Suggestions for Further Reading

THE *SOMERS* AFFAIR is one of the most sensational episodes in the history of the United States Navy. Many historians have written about it, but few of them, oddly enough, have devoted more than an article or book chapter to it. The story of the ill-fated cruise instead usually shows up in the context of longer sea tales. The two main exceptions are Philip McFarland, *Sea Dangers: The Affair of the* Somers (New York: Schocken, 1985), which is as thorough an account as can be found, and Frederic F. Van de Water, *The Captain Called It Mutiny* (New York: Ives Washburn, 1954). Both books, while very useful and enlightening, have their limitations. McFarland's narrative, accompanied by a good primary source bibliography, has an unusual style that sometimes confuses fact and conjecture; Van de Water's has a perhaps unavoidable bias born of the fact that he is the great-nephew of one of the alleged mutineers.

Other than these, the only book-length work is Harrison Hayford's *The Somers Mutiny Affair* (Englewood Cliffs, N.J.: Prentice Hall, 1959), which is largely a collection of excerpts from primary sources, especially the court of inquiry and court-martial. Passing reference to the episode, together with information on Herman Melville, the Gansevoorts, and the *Billy Budd* connection, appears in two recent biographies, Laurie Robertson-Lorant, *Melville: A Biography* (New York: Clarkson, 1996), and Hershel Parker, *Herman Melville: A Biography* 1 (Baltimore: Johns Hopkins University Press, 1996). A more complete primary account appears in *Proceedings of the Naval Court Martial in the Case of Alexander Slidell Mackenzie (1844)* (Delmar, New York: Scholars' Facsimiles and Reprints, 1992), which in addition to a transcript of the proceedings first published in 1844, also contains commentary by James Fenimore Cooper. Other early primary accounts include *Case of the Somers Mutiny: Defence of Alexander Slidell Mackenzie, Commander of the U.S. Brig Somers, Before the Court Martial Held at the Navy Yard, Brooklyn*

(New York: Tribune Office, 1843) and *Proceedings of the Court of Inquiry Appointed to Inquire into the Intended Mutiny on Board the United States Brig of War Somers, on the High Seas: Held on Board the United States Ship North Carolina Lying at the Navy Yard, New-York: With a Full Account of the Execution of Spencer, Cromwell and Small, on Board said Vessel* (New York: Greeley & McElrath, 1843).

One of the best and most thorough shorter accounts of the cruise and its aftermath is the chapter in Samuel Eliot Morison's *"Old Bruin": Commodore Matthew C. Perry, 1794–1858* (Boston: Little, Brown, 1967). While most writers tend to be at least somewhat critical of Mackenzie, the top-flight historian Morison—who also happened to be a highly experienced sailor—is the captain's staunch defender, denouncing young Spencer as "a prototype of what nowadays is called a 'young punk.'" The chapter is best read in the context of the entire volume, for Commodore Perry was a major player in the drama, and his story is largely the story of the early- and mid-nineteenth-century navy. A more recent biography is John H. Schroeder's *Matthew Calbraith Perry: Antebellum Sailor and Diplomat* (Annapolis: Naval Institute Press, 2001). Another thorough account that weaves the tale of Mackenzie and Spencer into a larger story of the service is Harold D. Langley's *Social Reform in the United States Navy, 1798–1862* (Urbana: University of Illinois Press, 1967). Like Morison's biography of Perry, Langley's whole book is essential reading for anyone who wishes to understand the *Somers* cruise and its context. Nearly the same is true of Claude H. Hall, *Abel Parker Upshur: Conservative Virginian, 1790–1844* (Madison: State Historical Society of Wisconsin, 1964), though earlier sections of this volume are more tangential than Langley and Morison.

Two other books mention *Somers* more briefly in the context of some crucial legal background: James E. Valle's *Rocks and Shoals: Order and Discipline in the Old Navy, 1800–1861* (Annapolis: Naval Institute Press, 1980) and the recent work by Jay M. Siegel, *Origins of the Navy Judge Advocate General's Corps: A History of Legal Administration in the United States Navy, 1775 to 1967* (Washington: Government Printing Office, 1997). Occasionally marred by small factual errors, Siegel's history is nevertheless basic reading for anyone wishing to understand naval law of *Somers*'s day, as is Valle's.

A number of other books paint the Old Navy in broader brushstrokes. For the reader interested in serious research into anything regarding the navy (old or new), the best available bibliography is Paolo E. Coletta, *American Naval History: A Guide,* 2nd ed. (Lanham, Maryland, and London: Scarecrow Press, 2000). Two general popular histories, each of which gives very brief mention to *Somers,* are Kenneth J. Hagan's *This People's Navy: The Making of American Sea Power* (New York: The Free Press, 1991) and Stephen Howarth's *To Shining Sea: A History of the United States Navy, 1775–1991* (New York: Random House, 1991). Older but still well worth reading is Harold and Margaret Sprout's *The Rise of American Naval Power, 1776–1918* (Annapolis: Naval Institute Press, 1966). Another essential read is a compilation of articles by Charles Oscar Paullin, *Paullin's History of Naval Administration, 1775–1911* (Annapolis: Naval Institute Press, 1968).

American society went to sea in more than warships. The ship-of-war's *raison d'être,* in fact, was the booming maritime fleet that was indispensable to America's financial well-being and blossoming economic might. Studies of the larger picture of the seagoing United States include K. Jack Bauer, *A Maritime History of the United States: The Role of America's Seas and Waterways* (Columbia: University of South Carolina Press, 1988); Andrew Gibson and Arthur Donovan, *The Abandoned Ocean: A History of United States Maritime Policy* (Columbia: University of South Carolina Press, 2000); and the excellent book by Benjamin W. Labaree et al., *America and the Sea: A Maritime History* (Mystic: Mystic Seaport, 1998). A more anecdotal account is Bill and Gene Bonyun, *Full Hold and Splendid Passage: America Goes to Sea, 1815–1860* (New York: Alfred A. Knopf, 1969).

The naval politics and personalities in the decades before the Civil War are the focus of a number of works. These include: James C. Bradford, ed., *Command Under Sail: Makers of the American Naval Tradition, 1775–1850* (Annapolis: Naval Institute Press, 1985); James C. Bradford, ed., *Quarterdeck and Bridge: Two Centuries of American Naval Leaders* (Annapolis: Naval Institute Press, 1997); and John H. Schroeder, *Shaping a Maritime Empire: The Commercial and Diplomatic Role of the American Navy, 1829–1861* (Westport, Conn.: Greenwood Press, 1985). Books focusing on a slightly earlier period, but good for grasping the mind-set of naval officers and policymakers, include Michael A. Palmer, *Stoddert's War: Naval Operations During the Quasi-War with France, 1798–1801* (Columbia: University of South Carolina Press, 1987); Eugene S. Ferguson, *Truxtun of the Constellation: The Life of Commodore Thomas Truxtun, U.S. Navy, 1755–1822* (Baltimore: Johns Hopkins University Press, 1956); William M. Fowler, Jr., *Jack Tars and Commodores: The American Navy, 1783–1815* (Boston: Houghton Mifflin, 1984); and Marshall Smelser, *The Congress Founds the Navy, 1787–1798* (Westport, Conn.: Greenwood Press, 1959). A more general account is Rowena Reed, ed., Robert Greenhalgh Albion, *Makers of Naval Policy, 1798–1947* (Annapolis: Naval Institute Press, 1980).

The Old Navy of which these books tell was drifting and aimless, without a clearly defined role, and the society that it represented and defended at sea was also going through serious change. Aside from the personalities of Mackenzie, Gansevoort, Spencer, and others, these two facts played the most serious roles in bringing about the *Somers* affair. To understand them, one must understand the nature of war at sea and America's mid-nineteenth-century spirit of ferment. As to the first, a fine introduction appears in the earlier sections of John Keegan's *The Price of Admiralty: The Evolution of Naval Warfare* (New York: Viking, 1988). A superb look at the upheavals in everything from logistics and strategy to seamanship and tactics that nineteenth-century technological changes caused is Bernard Brodie, *Sea Power in the Machine Age* (Princeton: Princeton University Press, 1943). The classic American statement of the philosophy of sea power—and one of the earliest—came a half-century after *Somers* with Alfred Thayer Mahan's *The Influence of Sea Power Upon History, 1660–1783* (Boston: Little, Brown, 1890). Mahan has justly been compared to Clausewitz; but while having had a huge impact on the American and other navies, and on the United States as a whole, Mahan's study is less systematic than Sir Julian Corbett's influential *Some Principles of Maritime Strategy* (London: Longmans, Green, 1911). Modern restatements of the subject include Colin S. Gray and Roger W. Barnett, eds., *Seapower and Strategy* (Annapolis: Naval Institute Press, 1989); Colin S. Gray, *The Leverage of Sea Power: The Strategic Advantage of Navies in War* (New York: The Free Press, 1992); and Clark G. Reynolds, *Command of the Sea: The History and Strategy of Maritime Empires* (Malabar, Fla.: Robert E. Krieger Publishing Company, 1974). If books such as these had enunciated the role of maritime power in the early nineteenth century—and specifically the role of the navy in American life—the *Somers* affair might never have happened.

All of these histories are helpful, but for the reader to understand what took place aboard *Somers,* a firsthand look at the ships and the men is required, without glossing by historians. By far the best glimpse into the sailors' world comes, firsthand, from two leading lights of early American letters: Herman Melville and Richard Henry Dana, Jr. Dana's *Two Years Before the Mast* (New York: Harper & Brothers, 1840) was one of the first books, and by far the most popular, to spell out for American landlubbers what the sailing life was like, as he recounted his mid-1830s voyages from Boston to the coast of California and back. Melville's *White-Jacket, or, the World in a Man-of-War* (Evanston and Chicago: Northwestern University

Press and The Newberry Library, 1970), part fiction, part autobiography, came out a few years after the *Somers* affair; it tells of Melville's life as a seaman aboard an American frigate. Both, and particularly Melville's account, are rich in the details of the life of the common sailor and the workings of large sail-driven ships. Other, less well-known accounts are also available, including Charles Roberts Anderson, ed., *Journal of a Cruise to the Pacific Ocean, 1842–44, in the Frigate* United States (Durham: Duke University Press, 1937); Tim Flannery, ed., John Nicol, *The Life and Adventures of John Nicol, Mariner* (New York: Atlantic Monthly Press, 1999); and Mackenzie's own *Popular Essays on Naval Subjects* (New York: George Dearborn, 1833). The maritime novel really began with Mackenzie's nemesis James Fenimore Cooper, who was the originator of the maritime novel, including *The Pilot* (1823), *The Red Rover* (1827), and *The Water-Witch* (1830). A survey of maritime literature is Haskell Springer, ed., *America and the Sea: A Literary History* (Athens: University of Georgia Press, 1995).

The type of ship on which Dana, Melville, and countless others sailed was the setting for much of the *Somers* story. Sailing ships were, and are, tremendously complex and functional works of art, and the sailor's language is its own, full of binnacles, preventer-braces, wearing, and reefing. To understand the *Somers* affair, one must try to understand the ships. One of the most prolific and useful authors in this department is Howard I. Chapelle, who has written three volumes, each complete with hull plans, that will help orient the reader to the heyday of American sail: *The History of American Sailing Ships* (New York: W. W. Norton, 1935); *The History of the American Sailing Navy: The Ships and Their Development* (New York: W. W. Norton, 1949); and *The Baltimore Clipper: Its Origin and Development* (Salem, Mass.: Marine Research Society, 1930). The purpose of a warship, of course, was to serve as a weapons platform. For a somewhat technical discussion of the main armament of *Somers*-era vessels, see Spencer Tucker, *Arming the Fleet: U.S. Navy Ordnance in the Muzzle-Loading Era* (Annapolis: Naval Institute Press, 1989). A broader look at the newer ships that were replacing sailing vessels, on which Mackenzie and others had served, appears in Donald L. Canney's two-volume *The Old Steam Navy* (Annapolis: Naval Institute Press, 1990) and Robert Gardiner, ed., *Steam, Steel and Shellfire: The Steam Warship, 1815–1905* (Annapolis: Naval Institute Press, 1992).

Somers, among the very last pre-steam warships, was heir to thousands of years of seafaring culture, technology, and strategy. For a well-illustrated, well-explained glimpse of that heritage, see John Harland, *Seamanship in the Age of Sail: An Account of the Shiphandling of the Sailing Man-of-War, 1600–1860, Based on Contemporary Sources* (Annapolis: Naval Institute Press, 1984); Veres László and Richard Woodman, *The Story of Sail* (Annapolis: Naval Institute Press, 1999); Gillian Hutchinson, *Medieval Ships and Shipping* (London: Leicester University Press, 1994); Frank Howard, *Sailing Ships of War, 1400–1860* (Greenwich: Conway Maritime Press, 1979); Robert Gardiner, ed., *The Line of Battle: The Sailing Warship, 1650–1840* (Annapolis: Naval Institute Press, 1992); Peter Goodwin, *The Construction and Fitting of the English Man of War, 1650–1850* (Annapolis: Naval Institute Press, 1987); and Peter Kemp and Richard Ormond, *The Great Age of Sail: Maritime Art and Photography* (New York: Facts on File, 1986).

The *Somers* affair, though, was about more than war at sea, warship design and handling, or even mid-nineteenth-century American culture. It was also about changes in American society, psychological pressures, the pressures of adolescence and of being confined in an insular, unescapable wooden-walled world. For recent popular insights into youth violence which may or may not have some bearing on Spencer's thoughts and actions, see James Garbarino, *Lost Boys: Why Our Sons Turn Violent and How We Can Save Them* (New York: The Free Press, 1999). A work focusing on changing notions of childhood in the nineteenth century is Bernard Wishy, *The Child and the Republic* (Philadelphia: University of Pennsylvania Press, 1968); a more comprehensive view appears in Joseph F. Kett, *Rites of Passage: Adolescence in America 1790 to the Present* (New York: Basic Books, 1977). For a more general view of antebellum social history, see Alice Felt Tyler, *Freedom's Ferment: Phases of American Social History from the Colonial Period to the Outbreak of the Civil War* (New York: Harper Torchbooks, 1944), old but still very useful. For the sort of life that Spencer thought that he wanted, see David Cordingly, *Under the Black Flag: The Romance and the Reality of Life Among the Pirates* (New York: Random House, 1995). A melodramatic contemporary account that might have helped fuel Spencer's own imagination is *The Pirates Own Book* (Portland: Sanborn & Carter, 1837).

Spencer's, however, was not the only mutiny in the world of the sailing ship. For a survey of some of the others, see Leonard F. Guttridge, *Mutiny: A History of Naval Insurrection* (Annapolis: Naval Institute Press, 1992). In addition to a good bibliography and a chapter on the *Somers*, this volume tells the stories of all the famous mutinies of recent years, including those aboard *Bounty, Hermione, Potemkin,* and the infamous events at Spithead and Nore.

No bibliography of this sort would be complete without an entry on the most basic element of all. While many accounts of seafaring have been penned through the centuries, Joseph Conrad's *The Mirror of the Sea* (New York: Marlboro Press, 1988) best brings the ocean itself to life in all its power, beauty, and cruelty.

Index

About the Author

BUCKNER F. MELTON, JR., holds a doctorate in history from Duke University and a law degree from the University of North Carolina at Chapel Hill, where he teaches at the School of Law. A specialist in American early national and constitutional history, Melton has published articles on topics ranging from *The Federalist Papers* to the history of eminent domain. His book *The First Impeachment: The Constitution's Framers and the Case of Senator William Blount* received national attention during the impeachment proceedings against President Clinton. During the impeachment Melton served as an adviser to several members of Congress and as a commentator for National Public Radio, *NewsHour with Jim Lehrer,* and MSNBC. He is also the author of the recent book *Aaron Burr: Conspiracy to Treason.* A native of Georgia, he lives in Durham, North Carolina.